RESEARCHING DIGITAL MEDIA AND SOCIETY

Simon Lindgren & Moa Eriksson Krutrök

RESEARCHING DIGITAL MEDIA AND SOCIETY

S Sage

Sage

1 Oliver's Yard
55 City Road
London EC1Y 1SP

2455 Teller Road
Thousand Oaks
California 91320

Unit No 323-333, Third Floor, F-Block
International Trade Tower, Nehru Place
New Delhi 110 019

8 Marina View Suite 43-053
Asia Square Tower 1
Singapore 018960

Editor: Natalie Aguilera
Content Development editor: Rhoda
 OlaSaid
Editorial assistant: Sarah Moorhouse
Production editor: Rabia Barkatulla
Copyeditor: Sharon Cawood
Proofreader: Christine Bitten
Indexer: KnowledgeWorks Global Ltd
Marketing manager: Elena Asplen
Cover design: Francis Kenney
Typeset by KnowledgeWorks Global Ltd

© Simon Lindgren and Moa Eriksson Krutrök, 2024

Apart from any fair dealing for the purposes of research, private study, or criticism or review, as permitted under the Copyright, Designs and Patents Act, 1988, this publication may not be reproduced, stored or transmitted in any form, or by any means, without the prior permission in writing of the publisher, or in the case of reprographic reproduction, in accordance with the terms of licences issued by the Copyright Licensing Agency. Enquiries concerning reproduction outside those terms should be sent to the publisher.

Library of Congress Control Number: 2023942555

British Library Cataloguing in Publication data

A catalogue record for this book is available from the British Library

ISBN 9781529605174
ISBN 9781529605167 (pbk)

CONTENTS

ABOUT THE AUTHORS

Simon Lindgren is Professor of Sociology at Umeå University, Sweden. His research is focused on politics, power and resistance at the intersection of society and digital technologies. Simon was trained as a qualitative sociologist but works today with mixed methods and has written extensively about developing approaches that integrate interpretive and computational techniques. He is the director of the DIGSUM Centre for Digital Social Research, and Editor in Chief of the *Journal of Digital Social Research* (JDSR).

Moa Eriksson Krutrök is Associate Professor in Media and Communication Studies at Umeå University, Sweden. Her main research interest centres on discourses and affective responses relating to personal and societal crises in digital spaces, specifically the expressions of trauma, grief and resilience in the domain of social media. Moa is proficient in predominantly qualitative digital methods. She is an affiliated researcher at Umeå University's Digital Humanities Lab (Humlab) and is also on the editorial board of the *Journal of Digital Social Research* (JDSR).

1

RESEARCHING DIGITAL MEDIA AND SOCIETY

Key Questions

- What does it mean that we live in a *deeply mediatised* society? How does this relate to *digital* media?
- What are some important shifts in the history of researching digital media and society? How has the field of 'internet research' developed over the years?
- How does the particular *data environment* of our digital societies impact on possibilities and challenges for research?
- What does it mean to work with mixed methods, within an *interpretive framework*?

Key Concepts

Deep mediatisation * internet research * reflexivity * data environment * mixed methods within an interpretive framework

Hi, hello, welcome! This is where it all begins. This is the book that we wish we would have had back in the days when we were students. It is the book we would have needed when we first started to explore the research field of digital media and society. It is also the book we wish we could have used when starting out teaching students on the courses that we now teach ourselves. We have been longing for this book, and now here it is! Hopefully, this book will make others happy too.

If you are a student just starting to learn research methods to study digital media and society, welcome! This book is a stepping stone to a wide range of options, ideas, concepts and methodological and ethical practices that are needed when delving into this field. The book not only provides a method-by-method run-through of what digital media research can consist of (Chapters 6–10), but it also covers the entire research process (Chapter 3), from beginning to end, including all the tricky issues involved in mixing methods (Chapter 2), and in approaching one's research and research subjects ethically (Chapter 4). In research in general, and maybe in digital media research in particular, there will always be sidesteps, redevelopments, and 'back to the drawing board' moments. The practical doing of research can be messy! We know. That's why we are doing this together. Simply come along for the ride.

In reality, every research project is different. This is mostly a good thing, as tailoring your approach to the specific task at hand will ensure that you get the best results possible. Even when you have been doing research for quite some time and are starting to get the hang of it, projects are never the same. Your starting points, your previous knowledge, your theoretical and methodological understanding, your ethical positioning, including your own self-reflective practice – all of these may vary. That is why this book can not only be helpful to beginners, but also to those that are already somewhat experienced in researching digital media and society.

We urge you to see this book both as an entry point into the field of digital media research, and as a handbook that you can use in a myriad of ways. Start with this chapter, move on to the next and then the next, until you've read them all. Or skip around, and mix and make connections between the chapters that you need the most right now. It's up to you (oh, but if this book is on your syllabus, listen to your teachers; they get to decide – OK?).

Most of all, this is a book that tries to make digital research methods less daunting, and more accessible and fun. Let it become a companion that you can relate to, return to, and allow it to ask those hard questions that can push your research forward. We want you to experiment with following the different methodological steps that are introduced throughout the following chapters, but also to make them your own. We want you to take ownership of what you are creating. Use this book as a map, while remembering that the map is not the territory. *You* decide which roads you will ultimately end up following or creating. Exciting, no?

RESEARCHING A DEEPLY MEDIATISED SOCIETY

First of all, why should we even study the relationship between digital media and society? To most people, it will be quite obvious that digital technologies (smartphones, computers, social media platforms) are no longer nerdy specialities. They are everywhere, and play some kind of role – sometimes a larger one, sometimes a smaller one – in a wide range of social settings. In fact, society has become entangled with the digital. So much so that most researchers no longer cling to the idea that what is digital and what is non-digital can be separated. The digital is everywhere, running through the various contexts of our society, our political beliefs and our personal networks.

As digital media researchers, we have still had to argue, many times, for the point of even focusing on digital technology when researching social issues, hearing from some non-digital scholars that it doesn't matter what people are saying online, that social media research isn't real-world analysis, and so on. By now, hopefully most people have seen enough evidence that what happens 'online' indeed has 'real-life' connections and consequences, not only personal, but also societal, cultural and political. Our social realities have become largely digital, while digital technologies have, to no small degree, become our social reality. Consider, for example, the new role of Russian social media influencers as propaganda machines on TikTok during the invasion of Ukraine in 2022. Or consider the spread of conspiracy theories concerning 5G and vaccine mistrust during the COVID-19 pandemic.

Claiming today that the digital sphere is something separate from the rest of society is simply missing out on the big picture. Media scholars Nick Couldry and Andreas Hepp have called our contemporary society 'deeply mediatised', meaning that our daily lives and the ways we make sense of the world are deeply entangled with the digital infrastructures we rely on for communicating. The title of their book, *The Mediated Construction of Reality*, draws upon the classic work *The Social Construction of Reality: A Treatise in the Sociology of Knowledge* from sociologists Peter L. Berger and Thomas Luckmann (1966), one of the most influential texts in the development of social constructionism. This book laid the groundwork for understanding how social concepts and roles are created and upheld within our social systems, at several levels.

Couldry and Hepp (2017) revisit these questions in light of the digital technologies present in contemporary society, to discuss how social theory and research can help us understand how the everyday world we now live in gets constructed both in, and through, digital media. In a deeply mediatised society, we need to take into consideration both more digital and less digital iterations of the social concepts we are exploring. The protests in the streets during a Black Lives Matter rally need to be seen alongside the digital traces of #blacklivesmatter social media content, discussions, or online backlashes from different political positions. We should, in other words, take the digitalness of such protests into account, just as we consider their other aspects. The main point is not where the digital begins or ends, but that it is present.

A HISTORY OF RESEARCH ON DIGITAL MEDIA AND SOCIETY

Digital media, and particularly the internet,[1] are technologically entangled, sometimes strange, and definitely ever-changing. And so are the methods used to research it. Studies may focus on people, technologies or devices, the platforms or apps, or the social spaces and uses of digital media. When it comes to what the actual study object may be, all of these different possibilities have also meant that research on digital media and society can look at its subject matter in a multitude of ways, for example seeing digital media as a social sphere where people interact, as a tool that people use, or as a field in which to collect data. Such complexities call for us to consider the ways that the digital technologies themselves have changed, in relation to how research around them has been conducted. Figures 1.1–1.4, partly drawing on Hooley, Marriott and Wellens (2012: 8–10), give a general, and non-exhaustive, overview of how digital media – focusing on the internet as the crucial technology – has developed, and how research interests and methods have followed along.

In Figure 1.1, we can see that the first version of the internet was launched in the late 1960s, followed by early iterations of email and mobile phone technologies in the early 1970s. Initially, the academic research around these things

1960s - 1980s	DIGITAL MEDIA	RESEARCH
	Early forms of computer-mediated communication	Technologically oriented research Computer science
	Birth of the internet (late 60s)	
	First email (1971)	
	First mobile phone (1973)	
	Early discussion forums	Early studies of 'information society' (Bell, Toffler).
	BBSs (1978)	
	Usenet (1980)	De Sola Pool: "Technologies of Freedom" (1983)
		First online survey (1986)
		First computer packages for qualitative data analysis

Figure 1.1 Digital media and research, 1960s–1980s

---

[1]Nowadays, researchers tend not to capitalise the letter i in internet, but for a long time it was customary to do so (written as 'Internet').

naturally had a strong focus on technological issues around their development and optimisation. This kind of research still exists, of course, and has become more and more developed when it comes to understanding the interplay between humans and technology (see, for example, Sharp et al., 2019). As more social and community-oriented uses of the internet emerged in the late 1970s and early 1980s, with early modes of computer-mediated communication similar to today's online discussion forums, more socially oriented research perspectives were also developed. Some key social science texts about the emerging 'information society' were published (Bell, 1973; Toffler, 1980), and Ithiel de Sola Pool (1983) wrote about the new electronic media as being potential 'technologies of freedom' that could enhance free speech. It was also during the 1980s that the first online survey was carried out (Kiesler & Sproull, 1986), and that some of the first software programs for qualitative data analysis were introduced (Wolski, 2018).

The 1990s was indeed a formative decade for the study of digital media and society, as research on social practices online took off. This increased interest and scholarly activity was due to the broad introduction and breakthrough of the World Wide Web (Berners-Lee, 1989). Books such as *The Virtual Community* by Howard Rheingold (1993), *Life on the Screen* by Sherry Turkle (1995) and *The Rise of the Network Society* by Manuel Castells (1996), provided stepping stones for studies to follow, by approaching digital media as social spheres. During the 1990s, the field of internet research started to take shape around emerging research centres, conferences and academic journals. Early on, discussions were

1990s	DIGITAL MEDIA	RESEARCH
	World Wide Web (WWW)	Pew Internet Research Center (1990)
	Public release of the Web (1990)	Rheingold: "virtual community" (1993)
	First web browsers and search engines	Methodological discussions about online interviewing (1994)
	Google search launched (1997)	*Journal of Computer-Mediated Communication* is launched (1995)
		Early mentions of 'internet ethnography'
	Early stages of social media	Turkle: "Life on the Screen" (1995)
	First weblog ('blog') (1997)	First debate over online research ethics (1996)
	First social network site (1997)	Castells: "network society" (1996)
		The WWW and Contemporary Cultural Theory conference at Drake University (1997)
		The Berkman Klein Center for Internet & Society at Harvard University (1998)
		The journal *New Media and Society* launches (1999)

Figure 1.2   Digital media and research, 1990s

revolving around methodological issues such as online interviewing (Brotherson, 1994), emerging forms of internet ethnography (Correll, 1995) and – notably – ethics (Allen, 1996; Boehlefeld, 1996; King, 1996; Thomas, 1996). This decade also saw the emergence of online formats and platforms that signalled the beginning of the era of social media, such as the first blog, *Robot Wisdom*, in 1997 (Djuraskovic, 2015), and the first social network site, SixDegrees.com, in that same year (boyd & Ellison, 2007).

The development of digital media, and digital media research, continued throughout the 00s (Figure 1.3). One important historical step for internet studies was the inaugural conference of the Association of Internet Researchers, held in Kansas in 2000. Initiatives, and research centres, such as the Berkman Klein Center for Internet and Society and the Oxford Internet Institute, helped to further cement the importance of the emerging field. Increasingly, a number of studies focused on people's everyday uses of the internet. For example, Wellman and Haythornthwaite's edited book *The Internet in Everyday Life* (2002) focused specifically on the social effects of the internet and how it fits into everyday lives, rather than seeing it as an alternate world. Studies like these considered different ways of being social in internet contexts, such as using email, instant messaging and blogging. While the field was still under development, Nancy Baym (2005) stressed that even though internet studies had generally been considered a scattered, interdisciplinary field, it should now be considered as its own discipline.

In 2004, sociologist Barry Wellman announced that, what he called the 'third age' of internet studies, had arrived. While early internet research had focused first on groups, and then on user studies, Wellman argued that an age of individualised

(20)00s	DIGITAL MEDIA	RESEARCH
	Mobile	
	Launch of 3G telecomms (2001)	Inauguration of the Association of Internet Researchers (2000)
	Development of VOIP (2004)	
	iPhone launched (2007)	Batinic et al.: "Online social sciences" (2002)
	Launch of 4G network (2009)	Hine: "virtual methods" (2005)
	Web 2.0 / Social media	Jenkins: "convergence culture" (2006)
	Wikipedia (2001)	
	Myspace (2003)	boyd: "networked publics" (2008)
	Facebook (2004)	Markham & Baym: "internet inquiry" (2009)
	YouTube (2005)	
	Reddit (2005)	
	Twitter (2006)	
	Tumblr (2007)	

Figure 1.3 Digital media and research, (20)00s

networks was dawning, as there was a move from a focus on community to a focus on social networks:

> [T]he evolving personalization, portability, ubiquitous connectivity, and wireless mobility of the internet is facilitating a move away from interactions in groups and households, and towards individualized networks. The internet is helping each person to become a communication and information switchboard, between persons, networks, and institutions. (Wellman, 2004: 127)

Likewise, danah boyd (2014) has narrowed down this very important change of the internet to the year 2003, when the big shift from it being specified around different topics towards it being focused on individual social networks, occurred.

As increasingly social and participatory platforms emerged on the web during the 00s, there was talk of a shift in terms of a move from Web 1.0 – a more static and mass communication-oriented web – to Web 2.0, based on participation, editability and user-created content (Cormode & Krishnamurthy, 2008). In what is often referred to as the original definition of Web 2.0, Tim O'Reilly (2005) lists a set of important differences between 1.0 and 2.0, such as a shift from personal websites to blogs and feeds, a shift from seeing web content as a one-time investment to seeing it as an ongoing process, and a shift from content management systems to linking based on user-driven tagging (so-called folksonomy; Vander Wal, 2007).

The field of researching digital media and society continued to develop throughout the 00s, with books such as *Online Social Sciences* (Batinic et al., 2002), *Virtual Methods: Issues in social research on the internet* (Hine, 2005),

2010s	DIGITAL MEDIA	RESEARCH
	Tools and platforms	Papacharissi: "the networked self" (2010)
	iPad introduced (2010)	
	Fitbit step counter (2010)	Morozov: "the net delusion" (2011)
	Siri and Alexa (2011/2014)	Bennett & Segerberg: "connective action" (2012)
	Samsung and Apple smart watches (2013/2015)	Rogers: "digital methods" (2013)
	Google Glass (2013)	van Dijck and Poell: "social media logic" (2013)
	First NFT (2014)	
	Launch of 5G network (2019)	First issue of *Social Media + Society* (2015)
		Lupton: "the quantified self" (2016)
	Social media	Chadwick: "the hybrid media system" (2017)
	Instagram (2010)	
	Snapchat (2011)	Couldry and Hepp: "deep mediatisation" (2017)
	Musical.ly and TikTok (2017)	Noble: "algorithms of oppression" (2018)

Figure 1.4 Digital media and research, 2010s

Netnography (Kozinets, 2015, 2020), and *Internet Inquiry: Conversations about method* (Markham & Baym, 2009) being published. Quite in line with the Web 2.0 era, key research at this time was focused on participation (Jenkins, 2006), peer-production (Benkler, 2006) and networked publics (boyd, 2008).

The digital media landscape evolved further throughout the 2010s, with developments in mobiles, tablets, and wearable technologies, as well as deeply digital forms and phenomena such as the Internet of Things (Thomas, 2006), blockchain, bitcoin and NFTs (Idelberger & Mezei, 2022). At the same time, the ecosystem of social media platforms had continued to develop with new additions such as Instagram, Snapchat and TikTok, adding new complexities in terms of visuality, ephemerality, and algorithmically governed user feeds (Bayer et al., 2016; Leaver et al., 2020; Bhandari & Bimo, 2022). Throughout the decade, research on digital media and society became more multi-layered and diversified with studies and conceptual developments around issues of identity (Papacharissi, 2011), politics (Bennett & Segerberg, 2012) and data-fication (Lupton, 2016). In light of the occurrence of hate-speech, racism and anti-feminism online, a more critical strand of research also grew stronger, counterbalancing the research on participation and democratisation by high-lighting also the more oppressive sides of digital media (Morozov, 2011; Noble, 2018). Methodological discussions began emphasising the importance of not merely adapting existing research methods for the internet, but also developing novel, natively digital methods (Rogers, 2013). Such methods, it was argued, are needed to analyse the increasingly hybrid (Chadwick, 2013), and deeply mediatised (Couldry & Hepp, 2017), digital society and its emerging media logics (van Dijck & Poell, 2013).

Today, this development towards (1) an increased complexity in terms of how *the digital* and *society* overlap (Couldry & Mejias, 2019; Kitchin, 2021; Nielsen & Ganter, 2022); (2) an exacerbated dualism between democratic gains and threats to democracy (Bail, 2021; Bennett & Livingston, 2021); and (3) the need to develop increasingly hybrid and novel research methods (Lindgren, 2020), pushes the field of researching digital media and society further. In this context, it is not the task of this book to take on the most intense challenges that may have to be faced in the years to come. Rather, we want to provide a steady platform for newcomers to the field. On the one hand, we will introduce a set of concrete methods (Chapters 5–10) that will be useful, each in their own right, when formulating research tasks and taking them on (Chapter 3). On the other hand, we also encourage you to think eclectically and dynamically about methods (Chapter 2), and to carefully consider the ethical issues involved in this (Chapter 4). Before we move on to the next chapter, and its discussions about mixing methods, we will deal in more detail with the research context that we are facing, starting with considering the role of datafication for digital media research.

A NEW DATA ENVIRONMENT

Throughout the past ten years or so, there has been much talk about 'big data', referring to the vast amount of data available through the increased number of volumes accessible online. Big data has been defined, by boyd and Crawford (2012: 663), as 'the cultural, technological, and scholarly phenomenon' that rests upon the interplay of technology ('maximizing computation power and algorithmic accuracy to gather, analyse, link, and compare large data sets'), analysis ('drawing on large data sets to identify patterns in order to make economic, social, technical, and legal claims') and mythology ('the widespread belief that large data sets offer a higher form of intelligence and knowledge that can generate insights that were previously impossible, with the aura of truth, objectivity, and accuracy'). In reality, however, the emergence of big data is only one of many transformations in our data environment, which affects opportunities as well as challenges when doing digital social research. For example, Kingsley Purdam and Mark Elliot aptly point out that what is commonly known as 'big' data is in fact data defined by several other things, rather than just its large size: it registers things as they happen in real time, it offers new possibilities to combine and compare datasets, and so on. Furthermore, Purdam and Elliot believe that even these characterisations are not sufficient. This is because those definitions still seem to assume that data is 'something we have', when in fact 'the reality and scale of the data transformation is that data is now something we are becoming immersed and embedded in' (Purdam & Elliot, 2015: 26).

The notion of a 'data environment' underlines that people today are, at the same time, generators of, and generated by, this new environment. 'Instead of people being researched', Purdam and Elliot (2015: 26) say, 'they are the research'. Their point, more concretely, is that new data types have emerged – and are constantly emerging – that demand new, flexible approaches. Researching digital media and society, therefore, often entails discovering and experimenting with the challenges and possibilities of ever-new types and combinations of information.

Different Types of Data

In trying to describe the ever-changing data environment, Purdam and Elliot (2015: 28–29) outline an eight-point typology of different data types based on how the data in question have been generated:

1 **Orthodox intentional data**: Data collected and used with the respondent's explicit agreement. All so-called orthodox social science data (e.g. survey, focus group or interview data and also data collected via observation) would come into this category. New orthodox methods continue to be developed.

2 **Participative intentional data**: In this category data are collected through some interactive process. This includes some new data forms such as crowdsourced data [...].

3 **Consequential data**: Information that is collected as a necessary transaction that is secondary to some (other) interaction (e.g. administrative records, electronic health records, commercial transaction data and data from online game playing all come into this category).

4 **Self-published data**: Data deliberately self-recorded and published that can potentially be used for social science research either with or without explicit permission, given the information has been made public (e.g. long-form blogs, CVs and profiles).

5 **Social media data**: Data generated through some public, social process that can potentially be used for social science research either with or without permission (e.g. micro-blogging platforms such as X (formerly Twitter) and Facebook, and, perhaps, online game data).

6 **Data traces**: Data that is 'left' (possibly unknowingly) through digital encounters, such as online search histories and purchasing, which can be used for social science research either by default use agreements or with explicit permission.

7 **Found data**: Data that is available in the public domain, such as observations of public spaces, which can include covert research methods.

8 **Synthetic data**: Where data has been simulated, imputed or synthesized. This can be derived from, or combined with, other data types.

The most important point here is that while social research traditionally relies on orthodox intentional data (1), such as surveys and interviews, digital media have enabled much more far-reaching registration and collection of participative intentional data (2), consequential data (3), self-published data (4), and found data (7). These are types of data that indeed existed before digitally networked tools and platforms but which have been expanded and accentuated. The remaining types – social media data (5), data traces (6), and, at least chiefly, synthetic data (8) – are specific to digital society. Therefore, researchers who analyse this society face dramatically altered conditions for the generation and gathering of data about social processes and interactions.

In today's world, large amounts of social data are registered and aggregated independently of initiatives from researchers. This is illustrated by work such as that of computational sociologists Scott Golder and Michael Macy (2011). Their research mapped people's affective states throughout the day as expressed via X (formerly Twitter),[2] in 84 countries, generating results of high interest to its subject

---

[2]Twitter, launched in 2006, was an often-studied social media platform among researchers up until its acquisition by Elon Musk in 2022. The change in ownership

area, but using a research design that was, by necessity, dictated by the availability and character of the time-stamped and text-based social media data. Examples of similar, highly data-driven, studies exist in several other fields. Researchers of digital media and society are often left to deal with data generated through platforms, rather than having the opportunity to elicit data in more conventional ways that are controlled by the researcher to a higher degree. While choosing an approach – for instance, opting for a survey or for in-depth interviews – will have continued relevance in some contexts, scholars are now increasingly facing the challenge of thinking up and constructing some of their 'methods' after the fact.

One of Purdam and Elliot's (2015) main points in the presentation of their typology is the argument that the complexity of today's data environment forces researchers to constantly think about the highly variable characteristics of data that they encounter or seek out. And one of the key challenges when entering this type of terrain is the need to constantly try out new methods for data gathering. In order to know that the data we elicit or download, as well as the strategies we choose to make sense of it, are appropriate, we may test our strategy to see whether it produces good research results. However, the dilemma is that in order to know that the results are good, we must already have developed the appropriate method. Because of this constant – and potentially endless – need for experimentation and discovery, investigations drawing on new tools and approaches risk becoming stuck and intellectually unproductive very quickly.

Imagine, for instance, that you are researching some aspect of social interaction on a platform like YouTube, and have decided that an analysis of user comments on videos seems to be the data-collection method of choice. Now, if this had been survey responses, or interview transcriptions, you could rely on an entire canon of literature on methods and well-established research practices in order to understand how to work with such data. Even though you might want to undertake new approaches or challenge the conventional ways of going about the research, you would at least have a sort of baseline or common practice to relate to and argue with. But, in the case of YouTube comments, you would have to do a lot more groundwork. First, for example, you would have to find a way of collecting the comments. If the number of comments was large enough for it to be inconvenient to manually copy and paste them – which is often the case – you would have to find some tool or another to automatically capture and download them. This risks the use of trial and error as you work your way through a variety of browser plugins, scripts or applications, none of which may eventually do what you want them to do. This process can be very time-consuming and it is not uncommon for the researcher to become so engaged with this very quest for a

---

came with new, much more restrictive, regulations around how scholars can download research data from the platform. In 2023, Twitter was rebranded as X.

tool that they – instead of doing the social research that was initially intended – start to devote a lot of time to searching for ever 'better' tools or learning how to code their own tools. And this is only the first step of several subsequent ones, where other challenges may throw you off track.

Once the comments are collected and ordered, there are wide ranges of issues as regards to how knowledge of the comments should be achieved as well as ethical issues to address. What are the comments actually? Are they individual comments or conversations? How should you, if at all, take the likes and dislikes of the comments into consideration? Do all of the comments relate to the YouTube video in question, or can the comment threads take on lives of their own, to become forums for the discussion of issues other than those insti-gated by the video? How can you, ethically, use these data for research? Do you need the informed consent of all the people who have posted in the thread? And so on. In sum, because of the inherent multidimensional complexity and unresolved questions, research on digital society must embrace research meth-ods as a creative act. Instead of relying on previous work, copying and pasting run-of-the-mill methods sections into our papers, researchers must 'reveal the messy details of what they are actually doing, aiming toward mutual reflection, creativity, and learning that advances the state of the art' (Sandvig & Hargittai, 2015: 5).

CHALLENGES IN RESEARCHING DIGITAL MEDIA AND SOCIETY

In other words, the complexity of today's data environment, alongside other par-ticularities and issues that arise when researching digital media and society, offers a set of challenges, which underlines the need for the kind of thinking around research methods that we want to engage with through this book. For example, the above-mentioned demand for reflexivity on behalf of researchers of digi-tal media and society operates on several different levels. Markham and Baym argue that research design is an ongoing process, and that especially in studying digital media within dynamic and exploratory projects, the latter will need to be reframed continuously throughout the process of research. They write:

> Different questions occur at different stages of a research process, and the same questions reappear at different points. Second, the constitution of data is the result of a series of decisions at critical junctures in the design and conduct of a study. [...] We must constantly and thoroughly evaluate what will count as data and how we are distinguishing side issues from key sources of information. (Markham & Baym, 2009: xvii)

As Jones (1999) emphasises, when researching the specificities of the internet, it is important to remember that its uses are always contextualised. Research subjects, both human and non-human are part of physical space as much as they are part of 'cyberspace'. This means, Jones (1999: xii) says, that '[n]ot only is it important to be aware of and attuned to the diversity of online experience, it is important to recognize that online experience is at all times tethered in some fashion to offline experience'.

So, while it is exciting to study the internet and digital society, it is also especially challenging. New platforms, concepts and social practices emerge fast enough to make the 'internet' itself a compelling area of inquiry. The field, Markham and Baym (2009: xviii–xix) write, has a 'self-replenishing novelty [that] always holds out the promise for unique intellectual spaces'. But, as discussed above, new terrains of research bring with them new challenges and difficulties. First, there is a need for constant reflection on the role of the self in the research. Processes of digital social research highlight that researchers are actually co-creators of the field of study. Our choices are made in contexts where there are no standard rules for research design and practice, and this makes such choices more meaningful. Furthermore, the often-disembodied character of digital social settings makes it important to think a little deeper about the relationship between the researcher and the researched:

> What decisions are we making to seek consent; what counts as
> an authentic self-representation? How are we conceptualizing the
> embodied persons we study? How are we framing our own embodied
> sensibilities? Do we approach what we are studying as traces left in
> public spaces or as embodied activities by people situated in rich
> offline contexts? We must consider how to interpret other people's
> selves and how to represent ourselves to the people we study,
> especially when we may not be meeting them in person. (Markham &
> Baym, 2009: xviii–xix)

Researchers and their subjects, Purdam and Elliot (2015: 47) say, increasingly bleed into one another. This is because 'as the proportion of our lives spent online grows, so the boundary between data and subject becomes less distinct'. In the same sense that offline identities of people are partially coming together in the minds and memories of others, our online selves are partially constructed in our intentional or unintentional data footprints.

Second, Purdam and Elliot argue, 'the activities of others also contribute to constructing these footprints, for example, a photograph of a person might be in the public domain as a result of being posted online by someone else'. Additionally, that photograph might also have been shared, tagged, liked or remixed by somebody else, and it may contain 'meta-identity information' (2015: 47). So, if a 'researcher' analyses this photo, posted by a 'research subject', then who or what is actually being analysed? Things are further complicated in the movement from orthodox intentional datasets to various types of data streams or synthetisations, which blurs the distinction between data and analysis.

Third, and finally, it is important to think about the quality of the data used in research. Conventional social science has a set of established mechanisms for quality control, which assess things such as the reliability, validity and generalisability of research results. The introduction of new types of data, and new modes of data gathering, demand that we ask ourselves questions about the most rigorous and robust methods of going about our research in order to avoid unnecessary errors or biases. When analysing different platforms, such as a discussion forum or X (formerly Twitter), and making claims about society, we must remain critical in understanding whose views – whose society – are being expressed on the platform in question, and in our own particular sample. Generally, however, conventional and established ways of thinking about such things can't be easily transferred to studies based on many of the new data types. The criterion of validity, for example, is about evaluating to what degree one is actually studying what one purports to study. Giving an example based on X (formerly Twitter), Purdam and Elliot (2015: 48) posit:

> For example, a tweet might be generated for fun, to provide information or to persuade or mislead; the motivation obviously affects the meaning of the tweet. With survey data and even, to some extent, administrative data, the impact of respondent motivations is, at least in principle, structured by (or perhaps mediated by) the data collection instrument itself. Thus, a well-designed social science research instrument can constrain motivational impact. But this is not so with Twitter data; here people's motivations are given full rein – a tweet might be designed to manipulate or obfuscate, to attract truth or to repel it. It might be designed to fantasize or 'try out an opinion', to provoke a response or simply to create controversy.

So, here we can choose different pathways: Do we want to find verification techniques with which to check the 'quality' of these data – for example, looking at a user's tweets over time to see whether a tweet is characteristic or not – or is it more feasible to argue that we are not studying the person, but something else? Society? Culture? The medium? These are the kinds of challenges and choices that we want to guide you through with this book.

AN INTERPRETIVE FRAMEWORK

After reading this book, you will be oriented in a set of different methodological approaches that can be drawn upon in a variety of different combinations, and with varying emphasis. For some research tasks, an approach that rests entirely on what is described in the chapter about qualitative text analysis might be sufficient. For other tasks, maybe a combination of social network analysis and digital ethnography will be the most suitable. To respond to other sets of research questions, one might be best off focusing on strategies described in the chapter about visual analysis, and so on.

We believe that – in research more generally, but particularly when studying something as dynamic, rapidly changing and socio-technical as digital media and society – methods must be used in creative and adaptive ways to best fit the object of study. More often than not, it is advisable to use mixed-methods approaches (discussed further in Chapter 2). As exemplified above, these may include a range of possible strategies, out of which we will introduce some useful ones throughout Chapters 5–10. While Chapters 5 and 6 introduce the more interpretive techniques of digital ethnography and qualitative text analysis respectively, Chapters 7 and 8 focus on some more computational approaches (to text and network analysis respectively). Chapters 9 and 10 focus on approaches to analysing visual content and the actual interfaces and infrastructures of digital platforms.

Two important points must be made here. First, that there are indeed significant overlaps between several of these approaches. To mention a couple of examples, visual analysis can be an aspect of digital ethnography, and social network analysis can be an important element in computational text analysis. Clearly, for pedagogical reasons, we introduce the approaches in separate chapters, but acknowledge, and actually embrace, the fact that they bleed together. In practice, as will be discussed in Chapter 2, we encourage the use of *methodological pragmatism* – a strategy which entails the researcher mixing and matching to combine a research strategy that best fits the task at hand, without feeling forced to adhere dogmatically to any particular 'school' of method. Second, it is important that we see the ethnographical approach from a two-fold perspective. On the one hand, *digital ethnography*, as a somewhat more narrowly described qualitative method for analysing digital media and society, is introduced in Chapter 5. In that sense, we see its set of tools and techniques as one of several methodological 'packages' that can be parts of a tailored mixed-methods combination. On the other hand, we propose a view where a broader ethnographic sensibility guides the entire research process, no matter which different methods are the parts of the chosen strategy at hand.

This idea – that an ethnographic mindset should guide the research, regardless of which specific method ('ethnographic' or not by actual name) – is key to this book. To distinguish between these two meanings of ethnography – (1) as a mindset for the entire research enterprise; (2) as the particular method of

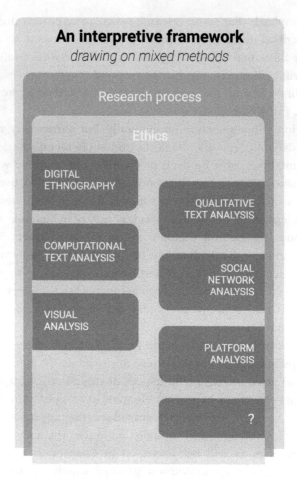

Figure 1.5 Elements in researching digital media and society

'digital ethnography' which is only one of many possible hands-on strategies for research – we will speak, on the one hand, of an *interpretive framework*, as in (1), encompassing all the methods that we introduce, and, on the other hand, of *digital ethnography*, as in (2), in Chapter 5. Figure 1.5 illustrates this.

As the figure shows, if we read it from the inside and out, research on digital media and society can draw on a number of different building blocks, as represented by the different approaches that this book introduces: digital ethnography (Chapter 5), qualitative text analysis (Chapter 6), computational text analysis (Chapter 7), social network analysis (Chapter 8), visual analysis (Chapter 9), and platform analysis (Chapter 10). The question mark in the lower-right corner of Figure 1.5 represents the fact that these methods – while common and useful – are not the only possible ones to use. They can be used, solely and in combinations (Chapter 2), both amongst each other and with other methods that are beyond the scope of this book.

We see these as hands-on methods, in the sense that they represent empirical and analytical approaches that are chosen by the researcher in their concrete work in exploring, mapping and analysing their object or area of study. As we will emphasise and introduce in this book, researching digital media and society – like doing any other research – demands elaborate thinking around issues of ethics (Chapter 4). Furthermore, as illustrated by the second outermost layer in the figure, any ethically guided hands-on methodological work must be set within the supporting structure of a research process (Chapter 3), which organises the empirical and analytical work according to a set of steps by which one advances from research questions to insights and results.

Finally, then, we see the entire research task as set within an interpretive framework – which means that we conceive of researching digital media and society as an enterprise aiming to achieve an understanding which is as rich as possible, drawing in strategic and fruitful ways on any possible tools that are at hand. Anthropologist Clifford Geertz wrote in his book *The Interpretation of Cultures* (1973) that the ultimate goal of the research is to provide a 'thick description' of the patterns, modes and functions of social life. The basic assumption on which this approach rests is that culture is 'semiotic' – it is made out of a complex set of symbols in the form of language, traits, customs, gestures, attitudes, actions, and so on, which are webbed together in systems 'within which they can be intelligibly – that is, thickly – described' (1973: 14). He wrote further:

> Ethnography is thick description. What the ethnographer is in fact faced with – except when (as, of course, he must do) he is pursuing the more automatized routines of data collection – is a multiplicity of complex conceptual structures, many of them superimposed upon or knotted into one another, which are at once strange, irregular, and inexplicit, and which he must contrive somehow first to grasp and then to render. [...] Doing ethnography is like trying to read (in the sense of 'construct a reading of') a manuscript – foreign, faded, full of ellipses, incoherencies, suspicious emendations, and tendentious commentaries, but written not in conventionalized graphs of sound but in transient examples of shaped behaviour. (1973: 9–10)

One of Geertz's key influences was the sociology of Max Weber (1922/1978: 4), which was focused on 'the interpretive understanding of social action' – on the subjective meanings that people attach to their social actions. Drawing on

Weber's idea of 'Verstehen' (understanding), according to which society should be analysed from a participatory and interpretive point of view, Geertz (1973: 5) famously stated:

> Believing, with Max Weber, that man is an animal suspended in webs of significance he himself has spun, I take culture to be those webs, and the analysis of it to be therefore not an experimental science in search of law but an interpretive one in search of meaning. It is explication I am after, construing social expressions on their surface enigmatical.

So, Geertz argues that ethnography is about analysing the meaning that people ascribe to their self-created 'webs of significance'. Similarly, Malinowski (1922: 9) said that ethnography should lay bare the unknown social and cultural principles that govern what previously seemed 'chaotic and freakish', 'sensational, wild and unaccountable'. As opposed to thin description, which just provides an account of facts, without interpreting them, thick description is characterised by specifying many details, the laying bare of conceptual structures, and the revelation of meanings. According to Geertz, it is the task of the ethnographer to not only present facts, but also to comment on and interpret them. The researcher must try to trace the ways in which meaning is ascribed. Against this background, it should be easy to see that ethnography – in terms of a broad interpretive framework – is highly relevant in researching digital media and society, not least because now, 'the Internet is the fabric of our lives' (Castells, 2002: 1).

As Figure 1.5 shows, we believe that researching the complexities of digital media and society demands an interpretive framework which is focused on issues of meaning-making, and on finding conceptual structures and social relationships. This then, once again, means to bring in strategies under the broader ethnographic umbrella, that are not conventionally associated with the ethnographic method. This is because – as we will also discuss in more detail in Chapter 5 – the notions of what actually constitutes the 'field' or 'the data' of ethnographic analysis are altered in digital society. This is in line with what Robert Kozinets has written about 'netnography'. In his writings about that approach, he argues that devising research methods for studying sociality online is about 'intelligent adaptation' and 'considering all options'. The root, he says, should be in the core principles of conventional ethnography, but researchers of digital media and society must also seek to selectively and systematically seize 'the possibilities of incorporating and blending computational methods of data collection, analysis, word recognition, coding and visualization' (2015: 79). We will argue in Chapter 2 that researching digital media and society should rely on methodological bricolage, and that it must move beyond any divisions between 'qualitative' and 'quantitative'. Kozinets would agree, and writes (2015: 53–54):

Consider that the images, words, Facebook profiles, Twitter hashtags, sounds and video files flowing through the Internet are composed of binary signals and various electromagnetically charged and uncharged blips of electrons and photons riding wires between various distant servers. Ultimately, they are zeroes and ones, already numerical and, in their own way, quantitative. We thus see fluidity and transferability, as analogue human experiences such as sitting and talking to a camera are transferred into digitally coded signals shared through a platform like Vine or YouTube, then decoded into densely pixelled moving images on screens and sounds emanating from speakers and headphones. This experience of audiencing can be captured as qualitative words and images experienced by a human listener and watcher, coded into fieldnotes or captured as a text file or visual screenshot, and immediately or subsequently optionally coded and transferred into a quantitative reading. Quant becomes qual becomes quant in this slippery shifting example.

CONCLUSION

In this first chapter, we have provided an introduction to this book and our ideas behind it. We have discussed, throughout the chapter, what it means to research digital media in a society that is mediatised to the degree that it is not always easy to see where different media begin or end. It is all complex and embedded. After giving a general outline of the parallel development of digital media technologies on the one hand, and digital media research on the other, we discussed the new data environment and some particular challenges that we face when researching digital media and society. Maybe the most important takeaway of this chapter is that technologies, society and research methods will all continue to change. Being a researcher of digital media and society means that you have to keep up and stay on your toes – open to new developments. We will talk about this flexible approach in chapters to come as well, so note this fact for now, as we will expand on it moving forward. The *methodological pragmatism* that we have begun to sketch out in this chapter, and its repercussions, are part of this. Any research method outlined in this book needs to be implemented in your study with care. The goal for your work should always be to stay creative, flexible and constantly informed. Your approach must always be adapted so that it fits your object of study (Chapter 3). Sometimes this will mean mixing methods (Chapter 2), and you must continuously re-evaluate your study as ethical issues arise (Chapter 4).

2
MIXING METHODS

Key Questions

- How can the researcher apply combinations of different methods in their studies of digital media and society?
- In what ways can methodological flexibility help us see things differently?
- What is triangulation, and how can it improve our research? What are its limitations?
- What benefits are there to applying a pragmatic approach to methods?

Key Concepts

the law of the instrument * mixed-methods research * multimodality * triangulation * methodological pragmatism * methods of the medium

It is a common view in research, particularly in the humanities and social sciences, that we should be flexible when it comes to the methods we choose in order to respond to the research questions that we wish to pose. One key idea, which is often reiterated in methods courses, is that we should decide on the research question first, and then choose the appropriate methods. This was formulated in the 1950s by sociologist Martin Trow who wrote that 'the problem under investigation properly dictates the methods of investigation' (1957: 33). And this does seem reasonable, no?

For example, if we want to analyse what people *feel* about gendered stereotypes on Instagram, it can be a good choice to use some form of qualitative, interpretive, method that allows for analysing what they write and say in more depth than sending out a questionnaire asking if they think Instagram is sexist: 'yes or no'. On the other hand, if we are looking to see which types of Instagram posts spread the fastest and furthest, it seems reasonable to choose a method which quantifies various measures of reach and virality. This latter research task would not demand any deeper form of analysis of the posts themselves. Yet again, if we are interested in *why* the posts that spread the most actually do so, we may want to look closer at the more fine-grained contents of the posts from a more interpretive, qualitative standpoint.

In this chapter, we will provide an introduction to how you can mix methods. While it is still common practice when teaching research methods to make a clear division between quantitative methods, such as surveys, and qualitative methods, such as interviews and observations, our argument is that there is much to gain from mixing methods. This goes for research more broadly, but is particularly pertinent when analysing digital media and society, which is a dynamic field where it can be especially challenging to capture enough of its complexity by using one single research method.

HAMMERS AND NAILS – THE LAW OF THE INSTRUMENT

While it is easily said that the thing we want to investigate should decide which method we choose, most researchers are still heavily reliant on the methods that they already know and use most often. If you have started to learn a particular method, and become skilled at it, it can be convenient, and easier, to continue to simply use that method over and over. But this can also mean that instead of looking for the most interesting and important research problems, we start looking for things that can be easily analysed using the methods we already know. And not only that. The risk is that we start to see and define our research problems in the terms that best fit our method of choice.

Let's say we face the research area of how disinformation spreads through social media, and we have become specialised in analysing emotions using sentiment analysis (see Chapter 7). Then, it is very likely that we start to think of disinformation as a whole in terms that we find fitting specifically for sentiment analysis. We might start looking for certain emotions in social media posts, and see those emotions as key to identifying how and where disinformation flows. Or, let's say that our speciality is within social network analysis (see Chapter 8) and we approach that same area of research: disinformation. In this case, we might begin to conceptualise how the spread of disinformation is a question of network relationships between different social media accounts. Or, if we are into visual analysis (see Chapter 9), we would instead be more likely to highlight the roles of imagery and memes in how disinformation propagates. Yet again, if we specialise in platform analysis (see Chapter 10), we might be prone to direct our research interest towards how the very architecture of the different interfaces of, say, X (formerly Twitter) and TikTok, impacts the spread of disinformation.

All of these different methodological pathways would very well work for producing some interesting studies, and relevant research results, no doubt! The point of these examples, however, is that in all of these cases it is the method, rather than an open mind that comes before the choice of method, which stipulates the focus of the study. To put it bluntly: just because the researcher knows network analysis, it does not mean that we need a network study of disinformation flows. We might! But it is not a given. Philosopher Abraham Kaplan wrote in the 1960s about what he called *the law of the instrument*, according to which a person that has a given instrument (read: research method) at their disposal, will start applying it to anything they face. Kaplan wrote:

> It comes as no particular surprise to discover that a scientist formulates problems in a way which requires for their solution just those techniques in which [they are] especially skilled. To select candidates for training as pilots, one psychologist will conduct depth interviews, another will employ projective tests, a third will apply statistical techniques to questionnaire data, while a fourth will regard the problem as a 'practical' one beyond the capacity of a science which cannot yet fully predict the performance of a rat in a maze. And standing apart from them all may be yet another psychologist laboring in remote majesty [...] on a mathematical model of human learning. (Kaplan, 1964: 28)

Many scholars have been concerned with this issue. Psychologist Silvan Tomkins wrote in a 1963 essay about computer simulations that there was a 'tendency of jobs to be adapted to tools, rather than adapting tools to jobs', and that 'if one has a computer with a storage capacity, but no feelings, one is more likely to concern oneself with remembering and with problem solving than with loving and hating' (Tomkins & Demos, 1995: 445). A recurring metaphor in many accounts of this tendency is that of hammers and nails, as formulated by psychologist Abraham Maslow in his 1966 book *The Psychology of Science*:

> I remember seeing an elaborate and complicated automatic washing machine for automobiles that did a beautiful job of washing them. But it could do only that, and everything else that got into its clutches was treated as if it were an automobile to be washed. I suppose it is tempting,

if the only tool you have is a hammer, to treat everything as if it were a nail. (Maslow, 1966: 15)

With this book, we want to encourage you to move beyond this narrow mindset when researching digital media and society. In Chapters 5–10, we will present six different tools – let's say a hammer, a wrench, a tape measure, a saw, a plier and a screwdriver (in any order). We hope that each component in this metaphorical toolkit will provide you with its own set of properties that might help you discover different parts of your research problem – because you may not only be dealing with nails that need to be removed with a plier, but also with enormous rusty bolts, tiles, boards, tubes, and so on. You might need to open up that toolkit in order to get to it all. So, basically, if you have more things than a mere hammer at hand, you might be able to treat the issues that arise with more nuance than by just taking out the hammer, and start banging away at whatever you see. Importantly, it's not about choosing the right tool before heading to the construction site. The key point here is that you often need to combine several tools in order to get the job done.

MIXED-METHODS RESEARCH

For quite some time now, mixing methods has been a specialisation in its own right. This scholarly area has its own journal – the *Journal of Mixed Methods Research* – and teaching textbooks that introduce students to it have been published before (Creswell & Plano Clark, 2017). While we may find scattered examples throughout the history of science of instances where researchers have combined different research methods, *mixed-methods research* is a more distinct methodological orientation that started to take shape and become more clearly defined during the 1980s (Creswell & Plano Clark, 2017: 3). In many accounts of mixed methods, especially the early ones, it was presented as a kind of third form of methods, alongside qualitative and quantitative ones. Simply put, the methodological landscape was presented as consisting of three choices: that of qualitative methods, that of quantitative methods, and that of a combination of the two. In line with this, very early efforts in the area of mixed-methods research were focused on trying to get mixed methods to be recognised and respected as one of three major research paradigms, rather than as an oddity on the side. This emerging orientation can therefore be seen as a kind of response to the dominance of the either-or of qualitative versus quantitative, and as a synthesis of ideas originating from the two. Mixed-methods literature offers many good ideas about the value of combining different methods, and about why we as researchers should try to do just that. In an early example, sociologist Tamotso Shibutani wrote about why it is important to maintain methodological flexibility in the face of a dynamic and changing social world:

> Societies, no matter how stable they may appear, are on-going things. The world is in a state of continuous flux, and as life conditions change, knowledge must keep pace. Crisis situations arise whenever new events are incomprehensible in terms of established assumptions. Existing expectations are violated; new sensitivities arise; and new ideas emerge to be tested. [...] Thus, the emergence of new hypotheses and their acceptance as part of a modified outlook is a social process. (Shibutani, 1966: 182)

Basically, as the world that we want to make sense of is ever-changing – something which might be particularly true when it comes to the transformative and rapidly changing character of digital media in society – it is key to realise that we must be correspondingly fluid and flexible when it comes to the research methods we choose. Between the two philosophical views that there are universal truths (as in quantitative methods), and that truths are multiple and relative (as in qualitative methods), the early forms of mixed methods were often aimed at trying to achieve a balance. That kind of mixed methods is not in any way groundbreaking or anarchic when it comes to producing knowledge about social reality, but rather quite simplistic. This means that mixed-methods proponents, in general, argue that there is something to be gained by using both qualitative and quantitative approaches within one and the same study. Even though the concept of 'mixed methods' was coined more recently, there were anthropologically oriented field studies of sociologists such as Lynd and Lynd, authors of the classic *Middletown* study (1929), and Hollingshead's study of *Elmtown's Youth* (1949), whose research analysed different communities through blends of qualitative and quantitative approaches.

Another key point in the prehistory of mixed-methods research is an often-cited article by psychologists Campbell and Fiske (1959) about what they called 'the multitrait–multimethod matrix'. In their late-1950s paper, which was in fact about analysing the psychological differences between individuals, the authors wrote about something called 'multiple operationalism'. They described this as an approach marked by *triangulation* – meaning that more than one method should be used and that the point of this was that results achieved through the different methods could validate each other. Basically, if both methods gave similar results, it strengthened the study as one could then know that the results were not those of any particular methodology. The goal, in other words, was that 'methods or apparatus factors' should not be allowed to impact on the research results (Campbell & Fiske, 1959: 104). In other words, using several different tools to analyse one and the same thing, and arriving at the same results, will better validate those results. As you can see, at this point in the history of mixed methods, the mixing as such was not really about being eclectic or playful with research methods, as in mixing a drink. It was rather about mixing in the sense of wearing progressive glasses, the benefit of which would be the ability to see clearly at different scales. A slightly less rigid definition of multiple operationalism was formulated by Eugene Webb and colleagues in the 1966 book *Unobtrusive Measures* where they explain that:

> Once a proposition has been confirmed by two or more independent measurement processes, the uncertainty of its interpretation is greatly reduced. The most persuasive evidence comes through a triangulation of measurement processes. If a proposition can survive the onslaught of a series of imperfect measures, with all their irrelevant error, confidence should be placed in it. Of course, this confidence is increased by minimizing error in each instrument and by a reasonable belief in the different and divergent effects of the sources of error. (Webb, 1966: 3)

What they say is that if we are 'combining different classes of measurement' (Webb, 1966: 30), or rather bombarding them with 'a series of imperfect measures', we will be able to be more confident in what we find. This means that our results will rely less on any single method, and it will be less important that the single method has imperfections, if we challenge the reality that we are studying with a variety of tools. Sometimes, one plus one doesn't just equal two. As we will discuss in the next section of this chapter, there is more to mixed methods than simply summing up method A and method B to some method A+B. In most cases, it is more exciting and motivating to go for more dynamic and experimental combinations, for example of different sub-methods within the big paradigms, and of more integrative combinations than is suggested in the mainstream mixed-methods literature.

MORE IS MORE

As we discussed above, the practice of combining several research methods within one and the same study is often used to try to mitigate any problems or biases that might come from using one sole research method. Sociologist Norman Denzin, who is the author of a range of books on research methods, directs our attention to four reasons why it is problematic to rely on just one method:

1 *Seeing things differently*. Denzin (1978: 292) argues that we must not conceive of the things that we research as being outside or external entities that we approach with a form of clinical distance. Rather, we must see the

things we study as 'social objects in the environment of the scientist'. When researching digital media and society it is, for example, quite likely that the scholar who is engaged in analysing a given social media platform will, at the same time, have a personal user profile on that same platform, where they also engage outside of their role as researcher. Many researchers use X (formerly Twitter) as their daily outlet, not only as part of communicating their research and work-related questions. Therefore, they may have stumbled upon important tweets, hashtags or people that they choose to include in their studies. Furthermore, even if that is not the case, the researcher is definitely part of the same society where their peers, to some extent, will engage with the platform in question, and part of the culture that gives the platform its meanings. Denzin explains that the objects that are studied are always part of the 'reality of the scientist' and that 'their meaning arises out of his or her experiences'. This embedded character of research and social reality demands that different methods are used. He writes:

> [E]ach method implies a different line of action toward reality – and hence each will reveal different aspects of it, much as a kaleidoscope, depending on the angle at which it is held, will reveal different colors and configurations of objects to the viewer. Methods are like the kaleidoscope: depending on how they are approached, held, and acted toward, different observations will be revealed. This is not to imply that reality has the shifting qualities of the colored prism, but that it too is an object that moves and that will not permit one interpretation to be stamped upon it. (Denzin, 1978: 292–293)

This is indeed key: just because we acknowledge that the social world is dynamic and fluid does not mean that 'anything goes' in terms of research methods. The point is, instead, that we always need multiple interpretations outside of our limited own interpretation.

2   *Seeing methods differently*. Another reason we should strive to rely on more than one research method is that every single method will always be used in different ways by different researchers. If, for example, two different scholars were to approach the same trending hashtag on Instagram, both using the same methodological literature in the area of visual analysis, we would still expect somewhat different results. This is because, as Denzin argues, each researcher will define the method in ways that will be unique to some extent. They would also have different ways of analysing the content due to their various understandings of the field, methods and theories within each respective approach. For example, say the two researchers are coming from the field of Political Science and Ethnology, respectively, they would be coloured by these academic traditions either way, especially through

which theories they use to make sense of the Instagram posts, and so on. Additionally, even if they were using the same method, they would still make different choices when it comes to sampling strategies, as to how rigid or fluid they would be in terms of how the analysis is carried out and documented, and in terms of what visual elements they would pay the most attention to. In the end, there will potentially be an 'endless variety of subtle differences' between the two studies (Denzin, 1978: 293).

3 *Being different researchers.* Yet another reason for using multiple methods is that we, as researchers, are different individuals. We have different points of reference, life histories, and views, and we will have our own individual idiosyncrasies and be in certain moods and modes when we carry out our analyses. If we are analysing lifestyle-focused influencers on Instagram, for example, our background and experience in relation to affluence, consumption, sustainability, body ideals and so on are likely to condition the study, through, for example, what we focus on, how we interpret it and, in the end, the results of our research.

In making this argument, Denzin points to a mid-20th century sociological community study in which Vidich and Shapiro found that results in a study of social prestige were biased by the researcher's background. While some of the community members were included in the study, others remained unknown, and the authors explained that 'the unknown group contains a disproportionate number of those with low prestige'. They wrote further about how 'the observer had made deliberate efforts to establish contact with lower prestige groups', but that their 'knowledge of community members was biased in favour of individuals with higher prestige' (Vidich & Shapiro, 1955: 31). Such patterns of selectivity, and selective association, of the researcher will impact on the possibility of reproducing research results. In other words, we can never count on the same method for producing identical results, which gives us yet another reason to strive to validate our interpretations by using more than one method.

4 *Being in a changing world.* A fourth and final reason for using multiple methods is, as Denzin (1978: 293) puts it, 'that the world of observations is in a state of continuous change'. This is especially true for those researching digital media and society, due to the ever-changing conditions of online platforms, their features and their users. Being a researcher in this ongoing shifting condition can be hard, especially if the platform you begin to research is suddenly morphing into something new, through the addition of new features – for example, when Facebook integrated the Reels function from its sister app Instagram, changing the features available for sharing visual content on the platform. Social reality is, as a whole, in a constant state of flux, meaning, for example, that analysing one and the same group

of people, using one and the same method, but in different periods of time or across various contexts, will produce different results. Staying flexible is key. This is especially true when it comes to the use of methods. By using several research methods, you are able to get a wider range of results, which will counterbalance any shortcomings that single methods may have in capturing the moment in time and space that you want to analyse.

All in all, it could be claimed that *more is more* when it comes to research methods. Of course, we should not use as many different methods as possible just for the sake of it, and the choices that we make when it comes to methodological combinations must be informed. The less-is-more approach, where we specialise in one single method and then use it for all intents and purposes, is frankly often not feasible.

TRIANGULATION

We have mentioned the notion of *triangulation* on a few occasions above, and it is indeed a key term when it comes to mixing methods. The word triangulation comes from the field of geometry, but refers in social and cultural research to the practice of using and combining different methods for research within one and the same study. Triangulation, as a concept, alludes to the idea of using multiple methods for the sake of validation, as discussed earlier. In geometry, if we have knowledge of two corners of a triangle, we can – given the right information – extrapolate the third. Similarly, in social science methodology, triangulation hints at the idea that if we have knowledge gained through two methods (i.e. two 'versions' of reality), we can extrapolate a more assured, third(!), point of knowledge. The idea behind practising triangulation is described in the following way by Cohen, Manion and Morrison (2018: 265):

> In its original and literal sense, triangulation is a technique of physical measurement: maritime navigators, military strategists and surveyors, for example, use (or used to use) several locational markers in their endeavours to pinpoint a single spot or objective. By analogy, triangular techniques in the social sciences attempt to map out, or explain more fully, the richness and complexity of human behaviour by studying it from more than one standpoint and, in so doing, by making use of both quantitative and qualitative data.

In other words, then, triangulation assumes – as we also discussed earlier – that there are generally two forms of method in the shape of qualitative and quantitative, and that mixing methods as such will then per definition be a combination of the two. The aim of this combination is to give a fuller picture or to cross-validate results by comparing them. In this book, however, we try to paint a less dichotomised picture of how methods should be understood and used.

As we introduced with Figure 1.1 in the first chapter of the book, we think of methods along a continuum and in a more integrative way. Indeed, the book involves both qualitative and quantitative approaches. Chapter 5 on digital ethnography, Chapter 6 on qualitative text analysis, and largely Chapters 9 and 10 on visual and platform analysis, are of the first kind; while Chapter 7 on computational text analysis, and Chapter 8 on social network analysis, are more of the latter sort. Our approach to mixing methods and triangulation in this book rests not on a view where there is always one qualitative and one quantitative component in the mix, but rather on the idea that methods vary on a continuum and are based on many other characteristics than whether they are 'qualitative' or 'quantitative'. We shall return to this kind of thinking, which is more integrative, and aims at mixing methods in more multifaceted ways, in the next section of this chapter.

Before we do so, however, it is worth noting that there are some good ideas in the literature about triangulation, that may be valid regardless of whether we are dealing in triangles, hexagons, squares or whatever. Denzin (1978: 294–304) offers a widely cited division of triangulation into four different types, which relate to strategies involving varieties of not only different forms of data, but of researchers themselves, of theories and of methodologies. The first type, *data triangulation*, refers to the possibility of using different data sources to respond to the same research question. This strategy has a connection to what has been discussed in terms of 'theoretical sampling' within the literature about so-called *grounded theory* methods. In the formative text for that field, its authors Glaser and Strauss explain that:

> Theoretical sampling is the process of data collection for generating
> theory whereby the analyst jointly collects, codes, and analyzes [their] data
> and decides what data to collect next and where to find them, in order
> to develop [their] theory as it emerges. This process of data collection is
> controlled by the emerging theory, whether substantive or formal. The
> initial decisions for theoretical collection of data are based only on a [...]
> general subject or problem area. (Glaser & Strauss, 1967: 45)

This strategy, whether we call it data triangulation or theoretical sampling, is about collecting data that we think may be useful in responding to our research question, and to then constantly evaluate if we need to explore other types of data, and if so which. Let us assume, for example, that a researcher embarks on a study of tweets using the #blacklivesmatter hashtag. While analysing these data, this researcher may find that a key pattern in their dataset seems to be that users are linking to a certain set of news articles. Depending on the research question, it may, in such a situation, be an option to – there and then – decide to also extend the data collection to those news sources. If, to extend the example, one was to find that interesting discussions were going on in the comment fields related to those news articles, or that certain TikTok memes were often mentioned in those news stories, it may also be relevant to extend data collection in one or two of those directions. As Denzin (1978: 295) writes: 'By selecting dissimilar settings in a systematic fashion, investigators can discover what their concepts (as designators of units in reality) have in common across settings'.

The second form of triangulation is that of *investigator triangulation*, which refers to when researchers work together based on the belief that their different perspectives will bring out different aspects of the object of study. It is fairly common in mixed-methods studies that different researchers take on the responsibility for the analytical work that relates to the method that they personally are specialising in. But it is a good idea, at least on some occasions during such a collaboration, to switch roles so that all researchers, regardless of specialisation, can become involved to some degree in interpreting the results produced through all methods used in the study. On the one hand, making interpretations may, to some extent, demand the particular methodological expertise in question. But, on the other hand, a researcher who is an outsider in relation to a given method may ask unexpected and exciting questions and force the expert collaborator to explain aspects of the method that may be taken for granted, but may still impact on the results.

In some methods literature, this kind of triangulation is discussed in terms of ensuring so-called intercoder reliability, which is usually done by involving more than one researcher to mitigate the effects of 'intraobserver disagreement or individual inconsistencies' (Krippendorff, 2004: 215). This reliability is important when several coders are involved in the process. For example, if several researchers were to manually code the same few hundred Instagram posts from famous 'outdoor brands', not all coders may be clear on how to decipher whether a picture of an individual on top of a snowy mountain was indeed depicting a person (1) hiking, (2) climbing, (3) mountaineering, or (4) skiing. These types of issues are important to sort out before starting the full coding process, and, often, a sample of the data is coded as a test, in order to see how different categories may be interpreted dissimilarly.

The third kind of triangulation is *theory triangulation*, meaning that one should ideally try to avoid a scenario where a small set of ideas guides the research. If we are too narrow-minded to begin with, we will collect data that relate only to a specific set of dimensions. Instead, Denzin argues that 'there would seem to be value in approaching data with multiple perspectives and hypotheses in mind' (1978: 297). This approach can be connected to the notion of 'theoretical sensitivity', as discussed by Barney Glaser (1978) and as developed by Lindgren (2020) in relation to digital research. This concept describes an approach based on an open relationship to theories, where we maintain great flexibility, and even eclecticism, when it comes to which theories we use.

First of all, to aim at theoretical sensitivity, we should try to start any research task having 'as few predetermined ideas as possible' (Glaser, 1978: 3). The point of this is that the researcher should be open to making new or unexpected discoveries when working through their data. In other words, rather than first selecting a theory and then viewing the data through the prism of that chosen theory, one should rather enter the field of research being as unbiased as possible by any interpretational terminology. When it comes to theoretical sensitivity, the key idea is that we should try to 'remain open to what is actually happening' (Glaser, 1978: 3), rather than to lock in on any fixed framework for understanding the object of study. As such, we should begin by being open to borrowing from others, by repurposing theories, as well as, frankly, inventing our own.

Sometimes we need to flip our preconceived notions all together and start to question what we thought we knew. Indeed, when 'the reality produced in research is more accurate than the theory whose categories do not fit' (Glaser, 1978: 4), we must first ask what our data themselves are telling us. In this way, research needs to stay flexible, and as a researcher, you need to stay open. Moving from theory to data, and back again, is essential here. And yes, sometimes frustrating. According to Glaser, there are different ways to accomplish this. One way to do this is through pure deduction, which is using data to confirm or disprove a predetermined theory. Another approach would be to analyse large amounts of data in an unsystematic manner and then describe the common-sense impressions gleaned along the way in suitable theoretical terms.

Another strategy for connecting theory and data is to develop a few major analytical categories systematically from the theoretical literature in the early stages of analysis and then proceed to describe them in detail with the aid of the data. Basically, this means deciding quickly on a set of headings and then seeing the rest of the analysed data strictly from that perspective. But this would not promote a theoretical sensitivity to the data itself. Instead, by analysing the data at hand, a theory would result, according to Glaser (1978: 16). Organising the ideas that emerge from the data, rather than the data itself, would aid a theoretical sensitivity to grow. Having arrived at a theoretical understanding, one may then use the data to illustrate the theory – regardless of whether the theory was developed by others, altered, or formulated in a new way (Lindgren, 2020: 150–151).

The fourth, final and most obvious kind of triangulation, in relation to the discussions thus far in this chapter, is *methodological triangulation*. It comes in two shapes, where the first one is *within-method triangulation* and the other is *between-method triangulation*. Within-method triangulation is used when the object of study is multidimensional, or, maybe more precisely – which is often the case when researching digital media and society – *multimodal*. As explained by Jewitt, Bezemer and O'Halloran (2016: 2), multimodality refers to the notion that the processes of meaning-making that we want to study do not have any strict 'division of labour' between different modalities (for example, images, writing, symbolism, sound, video effects, and so on). Rather, they say, we must study 'how different kinds of meaning-making are combined into an integrated, multimodal whole'. Basically, the analysis of a multimodal reality – a condition which has become 'more noticeable with the introduction of digital technologies' (Jewitt et al., 2016: 3) – demands the use of different variations of our methods. This can be achieved, to some degree, through within-method triangulation, where one might, for example, use different means and strategies within digital ethnography (see Chapter 5) to generate a richer picture of the context under study. This kind of triangulation is, however, seldom enough. Webb (1966: 35) emphasises this when stating that 'every data-gathering class', that is, every method, 'has specific to it certain validity threats'.

Because of this, it is most of the time recommended to turn to *between-method triangulation*, also referred to as 'across-method triangulation'. This is a more fully realised form of methodological triangulation which 'combines dissimilar methods to measure the same unit' (Denzin, 1978: 302). Different methods will have different strengths and weaknesses, and if we combine different methods, several strengths will be leveraged while the effects of weaknesses will be counterbalanced. Denzin (1978: 303–304) introduces four principles of this kind of methodological triangulation:

1   *Considering the research problem.* In deciding how to triangulate methods, one must always start from the research questions and from the issues that one intends to analyse. If we look, for example, to assess the emotional expression in TikTok posts, it would be reasonable to use some form of combination of visual analysis (Chapter 9) and qualitative text analysis (Chapter 6). If the study also wants to say something about emotional patterns and their spread at an overarching level, across a large number of posts, it would be advisable to employ forms of computational text analysis (e.g. sentiment analysis; Chapter 7) to assess emotional language, and social network analysis (Chapter 8) to map the spread. Starting from the research problem, and what we want to respond to, in this way will lead the researcher to draw on different combinations of methods in different ways, in different studies. Clearly, in some cases, the main emphasis will be on one or a couple of the methods, with the other ones fulfilling a complementary role, while in other cases there may be a more equal balance between the methods used.

2   *Considering the chosen methods in relation to each other.* When choosing
    the methods that we want to use in combination, choices should be
    made that take into account the various weaknesses and strengths of the
    different methods. Quite obviously, if one of our methods is better suited to
    interpreting the richer cultural meanings assigned to the TikTok posts, it is
    more likely that a method that catches breadth and spread rather than going
    deeper by interpreting meaning-making, will be a better complement than a
    method that is more similar to the first one, and so on.

3   *Considering the theoretical relevance of the methods.* The methods selected
    should be chosen with their varying forms of theoretical relevance in mind.
    As Denzin (1978: 303) explains, methods that have a broader and more
    quantitative focus 'are well suited to studying stable patterns of interaction',
    while more interpretive and qualitatively oriented methods are better at
    revealing 'interactions in their most complex forms'. Naturally, if we want to
    test a hypothesis about how TikTok posts spread based on their emotional
    content, we will need a method of the former type, while the latter type of
    method would better grasp the details and nuances of the responses to the
    emotions expressed. On the one hand, then, we should try to choose the
    methods that are the most appropriate for enabling the theoretical analysis
    that we aim to do. On the other hand, there is also sometimes value in
    'combining methods that initially seem inappropriate, much as contradictory
    theoretical propositions are brought to bear upon the same data' (Denzin,
    1978: 303). In other words, if we use unexpected methods, we may be able
    to bring out unexpected results.

4   *Continuously revising the methodological strategy.* Finally, it is important to
    always remember that when we start playing around with methods like this,
    we will have to think of innovative ways of deciding whether our research
    results are valid or not. There are already quite clear criteria in place, both
    for how to assess if a quantitative survey study is robust, and for assessing
    the rigorousness of a process of qualitative data analysis and interpretation.
    When we mix methods, sometimes even using just bits of methods, the
    nature of the considerations to be taken in these respects, changes. The
    practice of triangulation will take on a different form in each particular
    research project, which, by necessity, means that the methodological design
    is continuously modified and reinvented. As Denzin (1978: 304) puts it, this
    kind of research 'reflects the emergent, novel, and unpredictable features
    of ongoing activity'. As a consequence of this, researchers must remain
    flexible throughout the research process (see further Chapter 3), and
    maintain an openness to constantly re-evaluate their chosen methods in the
    face of the possibility that some major reconsiderations and changes to the
    methodological make-up of the study will need to be made.

Triangulation, thus, is a dynamic activity with lots of potential. It demands more work than relying on singular, ready-made methods, but can also bring many advantages. As researchers, we can often be more confident in our results if they have been arrived at through triangulated methods. Furthermore, the approach outlined above naturally drives the researcher in more innovative directions, as different methodological combinations will demand different, often creative, ways to collect data. As a consequence, data will be richer, while, at the same time, the combination of different methods – grounded in different theoretical traditions – will stimulate integrating and making connections between disparate theories (Jick, 1979). At best, if we arrive at largely different insights depending on the method of the moment, triangulation will help reveal contradictions that urge us to revise our research questions, or to pose different ones altogether.

METHODOLOGICAL PRAGMATISM

Thus far in this chapter, we have been writing about quite modular ways of combining methods, maybe even without truly mixing them. As you have seen above, the idea of triangulation, which sits at the centre of mixed-methods literature, sees methods as different elements in a setup where the weaknesses of one method are mitigated by the strengths of others, and so on. However, in all such combinations, the main point is that different methods contribute with different perspectives on one and the same object of study (Hammersley, 1996; Bruhn Jensen, 2012). In fact, most mixed-methods designs, described in methods textbooks, are sequential (doing one method at a time) rather than concurrent (Morse, 2003). We believe, however, in moving in the direction of mixed-methods approaches that are more open to integrating methods more fully, rather than combining them while still seeing them as fully separate.

Imagine, for example, that we collected a dataset of Facebook Reels from a specific advertiser, and we wanted to see how Facebook users respond to these ads by posting comments. At the beginning stages of this research, we might be fully interested in analysing the textual elements available in the comments section alone. In this work, we start to notice how the comments section is responding to, and politicising, content within the videos themselves, by connecting the visual elements in the videos to political issues and movements. This might mean that our textual analysis (see Chapter 6) of Facebook posts becomes much more multimodal, by incorporating visual analysis (see Chapter 9). Also, we might have to expand our understanding of how digital political action works in intertextual ways, where certain bits become incorporated, remixed and reimagined by users in different ways. Maybe a multimodal critical discourse analysis (MCDA) would fit the part (see Chapter 9).

In the preface to an early book on researching the internet, Steve Jones (1999: x) wrote that 'we are still coming to grips with the changes that we feel are brought about by networked communication of the type so prominently made visible by the Internet'. Actually, this is still the case. Research on digital media and society has continued to be a trading zone between conventional academic approaches and disciplines – it is truly transdisciplinary. In their book about 'internet inquiry', Annette Markham and Nancy Baym (2009: xiv) explain that:

> While most disciplines have awakened to an understanding of the importance of the internet in their fields, most do not have a richly developed core of scholars who agree on methodological approaches or standards. This absence of disciplinary boundaries keeps internet studies both desirable and frustrating.

This frustration, they argue, makes researchers of digital society push the boundaries of 'disciplinary belonging' in ways that most academic research would benefit from doing more of. Furthermore, they write that, as very few internet researchers have been specifically trained in how to do it well, one is by necessity forced to actively and critically navigate a landscape of old and new methods, in order to seek out ways of engaging with data that suit one's particular project. In other words, researching digital media and society can be seen as calling for particularly integrated and innovative methodological mixes. It is seldom workable in this field to simply apply previously existing methods – and theories, for that matter. Some perspectives and approaches can most likely be, and have also, to some extent, been repurposed for digital media research – for example, survey methods and interviews. But one must remember that the internet, and its networked social tools and platforms, is in many ways a different research context, possessing an 'essential changeability' that demands a conscious shift of focus and method (S. Jones, 1998: xi).

Because of this, researching digital media and society often demands that the person carrying out the data collection and analysis is even more critical, and more reflective, than what is already demanded by scholarship in general. The specific challenges of doing digital social research have, Markham and Baym (2009: vii–viii) argue, 'prompted its researchers to confront, head-on, numerous questions that lurk less visibly in traditional research contexts'. One such issue is the urgent need to address the longstanding dispute in social science between 'qualitative' and 'quantitative' methodological approaches, which has persisted, apparently unresolvable, for more than a century. Among researchers, there are still traces of a battle between case-oriented interpretive perspectives on the one hand, and variable-oriented approaches focused on testing hypotheses on the other. Scholars who prefer case-oriented methods will argue that an in-depth understanding of a smaller set of observations is crucial for grasping the complexities of reality, and those who prefer variable-oriented approaches will argue that only the highly systematised analysis of larger numbers of cases will allow scholars to make reliable statements about the 'true' order of things.

Today, however – as should be clear from the discussions in this chapter – there is an increasingly widespread consensus that the employment of combinations of 'qualitative' and 'quantitative' methods is a valid and recommended strategy, which allows researchers to benefit through triangulation from their various strengths and balance their respective weaknesses. The 'qualitative' tradition is seen as the more inductively oriented, interpretive study of a small number of observations, while the 'quantitative' tradition is characterised by the deductively oriented statistical study of large numbers of cases. This has given rise to the common notion that 'qualitative' research produces detailed accounts through close readings of social processes, while 'quantitative' research renders more limited, but controllable and generalisable, information about the causal relations and regularities of the social and cultural fabric.

When using our book as a toolbox for researching digital media and society, and combining its different approaches, we believe that the best strategy is *methodological pragmatism*, focusing, in the vein of Denzin's principles introduced earlier, on the problem to be researched, and on what type of knowledge is sought. Instead of engaging in methodological positioning within the existing field of methods literature, one can instead, as Denzin and Lincoln (1998: 3) have written, conceive of one's research strategy as a form of *bricolage*. They explain this further as 'a pieced together, close-knit set of practices that provide solutions to a problem in a concrete situation [...] It is a contraction that changes and takes new forms as different tools, methods, and techniques are added to the puzzle'.

Bricolage is a French term – popularised by cultural anthropologist Claude Lévi-Strauss (1966) – which refers to the process of improvising and putting pre-existing things together in new and adaptive ways. From that perspective, our research method is not fully chosen beforehand, but rather emerges as a patchwork of solutions – old or new – to problems faced while carrying out the research. As critical pedagogy researcher Joe Kincheloe (2005: 324–325) observes: 'We actively construct our research methods from the tools at hand rather than passively receiving the "correct," universally applicable methodologies', and we 'steer clear of pre-existing guidelines and checklists developed outside the specific demands of the inquiry at hand'. So, developing your method pragmatically, as a bricolage, means placing your specific research task at the centre of your considerations, and allowing your particular combination and application of methods to take shape in relation to the needs that characterise the given task.

CONCLUSION

In this chapter, we have introduced our thinking when it comes to mixing methods. We have discussed, first, the importance of not letting any favourite methods that one might have decide the research question. Even though it may be natural that we specialise in certain approaches, we must always make sure that the research question, rather than the method as such, is at the centre of the research process (see Chapter 3). Second, we have provided an introduction to some general ideas and practices in the area of mixed-methods research more broadly. We introduced some of the good reasons for using more than one single method, and explained how such strategies have conventionally been seen in terms of triangulation. This means using two, or maybe more, methods, and somehow weighing the results of the different methods together. While this may be a functioning approach, we have also, finally, encouraged you to think more freely, and pragmatically, in mixing and matching different methodological approaches, with a vision that maybe methodological combinations can be further integrated than what is the case in straightforward triangulation. So now, as we have both introduced the general field of researching digital media and society, and have worked through a conceptual discussion of what mixing methods can entail, it is time to move on to the next chapter of this book, wherein we will engage in more hands-on discussion of how to plan and carry out your research.

3

THE RESEARCH PROCESS

Key Questions

- What are the general steps of the research process?
- How can the researcher move from a general idea about what to study towards formulating a workable question to guide the research?
- Which is the best strategy for deciding on a unit or field of study – or several units and fields – and how might they be effectively delimited?
- What are some of the most important challenges faced by the researcher in gathering data to form the basis for empirical analysis?
- What are the key elements of data analysis?

Key Concepts

emergent research questions * multi-sited research * researching sites, topics, and people * logging your research process

As we have argued in the previous chapter, we see research on digital media and society as benefitting from drawing on a variety of different methodological approaches. The complexity of digital society and culture – as well as the multitude of differently composed platforms through which they exist – makes it both useful and necessary to be open and eclectic when it comes to choosing one's methodological strategy for approaching a given research task or project. Despite this, however, there are some key elements that tend to be part of any research process. These elements include the broad steps by which one progresses from the initial ideas to a completed study. This includes formulating a research question, delineating the field of study, collecting data, as well as analysing and interpreting it. In this chapter, we provide an overview – alongside some discussion – of such general steps. As will become clear throughout the book's different chapters, however, these steps, and particularly that of the actual analysis, take rather different shapes depending on the methods that are chosen.

This chapter will give you a hands-on approach for how to begin the journey of researching digital media and society. This framework may help you before you even begin choosing your methodological approach (in Chapters 5–10), and provide you with an orientation, inspiration and guidance as to what kind of methodological meat this structural skeleton can be used to uphold. This present chapter provides you with a fairly step-by-step discussion of the research process. In doing so, it focuses on the broader issues that relate to (1) formulating good research questions that will form a solid basis for your continued study – regardless of the actual method chosen to respond to them; (2) choosing your data and collecting it – which will be reliant on your choice of methods; and (3) analysing and interpreting it to arrive at the final research results.

WHERE DO YOU EVEN BEGIN?

One of the most important parts of the process is knowing what to look for. How will you be able to find it, and ultimately study it, if you don't know what 'it' is yet? This process of familiarising yourself with your field of study – whether it be a specific platform, a Facebook group, a hashtag – is initially about letting yourself get immersed in the material itself. And you need to do this carefully: give it time, figure out what it is you want to study, before deciding what data you will be collecting and how you will analyse it. More than once, both authors of this book have collected data that were missing some important components. Take, for example, a study of the tweets using specific hashtags on X (formerly Twitter) during a terrorist attack. What if you decide too quickly which hashtags to use in your searches and data downloads, based on the tweets you have read in your own personal X (formerly Twitter) feed, and miss out on one specific hashtag that was just as well-used, and just as important as the others that you have included in your study? Well, you can always collect more data later. This is perfectly fine as well, as sometimes we have to be open to research functioning as a pendulum – a movement back and forth between the data and the analysis. But if you can, try to avoid jumping too quickly into the data collection before finding out what you should be looking for.

Ultimately, you need to know what you want to know more about, and then start thinking about how best to study it. One of the most important things here, in the beginning stages of research, is just that – finding out what you are looking for. In Chapter 4, we will talk more about how important previous knowledge can be for being able to study something. While students might feel like their individual research ideas, based on their own digital practice and knowledge, is too simple for a research paper, it can be very helpful to have an immersive, lived experience of the context that you are going to ana- lyse. For example, if you are a student in Library and Information science, you might notice that your TikTok's 'For You' feed is full of 'BookTok' content, and this might interest you also as a field of study, in terms of how social media affordances may shape book reviews and connect users as part of finding net- worked connections. But some students may be surprised when such ideas are suggested by teachers, as if their relationship to the field is in itself unscien- tific, and would make them too biased, too immersed. Honestly, digging where you stand often just saves you a lot of time and energy. Instead of needing to relearn platforms, connections and communication patterns for a research paper, you are already 'in the know'. You are embedded in what you study, much like an ethnographer.

It is all about knowing the field. And familiarising yourself with a new field can take time. We will talk more about digital ethnography in Chapter 5, but this is basically what ethnographic fieldwork looks like in practice. This means taking a holistic and an interpretive approach to whatever aspect, dimension or charac- teristic of digital society you want to study. Drawing on different forms and levels of observing, taking part in, experimenting with, discovering and mapping your object of analysis, are a vital part of the strategy.

But research doesn't always begin in the same way. You may become inter- ested in your specific research idea for a number of different reasons. It can be empirical (finding a digital space that you want to explore), theoretical (reading theory and becoming interested in finding ways to test it through an empirical case study) or methodological (wanting to practically explore the use of a particu- lar method). Because of this, it is important to let different parts of your overall education guide you in ways that connect the literature you have read in differ- ent courses and to channel that knowledge into your own research project. In this process, do not be afraid to let your interests guide you. Being interested is a good motivator not only for designing your studies, but it also helps you keep going in actively doing the work of producing a finished project from that initial research idea.

Research is creative. We don't mean this in an artistic sense. But it is a con- tinuous work to adjust and find solutions to the many different issues that arise all throughout the research process. Research does not happen on its own. You yourself have to be the driving force through each step. So take that role seriously and let yourself be the guide. And remember that this can mean weaving your own personal interests and dispositions into the research, and letting these things guide you forward – just as long as you are also willing to rethink and question your own work throughout the process.

When you attempt to pin down what your study should be about, you must rely on literature to guide you. Many of the questions that students first start posing have already been answered many times over, in different studies and in different ways. This is why reading the literature not only in your own field, but also in surrounding areas, can be crucial at this stage. Look at any studies that have been published on your specific sub-topic before, and try to make your own focus specific! Let's say you are interested in finding out how local neighbourhood Facebook groups can facilitate spaces for communicating during ongoing wildfires. Now let's see what has already been done on this. Search for studies that have researched local neighbourhood Facebook groups (on any topic) – what are they often used for, how do they work, are they an essential part of the ongoing community communication, in what ways may they facilitate social interaction and make for better community spirit? Then, direct your attention to the scholarly work on digital forms of communicating during wildfires, regardless of platform. What research has been done on this specific form of crisis before, specifically in online settings? Facebook can be one such setting that may or may not have been studied before. Maybe all of the work that has been written on this has used X (formerly Twitter) as its main focus. If that is the case, that is in and of itself interesting. You might be on to something – you might have found a gap in the research that you may attempt to fill!

We researchers often talk about such 'gaps'. But beware of trying to find a gap simply for the gap's sake. Instead, try to be in conversation with previous studies rather than desperately trying to complement them with a study that has not been made before. You should focus on making your contribution – so what should it be? You might have to question yourself at this stage before moving on. Because, why should you look at Facebook groups anyway? Maybe people don't even use them that much during a crisis? Maybe not, so try and find out! What does the literature say about this? Can you find the latest statistics from other sources showing the numbers of daily users or their interaction patterns on Facebook, in order to see if the platform itself is even relevant nowadays? Take another look at that literature you began reading about Facebook groups: which years is it from? 2011–2014? That is indeed some years ago now. This might be your first doubting moment, and that is a good sign. It means you are on to something, and maybe you are able to use that momentum to strive even further.

You have thus far only looked at 'wildfires', but try also to lift your analytical view to understand this more broadly. What other forms of crises may have been researched in these ways: floods, tsunamis, earthquakes, pandemics? Start looking beyond the scope of what you have chosen as your specific subject and try to find connections with other contexts that may be more or less similar. At this stage, you might want to consider that 'crisis', rather than 'wildfire', is your analytical concept here, and that your study looks at 'crisis communication' specifically. Now that's an entire field to jump into, head first. Next, you may find yourself overwhelmed with the amount of studies, theories and positions that reside within this discipline. What are the essential studies that have been undertaken here? What theories are seminal in this field? This can take time – and you should let it. You are not supposed to rush to any conclusions or assumptions here too quickly.

Having trouble finding the literature? This seems to be a problem for some of our students. Of course, it can be hard finding studies that are relevant to your specific topic, but take comfort in the fact that doing this work may take time, and that some patience and effort must go into framing and delineating one's research focus. Talk to your teacher and ask for advice. Ask your local university librarian for similar studies that you could use. Ask a friend who recently graduated in an adjacent field that may have done course work on something similar. Maybe they can help you.

As a student, it may also be good to know that many published academic articles are paywalled, which means that they aren't but a Google search away. In fact, university libraries pay a lot of money to provide their staff and students with digital access to academic journals. You can start out by visiting the webpage of your university library and entering a fitting search phrase for the study you are trying to find: maybe the author name and specific words in the title. Find it? You might not be able to read the full study just yet. In most cases, you will have to log in with a university ID to access the paper, since only then are you verified via the university library that you are a part of this institution and have a right to access this paper through the licences that they have authorised for you. Find it now?

Furthermore, all academic journals may not be covered by the licences that your specific institution holds, and this is a cost issue, and a serious one. Let us not begin ranting here about the state of academic publishing, but licences are expensive, and not all institutions are able to afford all of them. While many papers have begun to be published freely available through open-access deals with publishing companies, these deals are also very expensive, especially for underfunded scholars or their institutions. This affects students, scholars and university libraries, in manifold ways. Don't worry! Honestly, most scholars are aware of these inequalities of publishing within academia, and often you are able to find papers in other ways. Do you have a network of other researchers on social media? Ask for help accessing the paper! Do you have a friend studying at another institution? Ask if they have access! Doesn't work? Just find the email address of the author of the paper, tell them about your project, and ask if they might send it to you.

A TOPOLOGICAL MAP

Depending on what you want to analyse, which questions you aim to answer, and what types of claims you want to ultimately be able to make, your research process will vary. We hope students will approach their chosen field of study as exploratively and consistently as an ethnographer would an ethnographic field-work practice, in the beginning stages of your research, no matter which of the methods you ultimately end up choosing (as outlined in Chapters 5–10). Robert Kozinets (2015: 101) writes:

> Are you ready to begin a netnographic research project? Pull that smartphone out of your purse or pocket. Flip open your laptop or uncover your handy dandy tablet. Double tap that app. Type some keywords into that search engine, pick your site and you should be good to go. You are just a few clicks away from finding a fabulously free-flowing online conversation about just about anything. And then you are off, entering the wonderful world of netnography.
> Or maybe not.

Or maybe not? The truth is that sometimes you need to reassess or redirect your focus once you have started to understand what this context you are studying is all about. You might begin with an idea that seems like a perfect plan – at first. Then you realise that it was something completely different than what you were actually looking for, and not at all as perfect as you believed at first glance. This is all part of the research process. Adjusting the scope of the study, or rethinking your analytical concepts, your theoretical framework or your whole field of research, are all part of the game.

When we have learned how to respond to crucial questions about the who, what and where, we also need to start reflecting on the how. We will look closer at Kozinets' approach in an upcoming chapter (5), but what is important for the time being is his notion that one must have a general sense of the response to such questions, rather than having things set in stone. Research needs to be fluid and adaptive to the detours that (surely will) arise. It is argued by danah boyd that one's methods should be a customised, evolving set of approaches and strategies. The main goal is to get a holistic picture of the object of analysis. She writes:

> Ethnographers use different techniques to interpret, complicate, and analyze cultural practices, situate complex cultural phenomena, and map social worlds from the bottom up. As a method, ethnography does not speak to individual traits or beliefs but to the complexity and interconnectedness of culturally driven practices and norms. Ethnography

produces a topological map of a particular set of cultural practices. (boyd, 2008: 46–47)

So the thing that the researcher should aim for is just that, a *topological map*. And to capture it, one must rely on a set of different techniques to analyse and situate the data. This is why the concept of 'methodological bricolage', discussed in Chapter 2, is so useful. It is all about being pragmatic and adaptive. Anthropologist Tom Boellstorff (2010: 129) also agrees that the research method for any project is constantly renegotiated and transformed. He writes:

Any claim that a particular method is the best (or the only valid) method [...] misses how research always involves a coming-together of research question and methodology. How one conducts research is not determined by some essential property 'out there;' it is determined by the research questions that one wants to investigate.

So, once again, even though we believe that the ethnographic approach is very well suited to unravel how digital society – or part of it – functions, the emerging data environment (see Chapter 1), as well as the complexity of social life, demand that one considers multiple methodological techniques to broaden the investigation. Such techniques will be further presented in Chapters 5–10.

FRAMING THE FIELD

The next step is to decide what constitutes the core unit of study. Then you need to start asking yourself: which setting, which group or which individuals will you study, and what are your delimitations in space and time? Basically, how should you frame your 'fieldsite'? The concept of fieldsite will be discussed in more depth in Chapter 5, but for now it suffices to say that it is a name for the context you want to study. Here, it is important to reflect upon not only which fieldsites may be important, but also their social contexts and relations to other fieldsites, including non-digital ones. Kozinets (2015: 118) writes:

[...] a research topic can be considered to be manifesting in a widely dispersed manner among a wide number of online and offline social experiences. A site such as a Star Trek or Samsung Galaxy wiki can seem at first glance to be a straightforward single location. [...] However, [...] my interest in a particular topic, such as Star Trek fandom, drew me to a variety of sites or groups. Sometimes, certainly, my entire study stayed on one site such as alt. coffee, but this was as much topical as it was a response to the relative concentration of the early Internet prior to the explosion of blogs and other social media forms. (Kozinets, 2015: 118)

This relates to the need to emphasise the 'non-digital-centricness' in your own research, as Pink and colleagues (2016) have referred to it. Since platforms, their users (the individuals or groups themselves) and their platform interactions (norms and vernaculars) change and develop, we shouldn't get too narrow in our understanding of these spaces. Instead, we need to take a broader approach to understanding what is going on, by accounting for the overall changes in society, including the changing norms and political practices of everyday individuals. In fact, seeing the digital as something completely different from the society that has shaped these fields, is somewhat of an old concept in this day and age. Our social worlds are highly entangled with the digital through our communication mediums, to the point where they can no longer be understood as separate. Such de-centring of the media itself as the focus of the study allows ethnographers to see these digital media expressions as inseparable from the social worlds they relate to.

Sometimes the field is actually several different fields, both on- and offline. For example, boyd (2008: 54) developed a 'multi-sited project' where her field-site, in practice, was a network of several different sites. In her case, these sites were both online and offline, which is quite often the case. It is common that the analysis of social things on the internet will urge the researcher to look for information in non-internet places as well in order to get a more complete picture. Furthermore, it can indeed be helpful to think about how we delimit and define our fieldsite – the boundaries between sites both on- and offline, and between online and offline as such, are perpetually unstable. Because of this, many studies end up encompassing both of these dimensions. As in boyd's case, the researcher may move between the online and the offline simply by following the field where it leads them.

Formulating the Research Questions

The research process, in most kinds of inquiry, tends to be iterative and reflexive, which leads to revisions of the choices that have been made, sometimes several times. But thinking about your research questions is a good place to start. Deciding on a research question, or a set of questions, is a fundamental and consequential part of the research process, and needed in order to get started. This is because it is the decision from which most other challenges and choices throughout the research will follow. Once the research questions are in place, at least some initial and preliminary ones, data collection can be started, guided by that question.

In order to arrive at your research questions, it is a good idea to start with some more overarching questions and drill down from there. Broad questions about the general area in which we take an interest will help us to explore the setting or topic we are interested in. Discussing her ethnographic work on youth and social media, boyd (2008: 44) reflects upon how her research question was repeatedly revised during the research process:

> My ongoing interest in identity, privacy, impression management, and social interaction shaped where I began, but my fieldwork also led me to explore other topics. While I had grown up at a particular point in the history of the Internet, it was tremendously rewarding to be able to watch a new generation of teenagers embrace an entirely different set of circumstances and technologies. I was well positioned to watch the phenomenon of teen engagement with social network sites unfold and I used that to my advantage. MySpace became popular with teens just as I began my fieldwork. I did not initially intend to focus on social network sites, but as teens turned their attention to these sites, so did I.

So, research questions are emergent. It is common that one starts off a project with a set of questions that are subsequently revised so that one comes out the other side with a quite different set of questions from the ones that were there at the beginning. You need to be adaptive here. If you fail to adapt the questions, the research will suffer. Sometimes we come across students who are so set on their initial questions that the resulting study does not compute.

While part of this process is about going along with the field, as boyd did, another part is about looking carefully at any previous research that has been done in this or related areas. Doing a literature review allows you to get a good picture of the domain to which you want to make a contribution, and mapping the state of the field will help sharpen your research interests. Boellstorff and colleagues (2012: 55) encourage researchers to 'just plunge in and start reading'. It's a good starting point for any research project, to get familiarised not only with the empirical field but with the field of research itself. Remember to think historically too about studies in related – even pre-digital – fields that may be relevant to frame your own work, and to think widely and to explore studies from less obvious parts of the research landscape.

Try to formulate your research question clearly: What is it that you want to study? Try writing it out and see how it lands. Sometimes, a good strategy can be to not focus on the full question, but on the words instead. Simply make a list of words that you are thinking about, in terms of the platforms, data and analytical concepts that you are interested in using. Through this list, you can add and retract words that might relate to the same concepts, be redundant in the larger scheme of things, and ultimately you may end up with a few 'finalists' in the word challenge. This becomes your first attempt at narrowing down your research focus. With this list, you can pick the most important concepts, and sometimes this process can surprise you! You might realise you hadn't completely figured out the difference between the concepts 'platforms' and 'media ecology', and you might have to do some more reading in order to narrow things down further. Or you may find that, even though you have been really interested in 'user practices on X (formerly Twitter)', the users might not be the most important concept in your list. Try out different combinations until you are satisfied – for now! It will likely change again. It's all part of the process, and staying curious will help you move forward. The general idea is to arrive at the research question through exploration. Look around, test ideas, discard some and hold on to others. However, this openness should not be mistaken for 'wandering around aimlessly', as having an adaptive approach still means that your work must be purposive.

What, how, why, where, who… Such basic question words can be just as tricky as the theoretical and analytical concepts. Try to use such words when narrowing down the aspects of the object of study that you are interested in exploring. For example, if you are interested in a specific online discussion group, or the group members, or their speech acts or discourses, you might be getting closer to finding the right question word to match the focus of your study. Narrowing down the field may also help you better understand what your question word may be. Kozinets (2015) suggests specifying which *sites*, *topics* or *people* are investigated in your study:

- Sites, then, are locations – any kind of social site, geographically, culturally or notionally. These are the places where people's social worlds take root and it is the job of the ethnographer to map them. Research into such sites responds to questions of *where*.
- Topics are conceptual, rather than spatial, and are related to language, knowledge, information and meaning. Focusing on topics helps the researcher respond to questions of *what*.
- People are what we analyse when we want answers to questions about *whom*.

Many of the phenomena that we study in digital society are relatively novel, emergent, and shift in their character, which demands that the researcher is prepared to modify questions based on what is encountered throughout the study. Back in the 1920s, anthropologist Bronislaw Malinowski (1922: 9) argued that the work of the ethnographer (just like that of any researcher) is 'worthless' unless they are prepared to be ungrudgingly casting any determination to prove certain hypotheses aside 'under the pressure of evidence'. So, the research question is often formulated iteratively throughout as 'an emergent process of discovery' (Boellstorff et al., 2012: 54).

It can be useful to think of one's research in relation to concepts and divisions such as these. Not only is it necessary to be able to break down and describe the research process to others afterwards in a comprehensible way, but it is also good to gain perspective on one's own relationship to the object of study, because, in practice, the levels and dimensions float into one another. Reflecting on this, boyd (2008: 55) describes her process:

> Instead of starting with one bounded site, I decided to approach my field site as a network. I focused my study on the intersection of American teenagers, their relationship to networked publics, and, in particular, the sociotechnical phenomenon marked by the rise of social network sites. I began my fieldwork from different angles and traversed the phenomenon using different approaches. My fieldwork includes mediated and unmediated environments and I moved across different social contexts and engaged with different relevant social groups to gain an understanding of what was taking place. Approaching this puzzle, I began broadly and narrowed my focus as I achieved clarity. As appropriate, I expanded my scope when following specific people or trying to make sense of specific spaces. This created many layers of awareness that allowed me to locate people, spaces, and practices in a broader context.

Research questions can be formulated on different levels of abstraction, and they can be more or less specific. Drawing on the previous chapters in this book, one can imagine a wide range of questions that would be interesting, relevant and important to study, as parts of the wider inquiry into digital society. One such question is: In what different ways are emotions and social support expressed in open and anonymous forums as compared to in closed and non-anonymous ones? Another one is: What parts of their everyday lives are people most likely to share with others in the form of photos posted on social media? Yet another asks: To what extent and how is hate speech countered when it occurs online? Or: How do 'amateur' creators of online content feel about posting their creations on privately owned, profitable platforms? No matter what our question happens to be, and what specificities about digital sociality, culture and interaction it is interested in, the mark of a really good research question is that it centres on issues that are important in relation to wider research communities (Boellstorff et al., 2012).

In general, it is a very good idea to make your research narrow while keeping your thoughts broad, which means formulating the question in a way that gives it the potential to produce results and generate knowledge that is relevant to larger debates in society. For example, we might study some aspects of online gaming and – nearly as a bonus – be able to say something more generally about, for example, intimacy and friendship in the 21st century. We may analyse social network patterns in posts hashtagged with #metoo, and also get to know new and important things about social movements and gender in today's world. A really good question will, if the research is successful, generate knowledge that is useful in more than one way. Boellstorff and colleagues (2012: 56) make a very important point when they say that it can't be overemphasised that, aside from its relevance, a research question is only as good as the level of passion the researcher has for it:

> All good science flows from a scientist's passion to learn something
> he or she is deeply curious about. Thus [...], although it is important
> for the work to be broadly relevant, the question should be personally
> interesting and exciting to us. It is vital to underscore this point because
> we are best served by honoring our own passions and intellectual
> journey when deciding on a research question.

We believe this is true, also based on our own interactions with students writing their theses. When they are not invested in finding out, even for themselves(!) the answers to the questions posed in their studies, they usually don't make the effort to reach for a more academically solid thesis. Once, we met a PhD supervisor in computer science who had eight PhD candidates at the time, and, through the years, he had been the supervisor on many a PhD thesis. They said that the most important part of their work as a supervisor was ultimately providing a space for the candidates to find their own set of questions, and ownership of their ideas, aims, questions and research scope. When the PhD candidates were able to, so to say, 'own' their problems, they were able to succeed. While it may be tempting to do a project that is decided at the department level, or by a specific supervisor, or someone else, getting excited about it to the point of feeling ownership of that research is key. Do you own your problem yet?

Narrowing Down: What's the Aim?

Counterintuitively, perhaps, now is a good time to narrow down what actually comes before the research questions themselves: your aim. So what is the aim? And why is it needed? The aim can be understood as the umbrella, hovering over the research questions, the chosen research method and your analysis. So if your aim should be stated first, why shouldn't you write it first? Of course, in theory you could. But it is most often easier to find the more specific, essential parts of your research first (by outlining your research questions), before lifting your gaze and taking a look at the horizon, asking yourself: OK, so what's the overall intent here? Why do we need to know this? These are the kinds of questions that the aim is intended to cover.

According to Johnson and Christensen (2014), there are five typical research objectives that will guide your research: 'exploration', 'description', 'explanation', 'prediction' and 'influence'. These will ultimately narrow down the type of study you are conducting, and hopefully help you to uncover what your aim should be. They describe these as follows:

- 'Exploration' involves using mainly inductive methods to discover a concept, construct, phenomenon or situation and advance understanding, hypotheses or generalisations.
- 'Description' involves identifying and describing the antecedents, nature and aetiology of a phenomenon.
- 'Explanation' involves developing theory for the purpose of explaining the relationships among concepts or phenomena and determining reasons for the existence of events.
- 'Prediction' refers to using pre-existing knowledge or theory to predict what will occur at a later point in time.
- 'Influence' relates to manipulation of the setting or variable to produce an anticipated outcome.

Before, we were interested in finding the right question word (why, how, what, when, who) but, now, you should instead focus on choosing your exploratory verb as the central part of your aim. So what's an exploratory verb? Have you set out to do some 'analysing', 'discovering', 'mapping', 'understanding', 'exploring', 'describing' or 'explaining'? These verbs tend to look different depending on the methodological framework, say Creswell and Creswell (2018), where a quantitative study may be more inclined to use words indicating directions, such as 'impact', 'determine', 'cause', 'affect', 'influence' or 'relate'. Remember, based on the research question, or questions, you have decided upon, you need to formulate an aim that overarches your research questions. Let us give you an example from a study of one of the authors of this book, where she wrote:

> The overarching aim of the study is to analyse the social media reaction after this [terrorist] attack and the way this may have shaped the collective understanding of it. The research questions aim to further the knowledge on the role of social media for the formation of cultural trauma discourses in relation to traumatic events:
>
> a   What different uses of this hashtag can be identified in the data? How did these modes of usage differentiate over time?
> b   How do different discursive understandings of the attack, expressed as tweets, affect how the event is constituted as cultural trauma (or not)? (Eriksson, 2018: 3980)

Oftentimes, we see students posing the aim as a question, but remember that an aim usually doesn't begin or end as a question. Instead, good phrases to use as a prompt for writing your aim are:

This research aims to…
The aim of the thesis is to…

However, let's be honest. In many studies that are published, 'aim' is not necessarily the word used. And that is usually OK. Let us look at a study by Sarah J. Jackson and Brooke Foucault Welles from 2016 where their aim is stated like this:

> We focus here on interrogating the role of initiators in the aftermath of Michael Brown's killing in Ferguson, MO, both because of the way their narratives may reflect counterpublic discourse and because of the importance of mapping the source of digital phenomena that so significantly impact the social and political agenda of our nation. (Jackson & Foucault Welles, 2016: 401)

When they write that they 'focus here on', this reads as their aim. They provide a backdrop for their analytical focus in this study, providing specific analytical concepts that give the reader a sense of understanding of, so to say, where they're coming from. For example, they aim to focus on the 'counterpublic discourse' during these protests, and through this study they will be 'mapping the source of digital phenomena' within these protests. They continue in the same paragraph (ibid.) with the following sentence: 'Drawing on quantitative and qualitative methods, this research is guided by three central research questions'.

Before we jump into their actual questions, take notice of the fact that the authors state (however brief!) how they will perform the study before stating their questions. Since they have provided us with an aim (however, not mentioning the actual word 'aim'), they state what type of methods will be used in order to provide a study that will meet the aim. Following this, they provide three research questions (shortened to RQ) that are stated as:

> RQ1: Who most centrally influenced the move of Twitter discussions about Ferguson from the margins to the mainstream, and what publics do they represent?

> RQ2: How did digital discourse about Ferguson change during the week following Brown's killing, and what does this reveal about the shifting identities of emergent crowdsourced elites?

> RQ3: How did the specific communication architecture of Twitter enable and shape the discursive strategies of the emergent crowdsourced elites within the Ferguson networked public?

First, let us begin by focusing on the numbered list. If you read through this list of questions again, do you find any patterns between them? What is the focus for each question here, and what level of analysis are they based on? Focus on the question words who (RQ1), how (RQ2) and how (RQ3). The second and third questions use the same question words, but the first one focuses very clearly on the smallest unit of analysis here: the individuals, right? The Twitter users themselves and their interconnections on the platform. How will they approach this in their study? Through a social network analysis (Chapter 8) of the users, by looking at all of the individual users as nodes in the network, and seeing how they interact with one another in this space.

The second question focuses not on the users, but on what they do. Now, we lift the analytical focus a bit further, to the digital discourse that is shaped by these Twitter users and that needs to be addressed using another kind of data, the tweets themselves, as qualitative text data (Chapter 6). The authors later state that this form of analysis will provide a 'thick description' (see Chapter 1) of human experience and affect in combination with the computational approach provided by the first research question.

The third question focuses instead on the platform itself, Twitter. See how the focus again has shifted to look beyond the users, beyond the tweets, in order to understand how this platform shapes the political communication of the most prominent users identified within the first part of the analysis. Here, they focus on how specific platform features are used in these conversations, such as mentioning other accounts, retweeting, and so on. This is both a quantitative and a qualitative endeavour, where they provide evidence of which tweets were the most retweeted, but also a qualitative analysis of the insights to these numbers: were they tweets from mainstream media sources, or other forms of elites? Who was mentioned, and how?

Now, research questions don't always need to correlate to different methods, as in the example above. But focusing on different aspects of the data you are analysing is a good strategy. Each of the research questions above showed a slightly different analytical focus, and starting with 'the small' (the users), moving to 'the broad' (the platform). You can use this same structure when you attempt to write your own research questions. How might you provide the reader with the same form of advancement from smaller to bigger units of analysis?

Collecting Data

After thinking about the field of study, the aim and the research questions, the next step is to collect the data to be analysed. As outlined in Chapter 1, these data can be of varying character. We are working on an ethnographic foundation here, so therefore 'qualitative' data (observation notes, interview transcripts and the like) will play an important role. As we have argued earlier, such data is enough in some cases. Sometimes, it will be useful to complement them with data which emanate from natively digital strategies for collection and analysis, what Rogers (2013) calls 'methods of the medium', such as search engine results, likes, links, tags, and so on. We may also be interested in 'quantitative' data to use in social network analysis, or large sets of downloaded text data to analyse with the help of 'quantitative' or computational text analysis techniques (more about this in Chapter 7). So, as discussed in Chapter 1, the emerging and increasingly complex data environment means that any researcher approaching digital society – or slices or bits of it – will want to access different data types that demand different techniques to capture them. Observational data can be registered through note taking, interviews may be recorded and transcribed, or done through email or text messaging, and will be automatically captured as text in that way. Digitally native data, social network data, and big text datasets will have to be captured through any means available – copying and pasting when possible, downloading when possible, and by scraping (using tools to automatically download it) or acquiring data from a variety of online services, databases, websites and resources according to different schemes from case to case. Part of becoming an empirical researcher of digital society is to embark on the learning journey of discovering tools, strategies and resources – mastering them and constantly adapting to their variable and changing functionality, availability and terms of use.

Similarly to the steps involved in the formulation of the research question, and framing the field, the step of data collection also lends itself to an open and explorative starting phase. Kozinets (2015: 167–168) describes this process in an engaging way:

> I am often asked which special software tool to use. Try everything out there, online and offline. [...] For the sake of illustration, you can simply use Google – and this includes additional Google features such as Google's Analytics, Trends, and NGram reader features. [...] Use several engines from Google, including the web, groups, blog and image search function. Then search YouTube videos. Search on Twitter, and on a forum search engine like omgili.com ('OMG I love it!'). Take a look at Facebook Groups, Wikis and LinkedIn groups. [...] Keep your search terms as simple and consistent as possible across sites and engines to start. Grab as many major overviews of data as you can, but always also stay as close to the interactions and direct experiences as possible. [...] Your main task at this stage is to first attune your perception to the various social media and other channels that might inform your research question. [...] For example, if you are studying the contemporary whale and seal hunts worldwide, then

consider entering variations on 'whaling', 'whale hunt', 'whale activism', 'whale management', 'conservation', 'hunting endangered species', 'animal rights', 'Native rights', 'Aboriginal rights', 'international markets for whale meat and blubber' and 'international hunting accords dating back over 1000 years'. Investigate everything. Look at every website that seems even remotely relevant. Read them, and follow all the trails and hints they bring to you. Take your time. [...] In the long run, you must choose particular routes and pursue those, seeing where they take you. [...] How and why you direct your research will be driven both by your research questions as well as by serendipitous discoveries that you make along the way.

After the exploratory phase, which may or may not be as wide-reaching and ambitious as that which Kozinets describes, a focused and structured phase of data collection – guided by the research question and targeted towards the chosen object of study (sites/topics/people) – must commence. As mentioned above, the actual process of doing this will probably include several different strategies, depending on the type of data. One important thing is to document your research thoroughly: 'If we fail to write it down, it might as well not have happened!' (Boellstorff et al., 2012: 82). So, it is important to take notes throughout the process, as well as keeping data organised. Make it a habit to keep a *research log*, where you note things such as the search queries you have made, what settings you manipulated and how, what day you carried out a research interview, which filter and layout settings you used in your social network analysis software – all of these things are useful to note. You will thank yourself for having kept that log when the time comes to write about your method and you are about to finalise your study. From the very start of the data-collection process, observational data, interview data and/or data gathered through any other methods must be neatly logged. Some researchers do this in notebooks, others in word-processing software, and others use databases. You need to take this type of note taking and documentation seriously. Boellstorff and colleagues (2012: 113) note that the handy possibilities for copying, pasting and downloading data in online contexts create a risk that other, researcher-centred, forms of documentation are forgotten:

> This ease of data capture can sometimes create the false impression that the methods enumerated earlier, such as taking fieldnotes based on participant observation, are unnecessary. Why go to all that trouble when we can just capture the data digitally? This temptation is false: we cannot stress enough that as useful as digital records are, they cannot stand alone without the rigor of a detailed accounting of interactions in the field.

Data collection in digital social research can and should be open, exploratory, and aim to get as complete an image as possible. It is useful to think about the concept of *saturation* when it comes to the issue of when one should stop data collection and move on with analysis. This concept, originally formulated by the originators of the so-called grounded theory method, Barney Glaser and Anselm Strauss (1967), postulates that once the research process has been going on for a while, the researcher will gradually develop a sense of whether a newly added piece of data points to any new insights. If the answer is yes, then the data collection continues. If the answer is no, the data is disregarded, since it only adds bulk to the dataset and nothing to the theoretical insights (Glaser, 1965). So, as Boellstorff and colleagues (2012: 59) write:

> When we start hearing the same reflections repeated in interviews, when we are no longer seeing new things or getting new insight while undertaking participant observation, when we have reached a point where we can anticipate answers, practices, and the general everyday unfolding of the field, we have likely reached the point of diminishing returns in our data collection and can consider that phase complete.

Basically, when we feel that we have enough data to be able to say something that is meaningful and interesting, and when our sample is sizeable enough to provide a solid foundation for the arguments that we want to make, then it is time to turn to the analysis phase.

Analysing and Interpreting Data

In the next step, the data that we have collected is used as the raw material for analysis and interpretation. Analysis is what we do when we break the studied phenomenon down into its component parts. Boellstorff and colleagues (2012: 166) explain that 'the key to data analysis is to interact with the dataset: read it, study it, immerse oneself within it, and let the data paint a portrait of the culture we are studying'.

As you will be able to tell from the approaches to be presented in Chapters 5–10, the methods for analysing data can indeed differ. On the one hand, they may be resting on a statistical foundation, as is the case in, for example, social network analysis and computational text analysis. On the other hand, they can be interpretive, as in cases where they draw on 'qualitative' observational or interview data. In line with this, Kozinets (2015: 198) argues that we should be open to using both hermeneutic interpretation and all sorts of computational elements. He (2015: 205) gives an example:

> Consider a collection of 3 YouTube videos, 4 pages of blogger text, 6 pages of newsgroup materials and 17 Instagram posts. Finding their

common elements, the key and core of their meaning structure, requires us to find the common elements between them. Locating these shared themes is the challenge of hermeneutic interpretation.

Hermeneutics is an interpretive strategy where parts and instances of the data are iteratively reassessed and interpreted in relation to a developing sense of what the data says as a whole. So, one starts to look at some of the data to arrive at some initial understandings. Those understandings inform subsequent readings of other parts of the data, and this process carries on in interpretive loops, while the researcher's understanding of the meaning of the entire context that is represented by the dataset takes shape.

Once one has arrived at the core themes of the context under analysis, the next and final step of the study is to develop arguments and conclusions that point to larger theoretical and conceptual insights. By necessity, the scope and type of the results that will emerge from your research will range from the narrow to the overarching, from the abstract to the concrete, from descriptions to applicable insights, all depending on what the study is about, and on the methodological choices made along the way. 'Ethnography' means culture writing, and the primary output of such research is the documentation and hermeneutic interpretation of the social setting that has been analysed. So, at the end of the research process, when insights have been channelled through codes and themes into broader insights that can be developed, discussed and positioned in relation to previous research and to theoretical concepts and debates, it is time to start crafting your text. In fact, the writing process is also part of the inquiry as one often arrives at important analytical insights through the process of writing itself.

RESEARCHING DIGITAL MEDIA AND SOCIETY: SOME POINTERS

1   In any social research, especially that which explores 'new' or uncharted phenomena, always strive to capture as much complexity as possible. Ethnography – striving for 'thick description' (see Chapter 1) – is a good basic philosophy, even though it can be scaled and adapted largely depending on the character of your study.

2   Drawing on an ethnographical basis, bring in other sources and techniques for getting a topological map of the analysed phenomenon that is as rich as possible. In studying the internet and social media, you can consider a range of methods such as those discussed throughout this book.

3   After your initial exploration, formulate research questions that are as concrete and sharp as possible. Don't worry if you have to revise them

continuously throughout your research. Aim to formulate the questions in such a way that the results of your study will potentially be useful beyond your specific empirical case.

4   Decide what you are going to study. Is it sites, topics or people, or more than one of these? Will your study be focusing on one delimited setting, or will it be multi-sited? What role will the 'offline' play in your study?

5   Collect your data with the appropriate methods. Make sure you keep a research log of all the choices – big or small – that you make and which affect the composition of your dataset in the end. Gather data while being open to following the research question and being led by where the field takes you. Combine several different strategies if needed. Stop collecting when you have enough.

6   Analyse your data in ways that follow from your research question and the type of data that you have. Systematise, code, mine and crunch the data with the help of your toolkit. Use techniques such as computational text analysis and social network analysis, and interpretive approaches, when suitable. Be open to the use of computational approaches when you don't necessarily think they are appropriate, and try to challenge 'quantitative' results with hermeneutic interpretation.

7   Draw on the ethnographic idea that writing up the research is also a key part of the analysis and interpretation itself. Write not only to publish, but also write as a research method.

CONCLUSION

Knowing where to start can be tricky. Because of this, we have provided you in this chapter with a walkthrough of each step of the process. We have emphasised throughout the importance of narrowing down the research focus, and of getting specific about what you aim to study. What is the unit and focus of analysis, and how can you delimit it clearly? We have discussed this in terms of a 'framing' of your 'field'. Starting out with your preliminary idea, we have asked you to specify the *aim* as well as the *research questions* for your study. Perhaps counterintuitively, we have asked you to write these backwards – starting out with the more specific research questions and working your way backwards towards an overarching, hovering aim. You can see this as an umbrella, that guards the research questions from above. Collecting the actual research data can be tricky as well. How can you know if you have managed to gather it 'all'? And should 'all' of it even be gathered? We have encouraged you to be open to following the data where it leads you, and to gather it there. Sometimes you need to use different methods to do so. But remember to keep that notebook close and to write down each decision you make as you move through the research process. It will come in handy when, months from now, you begin to wonder why and how you made this or that choice along the way. There are many decisions to make, so make sure to keep your future self up to date!

4

DIGITAL RESEARCH ETHICS

Key Questions

- What are some key guiding principles for ethically researching digital media and society?
- How can we ethically position ourselves and our studies through dialogue?
- What is the role of informed consent in digital social research?
- How can we anonymise our data without misrepresenting it?
- What particular considerations are needed when researching vulnerable communities?
- How might we share our research and data through an ethical practice based on open science initiatives?

Key Concepts

Digital research ethics * Ethics as dialogue * Informed consent * Anonymisation * Vulnerability * Open science

---

Hold up! It's easy to get ahead of oneself at the start of an exciting and engaging research project. You may have found something that you are really eager to analyse, and also some form of data that you feel will make it possible for you to do this. There are many exciting avenues of research in the field of digital media and society (Chapter 1), and with a range of different research methods at hand – which can also be combined in stimulating ways (Chapter 2) – it may be tempting to jump, head first, into the research process (Chapter 3). But before skipping ahead and beginning to outline each of these methods themselves, as we will do in Chapters 5–10, where you can start picking and choosing which methods and combinations are right for your own study, we need to make sure that we consider any ethical aspects of the research.

Why? Well, research can affect the individuals we study, and society around us, in a myriad of ways. While digital media research might deal with mostly public content on social media platforms, blogs or forums, this user-generated content is still representative of the users that have created it. Sharing it further, taking it apart through various forms of analysis, and citing it in publications must be seen in relation to the integrity of those who produced the content, and also in relation to overlapping sets of rules and regulations. In this chapter, we will give a practically oriented overview of some of the key considerations to make when researching digital media. We will discuss the need to see digital research ethics, not as something fixed, but as an ongoing dialogue. Furthermore, a set of general guidelines – even though they are always under healthy debate – for doing digital social research are introduced. We will also discuss, hands on, how to deal with a set of particular challenges relating to the issues of informed consent, anonymisation and vulnerable communities. Finally, we discuss how to extend the ethical reflection also into the practice of sharing research results and data.

A BRIEF HISTORY OF RESEARCH ETHICS

While research ethics as such has a long and evolving history, especially in the biomedical sciences and harking back to the so-called Nuremberg Code of 1946 in the wake of human experimentation during the Second World War, its history is somewhat shorter within the social sciences. While the American Psychological Association presented an ethics code in the 1950s (APA, 1953), and the American Anthropological Association did the same in 1967 (Nolan, 2002), similar practices have spread into other social science areas as discussions and regulations for ethical best practices have evolved. More generally, the so-called Stanford Prison Experiment, carried out at Stanford University in 1971, is often considered to be a key turning point – or at least a moral story – for the implementation of stricter ethics in research involving human subjects.

Led by Philip Zimbardo, a psychology professor at Stanford, the experiment consisted of a prison simulation with local students, who were each assigned the role of either 'prisoner' or 'guard', and was set to continue for one to two weeks. However, due to the increased brutality of the students assigned as guards, Zimbardo decided to shut down the experiment early. In the mock prison, set up in a cellar at Stanford University, the guards increasingly began to emotionally, physically and mentally humiliate their prisoners. Since the Stanford Prison Experiment, ethical guidelines have become more rigorous for studies involving human subjects, and ethics committees and institutional review boards are set up to review research studies before they are implemented, in order to judge whether the potential risks for harm outweigh the potential benefit of the scientific inquiry. The rise of internet research as a field in its own right in the late 1990s set in motion a new set of discussions about what particular ethical considerations must be taken when studying online interactions and environments.

As mentioned above, principles of research ethics, and how persons that are researched should be ethically treated, tend to be codified in various documents and policies throughout the academic community. Most of these codifications work best in relation to what Purdam and Elliot (2015; see Chapter 1) call 'intentional data'. And although ethical principles about maximising the benefits and minimising the harm of research are a good starting point – alongside the obvious need to respect the fundamental rights of human autonomy, dignity and safety – any kind of research demands consistent reflection. Indeed, issues that relate to how one should deal with the ethical treatment of data are highly context-sensitive. Markham and Baym (2009: xviii) emphasise that the context-specific uses of digital media demand that the researcher continuously and carefully reconsiders notions such as privacy, consent, trust and authenticity.

RESEARCH ETHICS AS AN ONGOING DIALOGUE

While research of the internet, platforms and digital spaces deal with human subjects through their content, the ideas of what is public or private, and how to differentiate between data and persons, are all issues digital media researchers need to be aware of, and to critically examine in their own work. On different platforms, different rules and social codes apply, where definitions of privacy are applied in different ways. Digital ethics scholar Charles Ess (2020: 22) underlines the difficulties in developing a 'digital media' ethics at all:

> At first glance, developing such an ethics would seem to be an impossible task. First of all, digital media often present us with strikingly new sorts of interactions with one another. So it is not always clear whether – and, if so, then how – ethical guidelines and approaches already in place (and comparatively well established) for traditional media would apply. But again, as emphasized in the term 'post-digital,' digital media remain analogue media in essential ways – the music arriving at our

ears remains analogue, etc. And so the lifeworlds of human experience that digital media now increasingly define remain connected with the analogue lifeworlds of earlier generations and cultures: this means that there remain important *continuities* with earlier ethical experience and reflection as well.

As Ess underlines here, there are many challenges stemming from digital media's evolving and constantly changing character. He also writes elsewhere that there will always be different views competing over defining how ethics should be done. In the excerpt above, he also emphasises that there are indeed potential relevant continuities with other discussions about research ethics, which points to the need to develop our ethical framework in dialogue with a number of different perspectives.

By asking a series of questions, in what Mustajoki and Mustajoki (2017) have called 'ethics by guided dialogue', where this dialogue requires us as researchers to both contribute and to listen, we can act ethically in regards to our research subjects. To discuss ethical issues and to decide the best course of action, they recommend collective ethical thinking and transparency among researchers. We should continually be asking ourselves how we can think ethically in each stage of the study that we are undertaking. Ethics is, indeed, a skill that can be learnt and acquired over time, and which should be constantly updated. We do this when we continually question our research, methods and predispositions. This chapter sets out to help in doing precisely that. Instead of providing all of the answers, we intend to give you a toolset to use as a starting point for developing an approach to researching in ethical ways.

GENERAL ETHICAL GUIDELINES FOR RESEARCHING DIGITAL MEDIA AND SOCIETY

The emergent and volatile character of the field of digital social research, a field which is in a perpetual 'beta state', makes it impossible to escape questions about ethical decisions. Such questions must be posed and responded to iteratively. Even though one might wish there were clear rules, issues like these must always be navigated inductively. In light of these concerns, the Association of Internet Researchers (AoIR) has put together an Ethics Working Committee, composed of internet researchers from a variety of regions and countries. The committee argues that ethical issues are complex, and that they can rarely be handled in any binary way. There is in fact 'much grey area' (Buchanan & Markham, 2012: 5).

The experience of privacy is important for researchers of digital media and society to take into consideration when carrying out their studies (Zimmer, 2018).

An individual's privacy settings are oftentimes unknown to themselves, or unconsidered altogether. Such insights raise the question of whether the public, user-generated content that is easily accessible online can be used in whatever ways the researcher sees fit. Of course it cannot. But a mere 10–15 years ago, some digital media scholars would have claimed that digital content found online should be used freely as it is in fact public (otherwise it would not have been found) – similar to how newspaper articles have long been used in the field of journalism and media studies. But digital media content is different, especially when it comes to its intended audiences. For example, bloggers might not keep in mind that their content could be sought after by parties other than the small number of followers that are actively reading and responding to their content. They may tailor their content, and make considerations about what they share and what they don't, based on their own assumptions of the reach and readership, even though the content is, in practice, accessible by anyone who comes across it. In these ways, content is most often not intended to be viewed or read by researchers and analysed without the consent of its originators.

In fact, researchers studying social media platforms should be aware of what these platforms themselves are demanding of researchers within their Terms of Service. While this is not always stated clearly, in fact they are generally vague about these issues, and these rules are continuously updated. For a research paper, Fiesler, Beard and Keegan (2020) studied the Terms of Service of 100 social media platforms to understand how researchers are prohibited from collecting data on these platforms. While they found that these prohibitions are in fact common, they also showed that they are ambiguous, inconsistent and often lack context. Because of this, the researchers propose that ethical decision making needs to extend beyond Terms of Service and to consider, in fact, the contextual factors of both data and research.

The transdisciplinary character of digital social research means that researchers and institutions confront many contradictions and tensions that are impossible to resolve completely. Instead, 'many competing interests must be negotiated by researchers, ethics review boards, and institutions' (Buchanan & Markham, 2012: 6). For the individual researcher, it is recommended, the committee writes, that ethical decision making is approached as a process, dealing with the issues in a contextualised fashion throughout the research. This is because different issues will be pertinent at different stages. This approach is in line with the perspective of the research method as a bricolage (Chapter 2). It is not only the methodological choices, but also the ethical considerations, that are emergent and unwinding. The AoIR committee arrived at the following key guiding principles (2012: 4–5):

> The greater the vulnerability of the community/author participant, the greater the obligation of the researcher to protect the community/author/participant.

Because 'harm' is defined contextually, ethical principles are more likely to be understood inductively rather than applied universally. That is, rather than one-size-fits-all pronouncements, ethical decision-making is best approached through the application of practical judgment attentive to the specific context [...]

Because all digital information at some point involves individual persons, consideration of principles related to research on human subjects may be necessary even if it is not immediately apparent how and where persons are involved in the research data.

When making ethical decisions, researchers must balance the rights of subjects (as authors, as research participants, as people) with the social benefits of research and researchers' rights to conduct research. In different contexts the rights of subjects may outweigh the benefits of research.

Ethical issues may arise and need to be addressed during all steps of the research process, from planning, research conduct, publication, and dissemination.

Ethical decision-making is a deliberative process, and researchers should consult as many people and resources as possible in this process, including fellow researchers, people participating in or familiar with contexts/sites being studied, research review boards, ethics guidelines, published scholarship (within one's discipline but also in other disciplines), and, where applicable, legal precedent.

While discussions about the concept of 'human subjects' in digital social research, about definitions of public versus private, about data protection and ownership, and about several other pertinent dimensions must be continuously reviewed, the AoIR committee presents the above points as general principles for research-ers to turn to as a starting point. The guidelines described in the quote above state that:

- The vulnerability of research subjects should decide how careful the researcher is.
- The rights of research subjects to be protected should be balanced against the importance of conducting the research.
- Research ethics must be continuously discussed among researchers and other relevant actors.

To this list, we can add some additional important things to keep in mind. Anthro-pologist Tom Boellstorff and colleagues (2012: 129–149) suggest the following:

- *The principle of care*: taking good care of informants and making sure that they gain something from their participation.

- *Informed consent*: making sure that informants know about the nature and purpose of the study.
- *Mitigating legal risk*: being aware of the relevant laws that govern one's research.
- *Anonymity*: avoiding the inappropriate revelation of the identities of informants – or any sort of confidential details or otherwise, that might lead to their identification.
- *Deception*: not pretending to be something you are not, and not using 'fly on the wall' practices to study sensitive topics.
- *Empathy*: trying to forge a 'sympathetic depiction of informants' lives, even when discussing aspects of informants' lives that some might find troubling'. This does not have to mean that the researcher 'agrees' with any actions or beliefs of the informants, but one must labour to 'grasp informants' own visions of their worlds'.

The AoIR ethics guidelines are constantly under revision, according to the dialogic framework discussed earlier. The overall guiding principles are 'ethical pluralism and cross-cultural awareness, coupled with the experientially-grounded view that ethics starts by asking and answering critical questions rather than taking a more deductive, rule-oriented approach' (franzke et al., 2020: 2). The recommendations that were introduced above were drawn from the 2.0 version of the guidelines (Buchanan & Markham, 2012), which in turn builds on earlier versions developed through work driven by an Ethics Working Group. In the most recent version (franzke et al., 2020), some developments are provided in terms of a discussion of ethics in relation to different stages of research, and to some challenges connected to big data research.

INFORMED CONSENT

One way of ensuring that research subjects are not harmed is by asking them all for informed consent, where each person taking part in the study – after having been informed about its context, aims and design, and how material about or by them will be used – has the opportunity to agree to partake in the study, and to withdraw this consent as they see fit. The 1.0 version of the AoIR guidelines (Ess & AoIR Ethics Working Committee 2002) states that, ideally, research subjects should be approached at the very beginning of the research to be asked for consent, but that this may also happen along the way as a project changes. As with other factors, the particular research setting must be taken into consideration when making the choice whether to ask for informed consent or not.

As an example, researchers in the area of news media research would, very rarely, if ever, ask journalists about their consent to analyse and cite what they have written and published. Similarly, political scientists analysing, for example, presidential speeches would also consider the speech as open for analysis and citation without the consent of the politician in question. But what then about a blogger, a YouTuber or an Instagram influencer? What about a public Instagram post by a lesser-known individual? The AoIR 1.0 recommendation is that the 'acknowledged publicity of the venue' should decide (Ess & AoIR Ethics Working Committee, 2002: 5). In many cases, even though the information is technically public, it may still be less ethical to use it for research without the informed consent of those who published it.

What does the notion of informed consent mean, for example, in the context of a study of X (formerly Twitter) users who use the same hashtag during a large-scale protest? Do we need to ask each and every one of them to confirm their consent before we undertake the study? In such cases, when we collect and work with large-scale datasets – of the kind that are commonly used in computational text analysis (Chapter 7) and social network analysis (Chapter 8) – it is very impractical, and not really at all possible, to obtain informed consent. There are several different ways of protecting the identity of individual research subjects in these cases (Bechmann & Kim, 2020). These include: (1) deleting names and other identifiable information from the dataset; (2) pseudonymising the data (replacing identifying information with placeholders or made-up names and information); (3) only analysing the data at an aggregated level, showing only general patterns and not exposing any sensitive information about individuals; and (4) asking for informed consent from a small number of research subjects, the posts of which one feels motivated to somehow reveal in the research.

Contacting Research Subjects: Getting Permission to Use Material

So, no matter whether one is doing interviews, observations or other forms of ethnography (see Chapters 5 and 6), or a kind of more large-scale analysis (Chapters 7 and 8), there may arise situations where you want to contact research subjects in order to get their permission to use material. However, as many of you know who have been active users of social media platforms, reaching out is not always easy, especially if the user is a medium to major content creator on a specific platform. More than once, we have reached out to content creators with queries of informed consent, only for them to never even see the message. They receive a lot of attention, and reading and answering direct messages (DMs) might not be their highest priority. Additionally, you may not always be able to DM them if they are not in fact following you back, meaning that you are exclusive friends on that platform, for example TikTok. This makes it even harder to get in contact with such people.

For example, you might, first, begin by commenting on one of their posts, directing attention to a message you have previously sent ('Hi, I attempted to contact you with an inquiry, check your DMs!'). But this sounds an awful lot like the messages they are bound to get from their collaborative partners, who want them to promote their products, no? Sometimes it's easier to move to a different platform instead. Often, content creators are present on several platforms, and sometimes with a whole different type of content, followers and communication opportunities. There, it might be easier to get their attention when sending a DM or comment, since they might have fewer of these interactions on that platform.

When researching, for example, political communication within marginal communities, such as Black, trans or gay, researchers may additionally have to question what role we assign these subjects. Are they solely faceless informants, or are they co-creators of the research we are doing? Jackson et al. (2020) have previously proposed that the content creators included in the study need to be included in an untranslated format, and thus accredited for their work. This means that consent is even more important when recirculating their content within the context of our studies. This position is especially important when we attempt to portray marginal groups' communication since their subjective experiences and contexts are important for how we, as researchers, are able to present our studies. By reaching out to these groups, we are able to show (list by Bridges, 2009: 120):

- humility in acknowledging one's own lack of understanding;
- respect for and sympathy with others' desire to construct their own understanding of their lives and practice;
- caution about importing external frameworks of understanding which might be oppressive rather than emancipatory;
- sensitivity in negotiating alternative and especially threatening understandings;
- wariness of the potentially exploitative nature of outsider inquiry, especially commercial and professional academic inquiry; and
- respect for other people's desire for privacy.

Practical example message to informants

Below, you will find a real-life example of communication between a researcher and an informant. Notice the different platforms and time frames in which this creator was contacted. First, you need to present yourself. For example, tell the informant about your job title, and link to any personal pages or profiles, and, as a student, it's important to include both your full name and information about the context of the study; is it a bachelor's or a master's thesis, what's the name of the course, and at what university are you taking it? What's your supervisor's name and how can the informant contact them? What's the preliminary title of the thesis, or what is the research subject you are addressing? All of these questions need to be answered in your communication with informants. Additionally, you need to be clear on their options, by stating that their

(Continued)

potential participation in the study is voluntary, and that they have the right to pull out from an initial agreement of participation.

Keep track of all communication in a separate document where you have your information letter template, and each message that you have sent, including the date and time, the exact platforms where it was sent, and follow-up conversations, as well as the final decisions of the content creators themselves.

Example message

Hi,

*I am a postdoctoral researcher in Digital Media and Social Movements at Umeå University in Sweden (www.umu.se/en/staff/moa-eriksson-krutrok), and I am contacting you in regards to a research article that I am writing about the #BlackLivesMatter movement on TikTok. The paper focuses on the uses of the hashtag #BlackLivesMatter on the social media platform TikTok in order to understand how victims of police violence are framed and circulated. For this purpose, we visually analysed the top 100 most circulated TikTok videos using this hashtag. In order to put protesters' own voices at the centre of this research, I want to accredit the creators of the videos I am analysing for this study. More specifically, I am asking you for permission to use **[THIS QUOTE]**, and if you want, I would like to include your username in the paper as well. I am happy to answer any questions you might have. Looking forward to hearing back from you!*

Kind regards, Moa Eriksson Krutrök

ANONYMISATION

Some users are anonymous online. For example, an individual's fake Instagram account (also known as Finsta) can be a space for them to be true to, for example, their sexual identity or political beliefs, but this anonymity does not mean that they cannot become well-known actors within their specific communities online. This is more common on certain platforms than on others. For example, on Reddit, individuals are mainly using aliases, but on Instagram or X (formerly Twitter), for example, there is a mix of users using their real names and users who are not. On Facebook, however, there is a strict real-name policy for all users, which still has not meant that there are no fake users on the platform. There have been political efforts to force social media users to use their real names. For example, in April 2021, the Australian government considered imposing a law that would require all citizens to provide official identification when opening social media accounts as well as dating apps. The reason for such a real-name policy was said to stop trolling, abuse and misconduct on social media. At first glance, this might seem like a reasonable idea. After all, would every single harasser online really want to be held accountable for sending unsolicited images (such as dickpics) to others on social media?

Well, research in this area has shown that the impact of such a real-name policy on online harassment is in fact low. Really low. We know this from the effects that real-name policies have had in various countries. For example, South Korea imposed a law that required citizens to provide their national identification number before posting online on sites with more than 300,000 daily visitors. The results of this law? The Korean Communications Commission found that hateful comments decreased by less than 1% during the first year (Thomas, 2021). Read that again. Less than 1%. Instead, one side-effect of this law meant that a cyber attack on these sites allowed hackers to retrieve the national identification numbers of 35 million South Koreans. Ouch.

Anonymity does not equal malicious behaviour. Instead, 'pseudonymity helps people foster creativity, playfulness and intimacy among compartmentalised audiences', said digital media researcher Emily van der Nagel at a seminar organised by the Digital Rights Watch in Australia in November 2021. There are in fact many different groups of people who are in desperate need of anonymity. For example, marginal communities, such as the trans or non-binary communities, or women currently in hiding from domestic violence and stalking, would be at risk not only of harassment, but also of political prosecution in some countries. Because of this, researchers on these platforms need to be aware of the importance of pseudonymity, even in their research output. Even anonymised accounts using pseudonyms should not be scrutinised for the sake of research. In fact, usernames and direct quoting should be more or less put off the table right away when we decide how to add quotations in our studies.

If you determine in this process that you are in fact dealing with data from individual accounts, for example, the Instagram posts using a specific hashtag (say #bodypositivity), exercise some caution. While the posts that you are able to see have been preset to 'public' (as opposed to 'private', where only the followers of the Instagram user are able to access and view the published photos on the app), these photos are nonetheless not up for grabs for the sake of research. Instead, as previously stated, the risks associated with using these pictures as research data needs to be outlined and reflected upon. But using these images as your data is, nonetheless, not completely off the table. Instead, you can use these images as data points that you are able to draw analytical conclusions and ideas from, using one or a combination of several of the methods detailed in this book (Chapters 5–10). But using them as data points is not the same as reproducing the original posts and scrutinising the content for the sake of research. This means that you should not include, for example, Instagram posts from individual users as part of your paper; instead, you should use methods for de-identifying this data.

In their study, Samuel Merrill and Simon Lindgren (2021) included Instagram images as part of their data plots, in a low-resolution and high-level aggregate form, where this ethical consideration aimed to offer 'limited possibilities to search Instagram captions and reduce the chances of identifying the original poster'. And this is one of the main points in much of the contemporary ethical guidelines of internet research, that the data (in the form of posts to Instagram, YouTube, Reddit, etc.) should not be, as Annette Markham (2012) has called it, 'googleable'. In fact, making sure that these data points of entry are 'ungoogleable' is a way in which researchers can make sure that the content used within their studies becomes anonymised. In their 2020 book *Instagram*, Tama Leaver, Tim Highfield and Crystal Abidin decided to use drawings of specific posts that they did not have access to the copyright of, but still wanted to include visually in their study. This does, however, mean that there is an extra workload to make these artworks themselves of the original posts. This is, nonetheless, an effective way to incorporate visualisations in published works.

Not all universities have the same regulations in regards to copyrighted materials in student papers. Make sure to check with your own institution what the regulations say about this subject. These issues can be even more relevant in relation to the General Data Protection Regulations within the EU (GDPR). University lawyers can be incorporated to advise students and course directors. At our local university, these issues have been raised on a number of programmes when students have wanted to incorporate visual representations of their data (screenshots of TikTok videos or Instagram posts, for example). In these cases, the university lawyers have been able to guide supervisors and course directors both in advising in individual cases, and in outlining precedent regulations for future inquiries. For example, some universities will allow published work to be 'quoted' in accordance with good practice if it is justifiable by the predetermined purpose of the study. However, make sure to include only the information that is needed, in accordance with your overall ethical consideration, i.e. make sure that the content you are incorporating into your analysis as visual representations of your material is not coming from individual accounts.

Markham's study from 2012 argues for the need for the strategy of *fabrication* as part of our data representation. Fabrication, in this sense, involves rearranging and replacing identifiable words, to change the content of the original text. Many students may raise their eyebrows at this point. We get it. It sounds more arbitrary than it really is.

And while it seems difficult, it really isn't. But let's practise this now so that it feels a little less daunting when you need to do this yourselves.

Practical Example: How to Anonymise Quotes From Social Media

Consider a study where you use a dataset of tweets using the hashtag #niewieder-krieg (meaning 'never again war') regarding the military actions of Russia against Ukraine – here, you might find such a tweet:

@username

The new anti-war movement needs to get LOUDER. We cannot tolerate these aggressions against Ukraine anylonger. This is the beginning of the END! (2022-02-15)

First, we need to be careful in our reading of this tweet. What does it actually contain, and how can we personify the contents of the tweet? Is it in favour of a Russian invasion of Ukraine, or against, or is it neutral to this issue? Second, what specific sentiment is inherent within the writing of this tweet? Does it express specific emotive states that need to be incorporated into our re-write of this tweet, and how can we do so? Third, are there specific characteristics of this tweet that we are able to work with, without the risk of disclosing the identity of the user?

Based on these three aspects of the text, we are able to find specific semantic characteristics here that we can work with. First, we find that this tweet is pro-Ukraine and in favour of an anti-war movement. Second, there are certain words written in capital letters ('LOUDER' and 'END'), and each of these is followed by, first, a full stop ('.') and an exclamation mark ('!'), which shows that these letters are not simply used as enhancers of the emotive state, but perhaps also of certainty and general persuasiveness. Third, we see that one word is misspelt, which tweets very often are, which can give more insights into the composition of this tweet – was it rushed? Is English not the user's first language? It may mean a number of things, which, nonetheless, can be important for the overall context of the tweet. Indeed, the use of the word 'we' is an additional aspect to consider. Who is the user referring to when using the pronoun 'we'? If the user had written 'We cannot tolerate aggression against us Ukrainians anylonger', what would we have known from that subject position instead?

These aspects are important for understanding the context within which the tweet was written. However, we are also able to rearrange the words within the tweet to avoid it being 'googleable', as described by Markham. In addition to this, we are able to exchange certain words to avoid them being identifiable. Let's consider some synonyms to the word 'aggression': *hostility, aggressiveness, belligerence, bellicosity, antagonism, truculence, pugnacity, pugnaciousness, combativeness, militancy, warmongering, warlikeness, hawkishness, force, violence, attack, assault, encroachment, offence, invasion, infringement.*

Some words in the above list are obviously too complicated, such as 'belligerence', 'pugnaciousness' or 'truculence'. But we can consider words like 'aggressiveness', 'invasion' or 'militancy' to get the general point across. What about the word 'movement' in the original tweet, then? Could that be additionally changed to a synonym, such as 'lobby' or 'coalition'? Taking all of these aspects into consideration, the tweet that we want to include as an example from our dataset in our analysis might look like this:

@username

We will not stand for this! An invasion of Ukraine cannot be tolerated and the anti-war coalition needs to speak-up and get LOUD. We are coming closer to the END! (2022-02-15)

As you can see, we have included a misspelling ('speak-up'), and two words with capital letters ('LOUD' and 'END'), followed by a full stop ('.') and an exclamation mark ('!'). We have kept the word 'we' as it is important for understanding the context. We have changed two of the words to their synonyms ('invasion' instead of 'aggressions', and 'coalition' instead of 'movement'). This example may, hopefully, help you to make your own fabrications of the quotes that you are intending to include in your analysis. In this way, we can protect the anonymity of our research subjects while still showing examples from our dataset in the writing of our study.

However, it is important to realise that there are no fool-proof ways of anonymising direct quotes. While this method is effective most of the time, sometimes the synonyms used in the examples are so obvious that readers can guess the quotes quite easily. Additionally, sometimes a post will have gained such notoriety already that the content of the quote is well-known beforehand, which means that the reader can decipher the source. However, it is our responsibility as researchers to do our best to keep research subjects safe, and this is not something that should be considered simply at the first stage of research planning. Instead, this needs to be an ongoing practice. As formulated by Svedmark and Granholm (2018), 'ethics is not a green card!' This means that while you may need to state your ethical considerations before you start conducting your study, that does not mean you don't have to consider your practices continually throughout the process.

There are exceptions to this rule. For example, public figure accounts or organisational accounts are sometimes used in research for understanding the rhetorical positions of a political leader on X (formerly Twitter) (for example, of Trump before he got suspended). Or you might be interested in how the police are portraying crime interventions on their TikTok accounts. If you are unsure about whether a specific user account can or should be named, and what you need to think of if you want to quote its content directly, in your study, Figure 4.1 provides some general guidance. This decision flow chart is inspired by, and in part directly based on, a similar chart created, specifically for Twitter research, by Williams et al. (2017).

As the figure shows, you must first think about the type of social media account that you are dealing with. It is, for example, generally fine to directly cite and reproduce content posted by public figures, such as celebrities and political leaders. When it comes to organisational accounts, the decision comes down to whether the account in question is posting in the name of the organisation in general, or if individual or private persons are expressing themselves through the organisation's account. In the many cases where we as researchers are faced with content posted by private individuals – even though their social media posts may be publicly accessible – there is the need to make a number of more careful considerations about both the vulnerability of the author and the sensitivity of the content. In general, you should never quote any individual – non-public figure and non-organisational – directly without seeking the consent of the individual in question. Furthermore, even if the originator of the post is considered to be public and not vulnerable, you also need to consider, before reproducing the content, whether it contains any sensitive information that may be harmful to people other than the author. For example, citing a hateful tweet by a political leader might be fine – since you would not be exposing a vulnerable author – but it is not necessarily fine to do so if the tweet, in turn, carries content that may expose or target vulnerable individuals.

VULNERABLE COMMUNITIES AND RESEARCHER REFLEXIVITY

While any research study demands ethical reflexivity on behalf of the researcher, and while we should always see our research subjects as potentially precarious, the need for these considerations come into particularly sharp focus when dealing with, what some have called, sensitive or vulnerable communities. In general, research subjects may be considered vulnerable when they, for example, include minors, political groups, or those dealing with trauma, illness, disability, and so on. However, who is defined as vulnerable or not is not as clear cut.

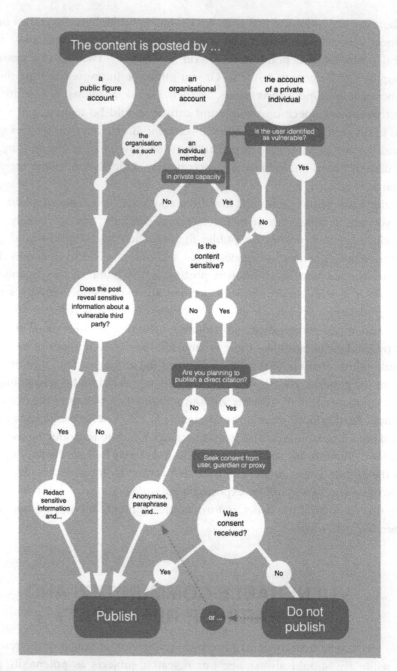

Figure 4.1 Decision flow chart for publication of digital media posts (partly based on Williams et al., 2017)

When conducting research, researchers must weigh up the potential dangers and negative effects on research subjects by judging their level of vulnerability. The National Bioethics Advisory Commission (NBAC, 2001) defines vulnerability as 'a condition, either intrinsic or situational, of some individuals that puts them at greater risk of being used in ethically inappropriate ways in research'. Such intrinsic or situational factors are important to relate to and be aware of during your research. Social media users may, for example, be underage, meaning their age defines them as being intrinsically vulnerable. On the other hand, an adult social media user may be situationally vulnerable by being in a specific emotional condition – for example, when mourning or being depressed.

Sometimes, methodological decisions are based on our own intent to act ethically as researchers. For example, we may not want to harm individuals in vulnerable positions by forcing them into an interview situation or subjecting them to other traditional forms of data collection that urges them to share. By, instead, assuming a 'fly on the wall' position, Svedmark and Granholm (2018) state that researchers may prevent negative effects on vulnerable communities by simply analysing them from afar. These forms of distant observation in online settings are often referred to as non-participatory fieldwork (which we will dive deeper into in Chapter 5 on digital ethnography).

In her work studying bereaved parents and their mourning practices in digital spaces, Hård af Segerstad (2021) reflected on the complexities of studying such sensitive communities, and especially what it means to study them as a participant within this community. In fact, her research sprung from her own interactions with this group, as a parent, herself, grieving the loss of her child. Due to her close ties to the group itself, the feelings expressed and the individual members, she realised she needed to stay true to this duality, and to centre herself and her experience as part of her methodology, writing: '[c]entralizing the researcher's experience and body in the study can provide detail and nuance not available through other methods of engagement with participants.' This was, however, not simply a methodological choice. In fact, it is deeply rooted in the ethical approaches of this research. Through this methodological choice, she was able to build ethically sensitive and situated knowledge that stayed true not only to the community, but also to her own personal relationship with the group. Another aspect of this dual role as researcher and research subject is not only the ethical responsibility towards the community of which she was a member, but also to herself, in terms of her own emotional capacity and challenges. Staying nuanced and unaffected was not possible, and arguably shouldn't be. Not all research can be done using an outsider's perspective. Sometimes the call comes from inside the building.

This kind of approach is based in researcher reflexivity and can involve a number of steps. Stating your own specific position in relation to the research subject(s) you are studying, which is sometimes referred to as one's 'positionality', can be important to share as part of your ethical practice. Having an affinity with your research subjects you have another relationship to both the people you study and their statements. However, this needs to be made clear to the readers of your study and not veiled behind a curtain of shame. Honestly, a lot of students express that they feel bad for wanting to research topics that are close to their own lived experience, but these studies are important and can create a space for dealing with ethical issues first hand. For example, gay students might find themselves interested in studying specific apps that they inhabit, like Grindr. Another student might want to study the Swedish Somali communities on Facebook, simply because they themselves identify as Swedish Somali. By disclaiming your own relationship to the field, you are able to clarify your specific role as a researcher and the connections you may or may not have to the community under study.

This self-reflective practice can be done at all stages of research, throughout the data collection, analysis and writing up of the study. It can be particularly important when researching groups you yourself are not a part of or don't identify with, especially if they are marginal groups, such as an Indigenous community. There can be cultural divides you are not aware of when you begin your study, and you might have to keep educating yourself in order to understand your informants and the research data. Deborah McGregor, Canada Research Chair in Indigenous Environmental Justice, advised white researchers in a 2021 interview in *Nature* to take intercultural, anti-racism or anti-oppression training when conducting studies on groups that they are not themselves part of (Gewin, 2021). In fact, certain communities have started to demand this approach from researchers positioned outside of the group. For example, non-Indigenous researchers in Australia are impelled to consider their own socio-cultural positioning before beginning any research on Indigenous populations, since it can influence their approach and analysis. Instead, developing partnerships where Indigenous and non-Indigenous researchers can work together can open up more opportunities for these marginalised groups (George et al., 2020).

As an insider, researchers have a much wider cultural understanding of the data they analyse in their studies. However, in an interview setting, that insider position might entail that the research subjects miss detailing specifics that may be interesting for the study, simply because these additional facts might appear unnecessary in these conversations. Because of this, a researcher may decide not to disclose their own experience when conducting interviews, in order to not position themselves as either an insider or an outsider. This was done in a study of Canadian HIV-positive men, where the first author of the study, Kinnon MacKinnon, who is Assistant Professor in Social Work at York University, Toronto, and himself part of the LGBTQ2 community, did not disclose his positive or negative HIV status, in order to enhance the rigour in the data collection (MacKinnon et al., 2021). In such ways, researcher positionality can and should be stated as part of ethical practice, as well as being a point of departure for showing research reliability.

Ethically Sharing Your Research

In wrapping up this chapter, we want to emphasise that there is an ethical element not only to carrying out your actual empirical research, but also to how it is being shared with the world around you. For example, not everyone has access to the kinds of academic publications that are locked into corporate platforms with hefty subscription fees. As a student or university employee, you usually have access to large databases of scholarly publications that are provided via university library agreements. The knowledge that is produced by researchers should, arguably, not simply stay within the settings of academic institutions. Therefore, it can be considered more ethical to publish your work in open-access journals, which are free for anyone to read online, and/or to publish early versions of your work on so-called preprint servers, such as arxiv.org and socarxiv.org, where researchers are able to upload their manuscripts in searchable databases.

As academic journals have become more and more hybrid (i.e. more extensively put online), publishers have started to provide open access as a way to encourage scholars to share their research in new and improved ways. Since these forms of publication are usually rather expensive for individual researchers, these fees are, in some settings, pre-paid as agreements between the university libraries and academic publishers, such as Sage. This is not the case for all research settings. Some of these licences are too expensive for certain institutions, and this disparity of access to open-access initiatives can have far-reaching democratic consequences. While, sure, the general public might be reluctant to read dull academic output (we are not well-known for our accessible writing styles), there is an important issue regarding the ethics of access to scholarly knowledge that needs addressing. This ethics of access is specifically about scholars 'recognising people's right to know what is known' (Willinsky & Alperin, 2011). In fact, scholarly knowledge is created by scientists and researchers who, themselves, are working in government institutions, such as universities, in order to create new understandings of these very societies. That has implications not solely for university staff and their students, but also for society as a whole.

Making the choice to publish through open access is in line with the ideal of open science, which is often used as an umbrella term that refers to both open-access publishing methods and open data. When it comes to sharing datasets so that others can access the data on which you base your conclusions – either so that they can make sure that your results are reproducible, or simply to use it for other purposes altogether – there are also online platforms available.

Two examples are Harvard Dataverse (https://dataverse.harvard.edu) and Kaggle (www.kaggle.com/datasets). The latter – similar to github.com and gitlab.com – also allows for sharing computer code alongside the data, enabling data science-oriented scholars to further enhance the transparency of their research.

Public outreach, finally, is also considered an important part of academic research, which means that researchers should promote public awareness of research outputs, and make informal contributions in accessible language in order to educate the public. This can include the writing of press release statements via the university, or answering media questions in interviews about one's research or on topical societal issues where journalists need commentaries from specific scholars. Public outreach can also be carried out through giving public lectures or partaking in panel discussions in non-academic settings, as well as being outspoken on social media about one's research findings. This all relates to what has been called the 'social impact' of research, and to how scholars are able to connect their results with non-academic settings. While the impact of research within the academic community can be, and is often, measured in terms of the quantity of citations acquired by academic publications, the more qualitative forms of broader social impact are important also for the sake of allowing the general public access to academic research. Providing knowledge to the general public should be an important part of every researcher's work. Generally, it appears to be the ethical thing to do to make one's research as transparent and useful to as many people as possible.

CONCLUSION

It has been argued throughout this chapter that research about digital media and society demands continuous critical reflection. This is true here to an even larger degree than in many other types of research, since this is a field without any fixed and established methodological tradition. The negotiations are ongoing, and as argued above, it is important to maintain continuous dialogue about research ethics, and for researchers to give others insight into their research processes. How the researcher navigates issues of research ethics will differ, depending on how the data in question have been generated and collected. Looking at the typology for data types presented by Purdam and Elliot (Chapter 1), new ethical challenges arise, especially in relation to self-published data, social media data, data traces, and found, as well as, synthetic data. New data types, and new ways of accessing and gathering data, demand that the researcher constantly navigates the data environment, and make choices in a critically reflective way.

Ethical reflection must sit at the core of each new study and be a key element in its preparation. Here, we need to be aware of how we gain access to the research data and where (through which platform, website, app, etc.) and whether we intend to interact with, or gather the data produced by, specific research subjects. We must also critically consider whom these research subjects potentially can be. Are they minors? Are they individuals representing marginalised groups in society? Are they politically active? All of these subject positions can mean that they are more subjected to potential harm. For example, when a political protest is ignited in the former Soviet state of Belarus, the tweets, Facebook or Instagram posts can potentially become weaponised by the military forces, and used against them in a political trial. Because of this, and a range of other eventualities, we need to treat each and every digital trace of each individual within our studies with ethical caution.

5
DIGITAL ETHNOGRAPHY

Key Questions

- What is ethnography and why is it useful for studying digital media and society?
- How can 'following the data' be a way to ethnographically trace different parts of the field?
- How must the notion of an ethnographic 'fieldsite' be renegotiated when research is done in 'virtual' settings?
- What are the main components of the *netnography* approach, and how does it differ from other forms of digital ethnography?

Key Concepts

fieldwork * participant observation * researcher positionality * following the data * lurking * netnography

Analysing digital media and society from an ethnographic point of view is about reading it as if it were a text, and trying to grasp the ways in which participants make meaning. In the words of Geertz (1973), the ultimate goal of ethnography is to provide a 'thick description' of the patterns, modes and functions of social life, as we previously described in Chapter 1. An ethnographer must not simply report observed events and details, but must also render and explain those observations in ways that help decode the webs of meaning from an insider perspective. In classic ethnography, the 'field' is understood as clearly delineated, and as an actual 'recognizable place to go to that contains the people we are interested in' (Hine, 2012: 24). In a digital world, however, these fields may be ever-floating, hard to grasp and difficult to define. In this chapter, we will explore how immersing ourselves in a specific fieldsite can look like, feel like and what it will result in for our individual studies. While each digital media researcher will, as was argued in Chapter 2, develop their own 'methodological bricolage' in different ways in relation to the tasks that might be at hand, an ethnographic exploration of some sort is often a very useful component.

Ethnography is not so much a single method as a bundle of methods. While participant observations may be somewhat of its signature method, ethnography may also include interviews, photographic content and video recordings, as well as other forms of non-participatory observations. An ethnographer may ask their research participants to make their own video recordings at home, showing how they wake up, put on their coffee maker and pour themselves a first cup of coffee. That can be one way of gathering data. In pandemic times, Zoom and other forms of video-conferencing tools have been used in the same sense – in the form of 'being there' without actually being there. In fact, ethnography is mainly about just that – being there. This is what typically gets referred to with the umbrella term of fieldwork, which takes place where the participants themselves live, work or simply hang out.

Digital ethnography, according to Varis (2015), should not be seen as a number of fixed principles but rather as an approach to the research process. We agree with this point and, in the introductory chapters, we have stated the relevance of digital ethnography for the beginning stages of all forms of digital research. Additionally, digital ethnography not only focuses on *where* the people studied are present but also on *how* research itself may be performed. In fact, the digital tools used for collecting, storing and analysing data from our ethnographic endeavours are all present within the realm of digital ethnography. As stated previously, video-conference calls may be used instead of in-person conversations. Specific hashtags, such as #metoo or #georgefloyd, may be where our fieldwork takes place instead of in physical spaces, to understand political discourse in the 21st century. As such, our line of inquiry – which communities we study, how they interact, and so on – is also shaped by the digital circumstances surrounding these research endeavours.

FROM ETHNOGRAPHY TO DIGITAL ETHNOGRAPHY

Ethnography means to write about people and culture (derived from the Greek words *ethnos*, meaning people/culture, and *grapho*, writing). In order to write about people in a reasonable way, we must get to know who they are and how they live – within their communities, in their homes and in their different social settings. This method started out as a reaction against 'ethnology' as the main means of anthropological inquiry during the late nineteenth century and early twentieth century, which involved comparing, contrasting and reviewing the accounts of missionaries and travellers from locations far away (Hammersley & Atkinson, 2019: 1–2). Because of this, they have been called 'armchair anthropologists', since they usually stayed put in their homes and provided grand theories of cultures 'out there'.

Armchair anthropologists studied their subjects from afar, most often people of distant civilisations. This colonial view of often non-white and non-Eurocentric settings was obviously flawed in many ways. While observational data from colonists and missionaries was often included in these descriptions, the anthropologists of this period did not themselves observe those they intended to describe. However, most researchers of this time were aware of the flaws in their data-collection methods, and of the need for newer approaches (for more on this topic, see Sera-Shriar, 2014).

Because of this, there was a need for change in the field of anthropology, which led to new methods of inquiry. The method of 'participatory observation', especially, was one of the most significant additions to the field and was popularised by Bronislaw Malinowski, who wrote several books about his 32 months of fieldwork in the Trobriand Islands off the coast of New Guinea (most famously *Argonauts of the Western Pacific*, published in 1922). Throughout his ethnography, Malinowski learned the local language and participated in the daily life of locals and could thereby see how their religious beliefs, ceremonies, customs and taboos related to the inner workings of their society. It was, in fact, Malinowski's work that pioneered the key ethnographic idea that the researcher should use participant observation to get 'the native's point of view'. Malinowski has, for this reason, been known as the 'inventor of modern anthropological fieldwork' (Hammersley & Atkinson, 2019: 4).

The underlying assumption of ethnography is that in order to develop an adequate understanding of what it is like to live in, or be part of, a setting, a balanced mix of immersion and detachment is needed on behalf of the ethnographer. The most classic ethnographies, predominantly carried out by anthropologists such as Malinowski, have tended to involve the researcher spending many months, even years, in the 'strange' or 'foreign' contexts that they wanted to try to understand. The key was long-term engagement, and the forging of deep and lasting bonds with people.

The method of ethnography has since been adopted into many disciplines. By observing individuals in their natural setting, researchers within these fields are able to understand, for example, their habits, socialities or beliefs. As our digital lives have become interconnected with our daily practical lives, these methods have moved and shifted into the realm of the digital.

Ethnography, then, is a pre-digital research strategy which is about creating detailed and in-depth descriptions and interpretations of people's everyday lives and social and cultural practices. This is most often done with the help of contextualised research data that has been collected through participant observation and in-depth interviews. Those data are then closely described, read and interpreted to carefully map out patterns of thinking and acting. What one might call digital ethnography, then, is an approach aiming to generate such knowledge about lives and practices in digital society – both online and in settings where digital media intersect and entangle with our offline lives. Two key scholars in this area are sociologist Christine Hine, who authored the influential book *Virtual Ethnography* (2000) and several follow-ups, and anthropologist Daniel Miller, who has developed a framework for what he has labelled *digital anthropology* (Miller & Slater, 2000; Miller & Horst, 2012).

As Hine points out, one of the pioneering studies of this kind was Nancy Baym's 1993 ethnography of a Usenet newsgroup where a community of soap opera fans was emerging (Baym, 1994). An even earlier example was Elizabeth Reid's (1991) thesis on internet relay chat (IRC). Not everyone was equally impressed by such studies, however. Instead, some scholars were quite sceptical about the possibility of doing anything worthy of being labelled ethnography through online-only analyses. For example, Wittel (2000: 6) argues that such studies stretch ethnographic practice so far 'beyond tradition' that it must deal with a number of serious difficulties. He identifies four problems:

- First, that the accuracy of information can hardly be validated.
- Second, that the key strategy of participant observation is about observing 'real people', and that this is not possible online.
- Third, that the shift towards an ethnography of networks makes it hard to do thick descriptions, as online links are an impoverished way of representing sociality.
- And, finally, that the lack of a physical fieldsite means that there is very little contextual data available.

Because of such shortcomings, Wittel calls for 'a modernised version of fieldwork'. He says that all of the problems are related to the fact that online-only ethnography seems to assume that there is a clear boundary between online and offline. Rather than emphasising the differences between material and digital spaces, we should introduce a more relational perspective and concentrate on the similarities, connections and overlaps.

In a 2016 blog post, Miller argued, rather refreshingly, that he has 'never, ever actually believed in "The Internet"'. He writes that ethnographic studies of online activity should focus on contextualising these activities from a holistic perspective: 'I study populations whose online activities are a growing element of who they are and what they do. Yet no one lives just online.' So, instead of 'fetishising' the internet, there is a point in the examination of the online setting as just one out of many places where people now live and interact. He makes the point convincingly:

> After overhearing a two-hour telephone conversation between your husband and his mother, for example, you would not remark, 'Oh, that sounded bad, but what is your relationship like in the real world?' Nor does online represent a consistent trajectory. What people call 'the Internet' has already meant entirely opposite things. The early debates – no one knows you're a dog on The Internet – were all about anonymity and creating specialist interest groups. (Miller, 2016: para. 2)

We should be open to finding that people online do entirely unexpected and contradictory things and that the same platform can do opposite things at different stages in its development. By contrast, current debates about Facebook are all about a lack of privacy and how it muddles work, kin and friendship. Middle-aged people used email to demolish the boundary between work and leisure; now young people use email to create a boundary between work and leisure. One of the main reasons new platforms become so popular may be connected to the fact that your grandmother still has not found it, and forced you to add her as a friend. In an impressive series of books, Miller and a number of his colleagues presented the results of fieldwork undertaken by nine anthropologists, who had spent 15 months in nine communities around the world, researching the role of social media in people's everyday lives. The project was called *Why We Post* and aimed, among other things, to show how problematic it is to assume that the internet and social media are the same everywhere:

> When we tell people that we have written nine monographs about social media around the world, all using the same chapter headings (apart from Chapter 5), they are concerned about potential repetition. However, if you decide to read several of these books (and we very much hope you do), you will see that this device has been helpful in showing the precise opposite. Each book is as individual and distinct as if it were on an entirely different topic. This is perhaps our single most important finding. Most studies of the internet and social media are based on research methods that assume we can generalise across different groups. We look at tweets in one place and write about 'Twitter'. We conduct tests about social

media and friendship in one population, and then write on this topic as if friendship means the same thing for all populations. By presenting nine books with the same chapter headings, you can judge for yourselves what kinds of generalisations are, or are not, possible. (Miller et al., 2016: v)

The key point here is that, from an ethnographic point of view, it is the content rather than the platform that is of interest. For Miller and Slater (2000), there is, for example, nothing inherently 'virtual' about the internet. Rather, the internet is only virtual in those cases when it is used or perceived as a virtual space. 'Cyberspace' is not always present as soon as the internet is around. So, from the perspective of digital anthropology, it is more useful to study a platform such as Facebook by exploring it as being contextually embedded from the eyes of its users than to study what is posted online. An embedded approach to an ethnography of the internet will lead the researcher to ask other questions beyond a cyberspatial point of view. The aim is to embrace the multiplicity of the internet and to pose questions about how it comes to mean different things in different settings among different people. Once again, this is because technology in itself does not have any pre-defined or given settings of use. Rather, different practices will generate different and divergent enactments of technology. Remember, however, that while some ethnographers may be interested mainly in the study of how the internet is embedded in people's everyday lives, this does not mean that online-only ethnography is irrelevant or wrong. As Hine (2015: 38) puts it:

There are still online spaces which develop distinctive and well-ordered cultures. It is still relevant and interesting to find out what people do when they are online, and what forms of identity, structure, and inequality emerge when people come together in online space. However, there are now also many ethnographers who want to study the embedding of the Internet in various dimensions of everyday life.

So, on the one hand, there are online-only studies that use milieus and platforms on the internet as fieldsites for ethnographic analysis, without going beyond what happens in those places. On the other hand, there are studies that focus on how the internet becomes meaningful through an analysis of how the internet is embedded in material and physical settings. Still, it is often a good idea for the researcher to move 'between mediated and unmediated spaces', since this often contributes to the contextualisation of the online interactions (boyd, 2008: 45). After all, 'people do not live in online communities, or not exclusively at least' (Hine, 2012: 27).

DIGITAL FORMS OF FIELDWORK

No matter what social or cultural issues we research, it is becoming increasingly difficult to avoid dealing with online aspects of communication and interaction at some point. It is important to note Hine's argument that the internet and social media do not just provide researchers with an additional arena where social things occur. Instead, she writes, the analysis of online settings is helpful to research social issues that extend beyond the internet itself. This is because the internet can be understood not only as a cultural artefact – a thing in the world – but also as a culture – an important aspect of the world itself. As people are simply going about their everyday lives in their use of the internet, by necessity, in the process, they leave traces that researchers will be able to draw on. Hine summarises her point:

> The Internet is, to summarize, increasingly reflective of broad swathes of the population and of diverse activities: it is readily accessible, it allows for imaginative new research questions to be explored and for previously hard-to-reach populations to be accessed. It offers rich data on almost every imaginable aspect of existence. Internet research has developed from being a somewhat esoteric and unworldly frivolity to serving as a route to explore significant and weighty social issues. (Hine, 2012: 11)

The internet makes it possible for researchers that use ethnography to observe a wide variety of social behaviours, patterns and phenomena, which were not nearly as readily available to see before. In a digital society, otherwise 'private' discussions take place in online public spaces, and many of the interactions persist as archived and searchable digital material. This makes it possible to carry out research that otherwise would be impractical due to the demanding, daunting work needed to negotiate access and traverse social barriers. As Hine (2012: 32) writes, it might not even be possible to decide about any exact limits of the fieldsite beforehand: 'As the research goes along, a deeper understanding of what the fieldsite should be, in terms of the contexts that the people involved use to make sense of what they do, is in itself one of the products of the research.'

Ultimately, sometimes a focus on online interactions alone may be enough, and sometimes such a focus will not be an appropriate choice. Obviously, however, no sociality between people can happen in total disconnection from any material reality, so it is to be expected that ethnographic projects in a digital society will force the researcher to look for evidence in various places. Some of these places may be located online and others offline.

Five Principles of Digital Ethnography

In the following, we introduce and discuss the five key principles for digital ethnography, as proposed by Pink et al. (2016: 8–14): *multiplicity, non-digital-centric-ness, openness, reflexivity* and *being unorthodox.*

The first principle relates to the *multiplicity* of the digital aspects of life. For example, these include physical and spatial characteristics, such as wifi connections, bandwidth, and social media infrastructures, essential for accessing these digital spaces. Not all humans are online, for starters. The digital divides between Western countries and the global South are persistent. Additionally, not all platforms are used by all people. Rather, we inhabit specific spaces in the digital world as part of our own individual lived experience. We are not all bingo players, so why would we all have the experience of being in a bingo hall? Conversely, not everyone knows the ins and outs of Reddit, YouTube or TikTok. One way of exploring platforms is by looking at the facts about them first. One way to find such facts is to look at user surveys, such as, for example, those carried out by *Pew Internet Research.* What demographics tend to use the platform? How do they use it – for reading articles or sharing food recipes? In that way, we can paint a broader picture of the social role of this specific space, before delving into the previous research on it.

Second, the *non-digital-centric-ness* relates to what Couldry and Hepp (2017) have called 'deep mediatisation'. Our social worlds are highly entangled with the digital through our communication mediums to the point where they can no longer be understood as separate. Such de-centring of the media itself as the focus of the study allows ethnographers to see these digital media expressions as inseparable from the social worlds they relate to. For example, there would be no use looking at a hashtag like #trayvonmartin without contextualising its history, intent and usage within the Black Lives Matter movement, in- and outside of internet spaces. Jackson and colleagues (2020: 103–4) have looked specifically at the way this hashtag has helped shape conversations about systemic racism and criminal liability in the USA. At another level, we may also have to look at the political contexts of internet platforms themselves. Look at TikTok, for example. Has this not been a platform subjected to much political discussion in most Western countries at this point? Starting with Donald Trump's famously named 'TikTok ban', to the ongoing negotiations over privacy issues and Chinese connections, it may be difficult to understand TikTok if we are not fluent in these contexts.

Third, the principle of *openness* in digital ethnography is based on the research process itself, whereby rather than interpreting it as a bounded method, researchers are encouraged to view it as a fluid and collaborative process. Here, we are encouraged to be open not only to other human beings but also to their input in our research. Rather than thinking about our sources as informants, we should see them as collaborators. What this means is that we give them the power to have a say over our research statements. We are no longer visiting far-away places and using people there as a basis for our own conclusions, as Malinowski did. Instead, we should incorporate their experiences in ways that they agree to. One question that arises from this practice, which we have encountered ourselves, is: does that mean that we jeopardise our own academic freedom? We usually answer: no. We invite voices in by, for example, letting them read the way we have used their quotes, content or otherwise, but we are not abided by law to let them have the last word. However, by seeing our sources as collaborators, rather than informants, we are at least willing to listen to them. We might not have to think they are 100% right, but we lend an ear.

Fourth, *reflexivity* is key to situating one's position in relation to the field. As expressed by Pink (2021), the place of the researcher in the material itself is a reflexive process that ultimately shapes how we come to learn and know the material and its field as researchers. Our existing experiences initially shape the study, but so do our gender identity, age, class and race. Therefore, Pink (2021: 48) urges ethnographers to interrogate the ways in which our own self is situated within the research. We will delve further into this point in an upcoming section on positionality (see below).

The last of Pink et al.'s (2016: 13) principles relates to how researchers are encouraged to find *unorthodox modes of communication*. In finding such alternative communication practices, researchers can 'seek out ways of knowing about other people's worlds that might otherwise be invisible'. Sometimes, we are guided to our fields by letting the algorithms take us there. We might not even know it is happening before we realise we have encountered a new space, and begin to seek it out. What spaces have you encountered lately? Which Taylor Swift Reddit forums have you tracked for years? What 'pro-ana' or 'pro-mia' content have you found on Instagram lately and found interesting? Have you subscribed to ContraPoints on YouTube since the start? Have you encountered lots of Putin jokes that seem kind of nationalist, but in a humorous way, on Telegram? Yes, you may be on to something.

Finding the Field

In terms of data collection, ethnography does not rely on any single approach. Instead, ethnographic understanding is developed by exploring several different sources of data in close detail. The most common methods for collecting ethnographic data are observation studies – where the researcher may or may not be a participant in the analysed context of interaction – and interviews. Ethnographic researchers may also collect other sources of data, the character of which may differ depending on the specific nature of the research setting. The notion of ethnographic fieldwork is often used as an umbrella term for all of the different strategies that a researcher employs to gain insight, as rich and detailed as possible, into the milieu under analysis. The primary source, however, tends to be observation studies, often in the form of so-called participant observation, where the researcher assumes a dual role of both taking part in and observing the setting. As linguistic anthropologists Jan Blommaert and Dong Jie (2010: 7) note: 'fieldwork is the moment when the researcher climbs down to everyday reality.'

But, even without taking the internet into account, ethnographers have had to deal with the fact that people of today very rarely locate their existence in pre-defined and fixed places. A history of increasing mobility, migration, tourism and commuting, as well as mediated communication, has relativised the ethnographic notion of the field. In a digital society, an ethnographer can be 'in the field' almost whenever and wherever they wish. But, Hine explains, the notion of a bounded fieldsite was always flawed. As new media researcher and anthropologist Andreas Wittel (2000: 1) writes:

> The idea of 'a culture out there', with the implication of being, firstly, a coherent entity and secondly, unique and different from other cultures becomes increasingly difficult to sustain given the developments and transformations we've been witnessing the last few decades.

The pluralisation of cultures, in general, makes the notion of 'the field' as a geo-spatially defined area of research problematic. This is further accentuated when one uses the internet, or parts of it, as one's ethnographic fieldsite. Instead of seeing the field in terms of spatially defined localities, the focus then shifts towards 'socio-political locations, networks, and multi-sited approaches' (Wittel, 2000: 8). In the years since writing *Virtual Ethnography*, Hine has increasingly questioned whether online settings should be used as ethnographic fieldsites in themselves. Is it enough to simply analyse online interactions in order to draw meaningful conclusions about social reality? Is it useful at all to adhere to the online–offline boundary when designing ethnographic studies? Hine (2012: 14) asks:

> Can the study actually be reliable if it is not rounded out by pursuing its concerns more deeply into the lives of participants? Would we be able to trust what participants said about themselves? Put bluntly, can a study that only looks at online phenomena be more than mere voyeurism?

And Hine does indeed think that 'online-only' studies can be justified. Many significant social things do happen in settings that are online-only, and as long as one is clear about which conclusions can be drawn with a given research design and object without becoming speculation, all is fine.

Sometimes, the sites we have decided to investigate turn out to be the wrong ones. Then, it can be important to leave room for revising our initial intent so that it clearly represents the area we are interested in researching. In a methodological paper, Vicari and Kirby (2023) discussed the limitations of their intended data collection on Facebook and Twitter when researching influences on middle-class understandings of food consumption in Brazil and South Africa. They explain how the initial interviews with stakeholders (phase 1), and later members of the middle classes (phase 2), shaped their understanding of which platforms to study during the third phase of data collection:

> This three-phase process was extremely important, not least because it soon showed that our initial plans to focus on Facebook and Twitter as key data sites did not resonate with the contexts we aimed to investigate. Both the interviews with stakeholders and middle-class users and our conversations with the country teams suggested that Facebook was indeed very central to the social media strategies of organisations and very popular with users in both Brazil and South Africa. Meanwhile, Twitter, tempting as it was to research due to data accessibility, was often a secondary part of the social media strategy of the activist organisations interviewed in phase 1 and rarely mentioned unprompted by consumers in phase 2 interviews in either country. Instead, Instagram soon emerged as a popular platform, especially in Brazil. As a consequence, we incorporated Instagram in our research design.

Usually, digital spaces such as platforms, apps and devices become the place where fieldwork happens in digital ethnography. The field may, as such, become however big or small the research becomes, but it can also become more or less digital. For example, this can be done by exploring the ephemeral traces of user interactions on social media, including their swipes and scrolls. Møller and Robards (2019) have suggested that our swiping or scrolling practices can be forms of ethnographic fieldwork in themselves. These ephemeral traces of user interactions connect our bodily movements to the media we use and incorporate into our everyday lives. Because of this, the authors proposed a:

> methodological framework of 'ephemeral, mediated mobilities' for representing less materialized ways of being with social media. The framework brings together small-scale media–body interactions – such as swipes and scrolls – that are often left unexplored due to them being between the intent of the user and a measurable action in the interface. The economic value of these small-scale interactions is also difficult to perceive. Our proposed framework is thus in other words concerned with somatic and digital movements, which, in our media ecology, remain largely untracked, unarchived or only precariously archived. Significantly, our framework places the user's action, experience and meaning-making as central to productive research inquiry. (Møller & Robards, 2019: 96)

This relates to the perspective of non-digital-centric-ness, as it takes into account the surrounding contexts conditioning our digital presence and interactions. In line with Møller and Robards, we would not only incorporate the social conditions of certain interactions but also the role of the bodily experiences of users in understanding their ways of using platforms. In Chapter 10, we will further investigate the ways in which interfaces of platforms allow certain forms of communication.

Positionality: Are You an Insider or an Outsider?

Classic anthropology and ethnography emerged from the academic discipline of natural history, and, typically, the early ethnographic studies were about allegedly 'primitive' cultures and people living in European colonies. Since then, however, an increasing number of studies have been made by researchers in the communities where they live and work themselves. What has remained, however, is the aim to identify and interpret the underlying meanings and principles of the social setting that one is analysing, as well as the idea of relatively long-term engagement in a fieldsite. This means that ethnography places a double demand on the researcher. It is assumed that in order to develop an adequate understanding of what it is like to live in a setting, one must become immersed in it and take part in it. But, at the same time, one must maintain the role of being a relatively detached observer.

The word 'relatively' is key here. The most important part of ethnographic research is staying reflexive. This means that we need to become aware of our own personal characteristics, histories and relations to specific fields, and make 'a deconstructive exercise for locating the intersections of author, other, text, and the world, and for penetrating the representational exercise itself' (Macbeth, 2001: 35). Because this is: exercise. We need to rethink the ideas we hold of ourselves again and again (and again). Our gender, age, race, nationality, sexuality and even our personal taste shape our positionality in research. It is not solely about introspection, though, as much as it is an exercise in accountability training, where we learn to see how our positions may affect our research findings. Sometimes, our positionality in relation to our research subjects presents relations and distances between us in ways we need to be extra aware of. In his ethnographic work on a black 'ghetto' area in the USA, Hannerz's (1969) informants joked about him being what the Black Muslims had referred to as the 'blue-eyed, blond devil', but he noticed that, because of being Swedish, he was given an out from the status as a real-life villain. The insider position can be a way 'in' to a field which may take a long time to penetrate. For Evelina Liliequist (2020), her own LGBTQ identification could facilitate the building of trust in the interview situation when conducting interviews as part of her ethnographic process for her doctoral thesis. But reflecting upon this, she writes:

> The, if not otherwise, imagined community that the informants believed we shared based on my person and my experiences, contributed, I believe, to creating a safe space where experiences could be shared. This trust, however, came with a heightened ethical responsibility. In cases where I sensed that the interviewees might have told more than they did with another researcher, to whom they did not feel some form of kinship, I have contacted the informant and double-checked whether certain quotes felt okay to use. In all cases where this has been relevant, the informants have then given their consent. (Liliequist, 2020: 36, our own translation)

Accessing spaces that we are familiar with can, in this way, be a straightforward way of conducting research. We already know the space so well – why not research it? Sometimes our students wonder if they need to focus on an app, a social context, or a forum that they themselves are not a part of or have not heard of before. But being part of these contexts over a long time may, instead, help them to find interesting viewpoints, research questions and potential informants. For example, researchers need to understand the specific forms of discourse, speech acts or platform vernaculars[1] of their chosen field of study, in order to ask the relevant research questions and explore them fully. Because of this need for prior knowledge of the field and the limited time offered for students to immerse themselves in fieldwork (for example, as the method for their BA or MA thesis, students may be better off researching the spaces they already inhabit since they understand them better). In a methodological paper about his own positionality during the research process, Gelir (2021) writes:

> This paper draws on [an] ethnographic study that investigated Kurdish preschool children learning Turkish and literacy (e.g. drawing, writing and numeracy) in a nursery in Turkey. [...] During my teaching years in that nursery (2009 and 2011), I wanted to study young children's learning, especially language learning. My students' (Kurdish) Turkish learning experience inspired me to conduct this research. Researchers having teaching experience highlight that classroom observations motivate them to conduct research [...]. *In other words, our past experiences play an effective role in shaping our future endeavours.* (Gelir, 2021, our emphasis)

---

[1]Platform vernaculars have been defined by Gibbs et al. (2015: 257) as 'shared (but not static) conventions and grammars of communication, which emerge from the ongoing interactions between platforms and users'.

Read that again: our past experiences play an effective role in shaping our future endeavours – also as researchers. We learn throughout our lives, both inside and outside of academia, what may be interesting scopes of research, and when we listen to our curiosity, we usually end up in fascinating places.

Being reflexive in our research practice also means coming to terms with the insider position we may hold in relation to the field we are attempting to study. The auto-ethnographic approach takes this position even further. Here, the researcher not only acknowledges, but also uses, their personal experiences in the analysis, along with their emotions relating to it (Ellis et al., 2011). It's a bold approach, that's for sure. Instead of hiding the personal connections to the data away, it highlights them. It can be understood as a form of theorised self-reflexivity where these divisions between self/society and distanced/personal are shattered (Reed-Danahay, 1997: 2).

We may also have to reflect upon our own being in relation to the research itself, the research participants, or our participation in the field. This can, definitely, stir up emotions. Liliequist (2022) has referred to the emotions stirring in her as part of her own inner journey of expanding her knowledge of digital LGBTQ spaces, which she herself had inhabited, but around which her understanding was further developed continuously through the ethnographic process. In addition to this developed knowledge of the space themselves and others inhabiting them, she was able to develop her own understanding of herself and her role within them. After publishing her PhD thesis, she reflected upon this developed relationship between herself, the research field and the research findings, saying:

> I was surprised by my own reaction when working with the digital material. All these happy, beautiful pictures of LGBTQ people living out in the country. On several occasions I burst into uncontrollable crying. Before starting my dissertation work, I never gave a thought to the fact that there could be a sadness in me related to the loss of a place. My research started a movement in me that has not stopped since. Ahmed whispers to me in a caring voice: 'You bring your past encounters with you when you arrive.' (Liliequist, 2022: 462, our translation)

While autoethnography and ethnography are separate approaches, there is a fine line separating the two, according to Pink (2021). As participants in a field, we relate to it in different ways, and we may include these experiences as part of our analysis. By holding ourselves accountable for the insider–outsider positions we may hold, we are able both to become ethically aware and to hold our research findings accountable for review.

Being familiar with the field can help in many ways to gain access to it, as well as for being able to interpret the data. However, Barley and Bath (2014) emphasised the danger of being overly familiar with the field, meaning that you no longer become surprised, or may fail to ask the right questions or be distant enough in your analysis to see patterns. In particular, Atkinson et al. (2003) stated that the 'culture shock' of doing fieldwork is, or should be, an important part of the journey of doing ethnographic enquiry. But is it necessarily better to be shocked, or is that view tied to an idealised image of ethnography? In her account of this 'culture shock' narrative, Irwin (2007) states that it has become a taboo topic within the wider anthropological community:

> For multiple reasons, researchers admitting to fear or depression during
> fieldwork may be ridiculed or dismissed as 'cowardly anthropologists'.
> I was once strongly encouraged to conduct fieldwork in a remote
> village rather than a larger town, so that I could be a 'courageous
> anthropologist'. Chiefly, I would argue that this is closely linked to a
> sense of academic bravado and competitive virility. I was given the
> idea that there is something inherent about studying anthropology
> that protects one against 'culture shock', and that anthropologists
> are 'naturally' better at negotiating unfamiliar situations than other
> sojourners. As such, anthropologists can feel a certain 'culture shock'
> within their own academic community, because their experiences of
> culture shock 'in the field' remain unacknowledged, and they are feeling
> something that they believe they ought not feel. Culture shock has
> become a taboo topic within the anthropological community.

We will continue to review ideals, norms and ideas of ethnographic fieldwork in the sections below. But, first, how do we find our data?

'Following the Data'

When you have decided on a specific digital context: a platform, an app, a forum thread, specific Instagram accounts, or what-have-you, you are ready to start exploring it. But as you explore, you need to figure out what type of material you have there, how you can access it and how you are able to analyse it. Pink (2021: 3) has highlighted the importance of focusing on the visual when researching digital spaces, saying 'it would be difficult to be a contemporary ethnographer without engaging with digital media, technologies and the social, material and infrastructural environments and practices associated with them'. While a qualitative text analysis (see Chapter 6) of a dataset of posts derived from any of these spaces may present problems of data retrieval and storage, a digital ethnography is mostly about being present in these spaces and taking fieldnotes. A lot of notes. And depending on the nature of the field, these notes can include different types of data. Hammersley and Atkinson (2019: 152) write on how to record and organise data from ethnographic studies:

> What is involved here varies considerably depending upon the nature of the data. As regards documents (online or offline), these may require copying or indexing, while it may be necessary to photograph, video, and/or describe material objects, in ways that make possible analytic coding. In the case of observing patterns of social interaction, the ethnographer's own reflections of participation, and other participants' accounts, the fieldnotes and/or electronic recordings produced will need to be written up or transcribed. This can be a very time-consuming process, and sufficient allowance must be made for it in planning ethnographic research.

Yes, sometimes note-taking may also look like copy-and-pasting specific posts, taking screenshots or downloading images that are specifically relevant. This fluidity – and some might say chaotic way of approaching your data – is actually part of the advantages of using digital ethnography as a method. By 'following the data' via, for example, hashtags, platforms and communities, instead of downloading a dataset and performing an analysis on that dataset alone, the researcher is free to follow along the ride instead of acting on presupposed ideas about where to find the data. This idea has been explored by Johanna Sumiala and Minttu Tikka (2020) as one of the key features of digital ethnography, which allows for a much greater scope of the multi-sited fields available online. They base this idea on the thinking of Marcus' (1995) methodological rule to 'follow the thing'. As digital worlds, communities and socialities are explored, researchers will, more often than not, be forced to stay aware of how digital cultural expressions and communities move and slide in between different contexts. While starting out on one platform, in one specific context, the researcher can move between different parts of the platform as well as move in-between different platforms for context. If you're an avid Instagram user, you might be familiar with the concept of crossposting content from TikTok, for example. If you, as a researcher, find specific TikToks being crossposted that seem relevant to the study you are conducting (for example, videos about body positivity when you are conducting a study about everyday political action in digital contexts), you might consider moving your analytical focus over to TikTok. This does, however, require the adaptability and skillset of being able to find and contextualise content from different platforms. This method of 'following the data' is one of the biggest advantages of digital ethnography and can even help to gauge the field as a first step, regardless of which other methods are used.

The point of gathering material in this way is to be able to analyse its implications on a larger level. Looking at the YouTube versions of Joe Rogan's podcast can tell us about more than just his show. It can tell us something about the politicisation of masculinities, the rhetorical practices of debaters within the realms of podcasts, and the importance of humour in politics. Maybe? This is a skill we may need to give a bit of time in order to develop, and in the words of Pink (2021: 155):

> This requires an openness to the unexpected, the ability to look beyond
> the obvious, to have an eye for those insights that enable us to get to the
> core of what we need to know and which will enable us to see things
> differently, and to follow them through the fieldwork and materials.
> This is not to sound mystical; visual ethnography analysis is not a skill.
> Rather it is learned with practice, and over time practiced with increasing
> confidence. Analysis in visual ethnography entails making links between
> different research experiences and materials such as photography, video,
> field diaries, ethnographic writing, participant produced or other relevant
> written or visual texts and objects. These different media and materials
> represent different types of knowledge and ways of knowing that may be
> understood in relation to one another, and which it is the ethnographers'
> responsibility to bring together to create meaningful narratives and
> connections.

Viewing, Lurking and Immersive Practices

Being a digital ethnographer may look somewhat like just being a normal person in the 21st century – constantly checking one's phone, keeping up with fast-shifting trends, and scrolling endlessly. It does not always look like real work. Sometimes students wonder if they need to pick something more difficult since it really does not look much like research at all. But what is going on underneath the surface is much more complex than that. While research of any type, in any context, can be overwhelming, the possibilities presented by the opportunities to search and get such huge amounts of data online will emphasise the feeling that one lacks the capacity as a researcher to account for the full complexity of it. Both the issues of ethics and those such as the one around reducing complexity in data are best dealt with through constant critical reflection and by being open about the 'messy details' of our research process.

In a special issue of the *Journal of Digital Social Research* (JDSR), Abidin and de Seta collected articles where researchers were allowed to 'acknowledge the messiness, open-endedness and coarseness of ethnographic research in-the-making'. Because it can be messy, for sure. They write (Abidin & de Seta, 2020: 1) that sometimes it can be more valuable to get insights into other scholars' messy steps of research, than reading the 'how to' genre of methodological literature, which is why it is important that:

> Laying bare our fieldwork failures, confessing our troubling epistemological choices and sharing our ways of coping with these issues [as it] becomes a precious occasion to remind ourselves of how much digital media, and the ways of researching them, are constantly in the making.

Doing this may be quite challenging, as it is not always easy to explain online fieldwork to outsiders. As de Seta (2020) writes:

> In my personal experience, the recurring question: 'what exactly did you do during your fieldwork?' becomes particularly awkward to answer, and often results in a jumbled mix of claims about using certain digital media platforms, collecting certain forms of online content, and spending time with a certain number of users in everyday situations. As a matter of fact, my 'doing ethnography' is grounded on several layers of involvement, and done through multiple forms of participation and observation.

As explained by de Seta, this question brought him to embellish the process in ways that may not stay true to the fieldwork itself. And, here, he relates to how this is just a new way of lying about ethnography, much in the sense that Gary Alan Fine wrote about back in 1993, in his article 'Ten lies of ethnography: Moral dilemmas of field research', where he states that while researchers are 'lone rangers, cowboys and individualists', they are also 'fundamentally honest, as lawyers, clergymen, doctors, and car salesmen are fundamentally honest'. However, he continues, we do present our work in ways that 'permit life to run tolerably smoothly – to engage in impression management' (Fine, 1993: 269). While using the controversial word 'lie', Fine's purpose was not to confront the real-life work of ethnographers, but, rather, the perceptions and ideals they are confronted with in their work.

In de Seta's (2020) rethinking of these lies, he presents the 'Three lies of digital ethnography', all considering the way we present our fieldwork, rather than flaws in the actual fieldwork. These three 'lies' are presented by de Seta as three researcher types: the 'networked field-weaver', the 'eager participant-lurker' and the 'expert fabricator'. The first of these relates to the multi-sitedness of research on digital media. We all know the different 'spaces' we inhabit which in turn relate to one another, and are difficult to grasp in one-sited field studies. We need to think about how going live on TikTok relates to the inner workings of content creation in the 2020s in terms of money flow, user interactions and follower counts. We need to see the histories of other contexts in the sites we reside in during our fieldwork, otherwise we would not be doing it correctly. Additionally, our digital ethnographic fieldwork is not only taking place in the digital, it is a continuous intertwinement of spatial and contextual circumstances. However, when we write up our findings, we usually claim to have performed a pre-set choreographed dance in between these spaces. Often, rather, we follow leads and are 'grasping at straws, and immediately cutting away most of what came along with them' (de Seta, 2020: 83).

The second lie of being an 'eager participant-lurker' relates rather to our participatory contexts within the fieldsite, and how we relate to our informants. Participant observation is, as we have stated above, one of the most crucial parts of doing ethnographic research. However, the internet presents us with many more different forms of participation than traditional fieldwork. Different platforms may allow for certain forms of interaction that others may not. We may float in and out of active use to non-active lurking, sometimes mixing approaches at the same time. Hine (2007: 625) stated that browsing webpages, following links and moving in and out of platforms should itself be considered part of the participatory actions of digital ethnography. The dichotomy of either being a participant or a lurker may be a false one:

> Rather than reflecting on what different modes of participation meant for me and the people around me (whom I ironically still called 'participants'), I preferred focusing on answering the 'what did you exactly do during your fieldwork?' question in a professional manner, flattening my involvement into easily understandable nuggets of interaction proving my active presence in the field. Confronted by the injunctions of participant observation, I wrote myself into an eager participant-lurker: a master of all modes of participation, portrayed as impossibly co-located across multiple fieldsites, surveying digital media use from a vantage of carefully crafted presence. Besides the false choice between naturalist lurking and active involvement, the issue of participation should become a central concern of digital ethnography instead of a purely methodological decision. We participate, just like our 'research participants', through a wide range of modes of participation tightly connected to social dynamics and technological affordances, that go from the choice of shutting down one's smartphone to the visceral need to sustain one's presence in a tense online discussion. Choices about these participatory modes punctuate our everyday engagement with digital media, and embracing the uncertainty [...] resulting from the way these situated decisions are negotiated and made sense of is probably of more interest than flattening one's own persona into the apologetic figure of an eager participant-lurker. (de Seta, 2020: 88)

The third lie — 'the expert fabricator' — refers to the tendency of online ethnographers to go so deep into the settings that they study, to the point that they become embedded in the community in ways that may impact negatively on researcher objectivity. We may then present our results in ways that show our 'expert' (insider) position rather than that of an outside researcher. Ultimately, we risk becoming bound to being experts at specific platforms and subcultures, rather than to carrying out the research itself. For example, de Seta recounts how his PhD thesis was read by outsiders:

> This process of expertise acquisition is part and parcel of the ethnographic mythology: in my case, both research participants and colleagues expressed admiration at my dedication to delve into the linguistic and semiotic repertoires of Chinese digital media – the former by praising my vernacular competence ('You know slang terms even I have never heard about!'), the latter by recognizing the time and effort needed to acquire the necessary sociotechnical literacy ('You must have spent a lot of time learning how to use all those Chinese apps.') (de Seta, 2020: 91–92)

Among all of these 'lies', we are encouraged to stay reflexive, attentive and flexible in our approach to digital methods. We need to find a way to balance these expectations and stay true to the research at hand.

NETNOGRAPHY: A PRACTICAL FRAMEWORK

As you will have gathered from the chapter this far, digital ethnography is not generally a set of ready-made tools or any prescriptive methodology. Rather, it is a flexible approach that incorporates various online research methods that share the ethnographic basis. In fact, its adaptability can be seen as one of its upsides and, as Hine (2000: 13) points out, 'the lack of recipes for doing it' may be seen as a strength, as there is much to gain from seeing ethnography as 'a lived craft rather than a protocol which can be separated from the particular study or the person carrying it out'. This, then, means emphasising the highly subjective and context-dependent nature of digital ethnography, which is heavily reliant on the researcher's reflexivity and continuous negotiation with variegated digital environments and online communities. Ethnographers have generally, Hine says, 'resisted giving guidelines for how it should be done'.

Starting out as a student exploring this method, it may, however, seem a bit scary and confusing to be without any set of clear guidelines to follow. This is very likely one of the key reasons why, when we supervise BA and MA theses, the methods chosen tend to be those that have clear and well-established protocols, such as thematic analysis or various types of quantitative approaches. But we must remember, once again, that the method should be chosen depending on what we want to achieve with our research, rather than because of how the method is generally described in methods books, and if the student – as in many cases – is in fact looking to explore quite complex interactions between people and technology, digital ethnography may be one of the most appropriate methods to choose, despite its lack of clear and concise protocols.

One exception to the principle of far-reaching openness in the broad area of digital ethnography is, however, the work of Robert Kozinets who has written extensively about the method that he calls *netnography*. This is certainly a form of digital ethnography, but quite different from the so-called virtual ethnography of Hine and others. Kozinets offers a highly structured way of conducting net-nographic research, arguing that even though flexibility is good – especially for experienced scholars – such flexibility 'assumes a type of hands-on mentorship and a basic level of knowledge and ability that is not always the case' (Kozinets, 2020: 7).

So, even though there is much to recommend the flexible and adaptable frame-work of digital ethnography, it may be useful when starting out to have some firm principles or steps to guide the work. As you become increasingly comfortable in your role as a digital ethnographer, however, it is quite likely that your need for such principles will diminish, so that you can move towards a more flexible and open approach. But, for now, let's dive into the 'basic recipes' for doing netnog-raphy that Kozinets provides.

Forms of Data Collection

When it comes to data collection, Kozinets (2020) identifies three types of opera-tions: *investigative*, *interactive* and *immersive*. Investigative data operations are about collecting the empirical material for research by gathering a sample of information that was created by others and posted on digital platforms. This is done, Kozinets explains, by conducting desktop research using search engines and other digital tools. The process moves through five general steps: (1) *simplifying* your research questions by translating them into search terms and keywords; (2) *searching* based on those keywords in relevant places; (3) *scouting* – clicking, following reading, watching, listening to the material that results from the searches; (4) *selecting* which of the data to save into the dataset for your study; and (5) *saving* it.

Interactive data operations happen when the researcher somehow engages in questioning or interference. Examples of interactive data collection include online interviewing, posting public questions, posting comments to get reactions, asking things via email or direct messaging, using a research webpage to which participants are invited, and so on. Kozinets (2020: 250) suggests that this kind of interaction, whether it be through interviews, making posts, or any other mode, can happen according to five different 'engagement strategies'. The researcher can engage (1) *intellectually*, by deliberately trying to get a more far-reaching conceptual understanding of the context and people; (2) *culturally*, by paying attention to important practices, linguistic terms, rituals, symbols, abbreviations, and so on; (3) *historically*, by trying to understand the context in terms of its past history, traditions, myths, narratives and so on, that made the context what it is; (4) *emotionally*, by engaging with the feelings of the participants and trying to understand the emotional experiences that shape their interactions and practices; and, finally, (5) *socially*, by being directly involved such as in participant observation – openly communicating and interacting.

Finally, immersive operations are focused on collecting rich and descriptive data while also preserving the original context, according to a more anthropological model, by 'living' in the environment to be studied. In doing this, the researcher takes fieldnotes and begins making connections according to four sets of skills that are outlined by Kozinets (2020: 284): (1) *mapping* or, in Kozinets' words, 'reconnoitering', the territory to be studied, conceptualising and beginning to understand the ecosystem of the online context under analysis; (2) *recording*, which involves *logging the process* of search and investigation, noting down observations and impressions; (3) *researching*, in the sense of beginning to draw on existing theory and conceptual frameworks to gradually make sense of (1) and (2); and (4) *reflecting* by incorporating one's own experience of the immersion into the analysis, as well as one's own role in what is found and how it is interpreted.

Analytical Steps

Once the data is collected, or in fact partly also while it is collected, the researcher then moves on to analysing the data in order to make sense of it. Kozinets (2020: 332–333) introduces five types of operations that the analysis consists of, in various forms and combinations. He writes about the acts of (1) *collating* the data, which is about preparing it by getting it into codable form, through steps such as filtering, formatting and filing; (2) the crucial moment of *coding*, by which data is broken down into chunks that are assigned meaningful labels (see the description of thematic analysis in Chapter 6); (3) *combining* the codes into categories and themes to patterns that are more abstract; (4) *counting*, which does not necessarily mean numerical quantification, but can also be about describing found patterns with words that allude to quantity such as 'more', 'less', 'often', 'commonly', 'decreases', and so on; and (5) *charting*, which is the act of visualising, mapping and displaying data with tools such as tables, graphs, networks, word clouds, and so on.

Interpretation and Summarisation

The analysis is followed by the interpretation of results which, according to Kozinets' (2020: 364) description of netnography, can rely on a number of strategies from which the researcher may draw inspiration. Two important strategies are those of *theming* and *translating*. Theming is about trying to bring the different pieces of the abstracted analysis back together again in an analysis that forms 'a new conceptual whole'. By such theming, we can synthesise the different patterns and codes that emerged from data analysis in order to produce a somewhat coherent picture of what the data is saying. Translating, as described by Kozinets, is about 'moving between the worlds of data and theory' (see also Lindgren, 2020) and using the data to challenge, refine or extend the existing theoretical concepts. This can just as well also be about challenging our interpretations of the data with concepts from existing theories.

Kozinets also describes the strategy of *troublemaking*, which is a useful counterpart to the work of finding order and structure, as it involves critically examining the findings to identify the inconsistencies, contradictions and exceptions that may challenge or complicate the identified themes. This approach ensures that the analysis is not oversimplified and acknowledges the complexities of the data. Additionally, Kozinets invites the researcher to also engage in other strategies that may help move the interpretation of results forward. He then writes of using various modes of artistic expression to explore the results ('talenting'), and of 'holding the telescope backwards' (Kozinets, 2020: 375) to try to reconnect the data to the contexts from which it was taken ('turtling'). Finally, the strategy of *totalising* is about bringing together the different strands of analysis and interpretation in order to explore the conceptual whole that the analysis and interpretation have resulted in, and to engage in broader discussions about what it means to the world.

CONCLUSION

Ethnography is an important practice within the field of anthropology, but, as we have argued in this chapter and previously in Chapter 1, an ethnographic sensibility can guide the researcher through the entire research process, no matter the method chosen. Before beginning any form of study, collecting data and delimiting the research field, you may need to 'immerse' yourself in the field first. In this chapter, we have discussed different aspects of, and challenges in, doing a digital ethnography, from beginning to end, from the perspectives of different scholars in the field. We hope you will find your own way through these perspectives and enter the field with a backpack full of tools to incorporate into the analysis. While the field may differ in scope, size and connections, digital ethnography provides possibilities for studying digital media and society in deeper ways.

6
QUALITATIVE TEXT ANALYSIS

Key Questions

- What different types of qualitative methods can be used for analysing textual data?
- How does coding work, and how can themes be found within coded text material from digital sources?
- What different approaches of discourse analysis can be utilised for the study of digital media and society?
- How can a critical approach be implemented, where power and the ideas that are seen as 'common sense' are scrutinised?

Key Concepts

qualitative content analysis * thematic analysis * discourse analysis * genealogy * archaeology * subject positions * nodal points * floating signifiers * CDA * building tasks

There are many different approaches to dealing with text data, and while some strategies may be quantitative or computational (see Chapter 7), others take a more qualitative or interpretive approach. It is methods of the latter type that we discuss in this chapter. Because no matter if you want to collect a dataset of tweets during a US presidential election, or work through a Reddit thread on prepping, or any other text-based digital media dataset, you will often have to qualitatively analyse these texts in some way, shape or form.

The available methods for qualitative text analysis are essentially non-digital. What we mean by this is that you have probably heard of all of these approaches before in your traditional methods classes, as these strategies for close reading texts and finding their broader meanings have been used for decades in humanities and social science research, and they were not developed for use on digital media content in particular. After all, a text is a text. However, because of the sheer volume and diversity of digital text data that are available today, and not least because of the risk that researchers become too enamoured with, or too convenient in relying on, the constantly developing computational techniques, qualitative text analysis methods are today becoming more important than ever before.

But just because the methods to be discussed here have a pre-digital history, this still does not mean that digital contexts don't matter. The digital aspects of the texts that you analyse are an important part of the ways in which you will be able to interpret them, situate them and ultimately make sense of them. In this chapter, we focus on a set of frameworks for qualitative readings of text data, namely qualitative content analysis, thematic analysis and discourse analysis. These approaches can, and sometimes must, be combined with the computational methods discussed in Chapter 7. You may, for example, want to explore at a large scale the interconnectedness of different hashtags used by activists during the Mahsa Amini protests in Iran in 2022, but, while exploring those connections using a computational method, you may come to find that you need to read a selection of the posts closely in order to get the full picture. This is why, throughout this book, we try to encourage you to think pragmatically about which methods you use, and when.

QUALITATIVE CONTENT ANALYSIS

As we will discuss further in Chapter 7, the method referred to as 'content analysis' is mostly associated with quantitative approaches that entail counting various elements in texts. However, for the purpose of this section, we will focus on *qualitative* content analysis, which is one of the more straightforward ways to approach text content, through reading it. Mayring (2000, Section 1) presents qualitative content analysis as an empirical and methodologically controlled approach to analysing texts within the context of communication, which does not deal with the 'rash quantification' of text. Qualitative content analysis is rather about identifying patterns, themes and meanings through a careful and systematic examination and interpretation of the given text.

Klaus Krippendorff (2019), a scholar who is mostly known for writing about the quantitative forms of the method, has discussed – more broadly – the variety within the field of content analysis and that 'content', in itself, may even have been a bad word to use in the first place for this type of analysis since it can be understood in so many ways. Is it referring to content which is contained in a text? Is content a property within a text? Is content what is emerging in the analysis? Such different ways of defining content could lead to wholly different analytical procedures. Krippendorff (2019: 28) clarifies that texts can, and will, be read differently by different readers, otherwise 'content analysis would be pointless'. If interpretations were obvious, everyone opening up a newspaper would be a researcher. So, to analyse the content of text data, some methodological procedure is needed.

Mayring (2004) writes about four key procedures in content analysis: summarising, inductive category formation, explicating and structuring. The approach of *summarising* reduces the material into a manageable short text while preserving essential contents. *Inductive category formation* gradually develops categories from the material. The strategy of *explicating* seeks to collect additional explanatory material to make unclear textual components understandable and easier to interpret. This could for example be about an analysis of a meme, leading you on to read up about the origins, meanings and further contexts of that particular meme in order to be able to move forward with your content analysis. Finally, the strategy of *structuring* is about filtering out particular aspects of the material and categorising it based on some ordering criteria that have been decided beforehand. All such strategies may be used as tools for abstracting the content of texts to move your research process into a stage of systematic classification and identification of themes or patterns, which is what is at the core of qualitative content analysis.

Such strategies, however, do not in any way guarantee that interpretations will always be the same. Some of our students were quite cross when reading an academic article for a seminar in a course on Media and Popular Culture, where the authors had interpreted elements of the Netflix series *Stranger Things* through the lens of psychoanalysis: 'The Demagorgon's head resembles a vulva; when its face opens to consume its prey, the various layers described by Setrakian bear a likeness to the vaginal opening, labia minora, and labia majora' (Lu et al., 2022).

But these interpretations were not made out of thin air. And the students came to the realisation that since the writers of this text themselves were psychoanalysts, or trained in the psychoanalytic tradition, they would interpret the Demagorgon this way. After all, the Demagorgon looks sort of like a vulva – if you think about it. Aligning with such insights, Krippendorff points out that texts do not, in fact, only have one meaning, and meaning should not be 'seeked out', or 'found', lying around waiting for you to dig it up to the surface. It is much more fine-grained than simple excavation. It demands you look at individual parts and question them – how can we understand this? How would my interpretation be read by someone else? What does this mean, in a higher analytical sense? Meaning, additionally, should not be understood as something that texts simply 'contain' or 'have'. They need context, and as analysts, we can provide them with such. Krippendorff (2019: 28) elaborates that texts are not reader-independent, meaning that 'data arise in the process of someone engaging with them conceptually'. But texts do not themselves contain meaning. Instead, he makes clear that '[t]exts have meanings relative to particular contexts, discourses, or purposes'. Start examining the pieces one by one, then all together, then one by one again. How can you interpret these individual parts, and the totality of them?

Drisko and Maschi (2015) differentiates between three different approaches to content analysis: basic content analysis, interpretive content analysis and qualitative content analysis. Basic content analysis, then, is one of the more quantitative types that we discuss in Chapter 7. Interpretive content analysis focuses rather on the different levels of content that can be analysed – both manifest and latent content. Manifest refers to what is actually there, the actual words, phrases, uses of metaphor, and so on, while the latent has to do with what is implied or implicitly there in the text. The latent parts of the material make out the interpretation of what is being communicated. We use this form of analysis in everyday life as well. Imagine your partner asks you to pick your dirty laundry up off the floor. Are they implying you are messy? Is this question a form of criticism on their behalf? Should you be offended? You tell us.

What is important here is the interpretation itself, as you perform it within your analysis, not the number of times a word has been used. Instead, the analyst can use a code sheet when reading the text, and tracing where, and how, certain concepts or contexts may appear. Imagine you are interested in user migration from Twitter to Mastodon, due to Elon Musk's acquisition of Twitter in 2022. Taking a stand against new user policies due to this power shift, many users decided to close down their account on Twitter, or keep their account on Twitter while moving their activity to Mastodon. Imagine you want to track this move by looking at users' first interactions on the new platform by seeing what they are posting. Are they expressing critique against Elon Musk? Are they exhibiting signs of nostalgia? How are they talking about their old platform, now that they have joined their new one? Consider this quote as an example:

> Jeez I finally made it to Mastodon, but what is up with this place? Where is everyone? HELLO????

How would you code this? On a manifest level, this Mastodon user is posing several questions regarding the platform and its users, especially in an attempt to find others. The user is including several words or symbols in order to convey something about their emotive state, such as 'Jeez' or writing in capitals 'HELLO' and adding '????'. What might this imply on a latent level? That this individual has moved over from another platform, say Twitter? Could this be a sign of critique, maladaptation or discontentment? How might we understand such discontentment by providing any form of context to this post? Can we connect this emotive state with other, previous, research regarding any form of digital migration from one platform to another? In their study of digital migration patterns of online fandom communities, Fiesler and Dym (2020) identified both technical and social challenges to digital migration, in terms of, for example, experiencing a steep learning curve (that sometimes is never overcome) and that communities from previous platforms splinter, since not everyone migrates, or migrate to different places.

THEMATIC ANALYSIS

Another often-used method for analysing qualitative text data is known as thematic analysis, and was introduced by Victoria Clarke and Virginia Braun (2006). The basis of thematic analysis is uncovering and identifying themes in qualitative data materials. While this might seem easy, for example reading tweets regarding the rebooted version of *The Little Mermaid* and easily putting them under the two themes 'celebratory' and 'racist', it goes deeper than that. In fact, the researcher needs to be aware of all possible versions of these interpretations. Especially important is the realisation that themes do not just 'emerge' from data, instead 'theme development is an active process; themes are constructed by the researcher, based around the data, the research questions, and the researcher's knowledge and insights' (Braun & Clarke, 2022: 35). This speaks to a more general understanding of the researcher's need to stay reflexive, in many different senses of the word. On a personal level, we need to take into account our own values and how that may shape our research and knowledge production. We have already discussed this in Chapter 4 as an important part of the ethical reflections, especially as it is connected to 'positionality' in relation to the field of study we have chosen – for example, how does your race, gender, ethnicity, abilities or age play a part in how you are able to understand, or contextualise, a specific research topic? Will you understand the people you study better because you have gone through the same thing before? Will you interpret a statement differently if you hold the same political views as the individual expressing it?

Additionally, we need to consider other kinds of reflexivity: functional and disciplinary (Braun & Clarke, 2022: 13). Functional reflexivity means thinking critically about our chosen methods, while disciplinary reflexivity relates to how we may have been conditioned by different academic disciplines towards prioritising specific methods or research questions. Here, we need to consider not only our personal dispositions, but also the systems within which we have learned, and been exposed to, specific forms of research.

The level of reflexivity is especially important for thematic analysis, and while it always has been, Braun and Clarke have attempted to make this even clearer by calling the method 'reflexive thematic analysis' in their later work. While the method was introduced in the mid-00s, they have further developed and clarified the need for reflexivity within this particular method. However, we would suggest that these are important questions to pose for any type of researcher, using any form of method. The authors suggest that one important part of beginning to analyse a piece of material is not only performing the analysis itself and presenting it well; a lot of the work should be done by keeping a 'reflexive journal' outside of these rigid forms of analysis work. This could be a physical notebook that you keep at hand while doing the analysis, where you can jot down incoherent thoughts, notions, words, or ideas that you might get during the process of research. It could also be a digital document or note where you allow yourself no structure. And we will return to the relevance of being messy in just a bit.

Thematic analysis is done in six steps, according to Braun and Clarke (2022: 35–36), beginning with the initial familiarisation with the data, which means you need not only read but also re-read your data several times over, while making notes about what jumps out to you in these first attempts to understand what is there. Second, you need to start coding. Now, people generally understand coding in the sense of writing computer code, but, here, we are simply looking for analytically apprehensive descriptions of the dataset that range from the word-level (semantic) to the more analytical (latent) meaning of the data. One important thing to remember is that your code labels should not simply summarise what is there, but also capture something within the data that is important for the total picture. For example, when researching the meaning-making discourse on Twitter after the 2011 Norway attack on the island Utøya outside of Oslo, one quote read (altered for anonymity):

> Media calls him a 'gunman' but if its a muslim, he's a #terrorist along with all other muslims! #hypocrisy #oslo

This quote could, at a surface level, be interpreted as a critique on a vocabulary level, focusing on what type of word is used for different perpetrators of violent crime. However, there may be a wider form of media critique embedded in this quote, relating not only to the explicit word choices but also to racist biases within the news media. What is important at this stage is not to set your analytical standpoint in stone just yet. When supervising students, we encourage them to be messy, and actively tell them when they hand in their first draft of their coding: 'This is a hot mess, well done! Now you can start connecting all of these dots. Let's see where you end up!'

When you have gained a big-picture mess of codes that may or may not become part of your final write-up, during this third step of the analysis, you are ready to start reviewing codes and deciding which are important enough to constitute the themes in your study. Try adding codes together and see what happens. One of my (Moa) research papers came from a dataset of tweets made after a terrorist attack had occurred in central Stockholm in 2017, where some of the codes – 'help', 'spread the word' and 'offering lifts' – could be added up and made comprehensive within one and the same theme, 'coordination'. In this way, these initial codes may speak to a wider theme that becomes central to the analysis, in a way that each individual code may not.

What now, you have your themes, just write the paper, no? Hold up, not so fast. You are ready for the fourth step of your analysis. Now is the time to review your themes and check if they make sense. Themes that might have made sense when you were deep-diving in the dataset might not anymore, so what does that say about those themes? Braun and Clarke (2022) are clear on this point: now is the time for revision, even radical revision. Be harsh. Killing your darlings is one major step when it comes to this type of revision, and it can really feel like a murder has taken place – especially if your supervisor is the one that has asked you to pull the trigger. Just remember that this is part of the process and an important part of it.

Be attentive to what your themes represent, and most often, this is where you will need to return to the books – get searching! Because what you are deciding to keep will have to be written in relation to what others have done before you in previous research. Also, how can you understand these themes in relation to bigger analytical or theoretical concepts? This is a form of 'library stage' of analysis; you need to take your time with this and start looking around. Maybe you have missed one major theoretical book that would help you build the argument for a specific theme you are working with. Ask around, especially your local librarian. They can be a godsend in moments like these.

The fifth phase sets you up for further revision. Review your themes and try to be clear, if just for yourself: what story is this theme telling? How does it relate to other parts of your argument? Additionally, now is the time to get real about naming our themes, shall we? Because finding the absolute most to-the-point heading can take a long time. Where you have identified the theme 'security politics', what are you really talking about? Dig deeper. What have you read in the literature? How can you sharpen your analysis? Could it really be about a 'politics of fear', as you read in Altheide's 2006 book? Is it about images of threat, where you can talk about affectivity? Which might make you think of that book by Sarah Ahmed where she talks about the concept of 'stickiness'? Maybe your headline should be 'The stickiness of fear'?

The sixth and final step here is the write-up of your analysis. But let me be clear, you need to write your way through each of these steps. This is just the final, polished, version of the analysis, where you write for an external reader that has not partaken in the research process and knows what you are trying to say. Clearly state what your analysis shows, and how it relates to your research questions. And voilá, you have made a thematic analysis from start to finish!

DISCOURSE ANALYSIS

The previously discussed approaches, qualitative content analysis and thematic analysis, are two quite structured and intuitive methods for working with text. They are both, in their own respective ways, drawing on what our brains do when reading text – summarising, abstracting and seeing themes and patterns in content. This immediacy is the power of those two techniques, and they are especially powerful when combined with other methodological approaches, such as, for example, digital ethnography, network analysis, computational text analysis or any other method, for that matter. By using these approaches, you can effectively analyse textual data systematically to gain a deeper understanding of the content and context of your data and to identify patterns or themes within it that a more unstructured reading would likely miss. Sometimes, however, qualitative text analysis is more about 'reading between the lines', and about finding some form of underlying meaning of a text, or problematising the potential consequences, in terms of power and politics, of what is said and how it is said. In those cases, the method of discourse analysis comes in handy.

Discourse analysis, however, is not as much of a hands-on method as the previous two. Rather, it mixes theory and method to form a rather abstract framework for exploring the ways in which our use of language shapes and is shaped by social contexts, power relations, ideologies and identities. In other words, while techniques like qualitative content analysis and thematic analysis are more structured and intuitive in nature, discourse analysis is a method that involves exploring language use in a way that focuses on the deeper underlying meanings and social implications of text. This also means that the method is more challenging and less formulaic. In fact, in order to fully grasp discourse analysis, we must delve quite deep into areas such as linguistics, political theory, social psychology, cognition, and so on. Our aim in the following, however, is to introduce you to a set of different approaches within the broader area of discourse analysis, which can provide a good starting point for you to better understand the method and how you could potentially make use of it in digital media research.

But, first, let's turn to the very concept of 'discourse'. In everyday speech, the term is often mistaken as a synonym for 'discussion'. Sometimes, when we ask our students to identify a discourse as part of an assignment for class, many of them return with examples from controversies in the media, such as tweets or

TikToks using specific hashtags. While public debates certainly can uncover specific discourses, these debates are not synonymous with what we call discourse. An abortion discourse, for example, may be shaped by a midterm election and the ways pro-choice organisations agitate during it. But an abortion discourse is much wider and broader than those specific moments in time. Instead, it continues and morphs through different time periods, in different contexts and in different political climates. Therefore, when our students seek out specific activist hashtags or groups, as part of the assignment to identify a specific discourse, they tend to focus more on the controversies rather than the discourse itself. In these cases, we usually ask them to specify: what is the discourse at hand here? Is it a political discourse? Is it a libertarian discourse? Is it an activist discourse? Or is it an abortion discourse?

Discourse is commonly understood as both constitutive and constituted in the sense that it allows us to speak of, and see, the world in specific ways, but it is simultaneously shaped by individuals through their social practices – it goes both ways. Discourse, as such, can shape many parts of our social world, such as our social relations, social identities and, on a wider level, our systems of knowledge.

But where does a discourse start or end? According to Ernesto Laclau and Chantal Mouffe in their 1985 book *Hegemony and Socialist Strategy: Towards a Radical Democratic Politics*, discourses are shaped through articulation. Certain ideas may become 'fixed' within a discourse – for example, *democracy* is generally understood as a central and important component of politics, and we tend to understand it as a political right to vote, organise and speak out against oppression. However, what something like *rights* really means in practice can be debated by different parties and in different contexts. It can be, both, a woman's right to choose to have an abortion, as much as it can mean the right to ban sex education in primary school in specific states in the USA.

Such are the kinds of issues, and conceptual discussions, that a discourse analysis perspective urges us to face. In order to untangle these complex relationships between how texts produce knowledge, and the power relationships built into that knowledge, different directions within the broader field of discourse analysis have introduced some different sets of frameworks and concepts. In the following, we discuss Foucauldian discourse analysis, discursive psychology, discourse theory and critical discourse analysis (CDA).

Foucauldian Discourse Analysis

Michel Foucault, generally seen as the founder of discourse analysis, describes discourse as '[...] practices that systematically form the objects of which we speak' (1972: 49). In other words, a discourse is a set of statements, practices and beliefs that shape our understanding of the world around us. Discourse analysis of texts, then, is about mapping and analysing such statements, practices and beliefs as they are expressed in the text. Foucault (1981) used both a genealogical and an archaeological perspective in order to uncover discourses.

Genealogy, as developed by Foucault, refers to his method of historical analysis that aims to uncover the contingencies, power dynamics and historical conditions that shape the present. It seeks to challenge established narratives and reveal the historical processes that have produced existing structures of power and knowledge (Foucault, 1989). Discourse is a central concept here, as it refers to systems of power-knowledge that regulate and produce social practices and identities. Discourses are not merely linguistic or intellectual structures but encompass a broader network of practices, institutions and power relations that shape and govern our lives. Furthermore, discourses are deeply intertwined with power, as they operate to define what is considered true, acceptable and normal within a given social context.

Genealogy and discourse are connected in the sense that Foucault's genealogical method seeks to trace the historical development of discourses. Instead of assuming that knowledge or power is based on timeless truths or universal principles, Foucault argues that discourses are historically contingent and shaped by specific power relations. Genealogy examines how discourses emerge, evolve and become dominant over time, revealing the complex interplay between power and knowledge in shaping social reality. Through genealogical analysis, Foucault aims to challenge and disrupt the dominance of particular discourses by unveiling their historical conditions and exposing the mechanisms through which they operate. By understanding the historical contingencies that underpin discourses, Foucault opens up the possibility of questioning established truths and power structures, thereby providing a critical perspective on dominant forms of knowledge and power.

All this talk of historical patterns may seem out of place in discussions of contemporary digital and social media, but Foucauldian discourse analysis can in fact be a quite valuable tool in uncovering how power operates through language, also in the online setting, not least because today this is where people's lives and social relations are increasingly mediated. Imagine, for example, if the genealogical perspective was to be used in a study of YouTube. This could, then, be about tracing the emergence of certain discourses about gender, race or sexuality within certain genres on the platform and how they have been reinforced and challenged over time.

This also aligns with Foucault's notion of *archaeology*, which refers to a method of analysis that aims to uncover the epistemic and discursive conditions that govern the emergence and functioning of various forms of knowledge. It focuses, however, on the internal coherence and logic of discourses, rather than their historical development. It seeks to understand the rules, concepts and categories that define what can be said, thought and known within a particular historical epoch. But the application of this perspective need not be limited simply to historical epochs. In the context of researching digital media and society, it could also be used to explore the ways in which digital technologies themselves shape and influence knowledge production, as well as the forms of power that are embedded within them. Or, more narrowly, one might design a study of a particular digital subculture, or a certain kind of content or community on a given platform, and approach that object of study from Foucault's archaeological perspective by looking at the underlying assumptions, categories and rules that shape the discourse within that specific context.

Foucault's archaeology is about uncovering the 'episteme' of a particular era or context, which refers to the specific set of discursive rules and conditions that define what is considered valid knowledge and permissible discourse at a given time or place. The episteme shapes not only the content of established knowledge but also the boundaries of thought and the conditions for the emergence of new discourses. Through the archaeological analysis, Foucault aims to unveil the discursive formations that operate within a particular episteme and examine how they produce and regulate knowledge. By understanding the underlying structures and rules that shape discourses, Foucault challenges the assumed universality and neutrality of knowledge claims, revealing the historically contingent nature of discursive practices and opening up space for critical inquiry. Imagine, for example, the way TikTok has been understood as a threat to Western society due to its connection to China – and by extension the Chinese government. These types of knowledge claims can be the focus of a discursive study, for example, by looking not only at the documentation from TikTok itself, but also at the legislative proposal put in place in different countries, and news articles written about TikTok. These types of materials, too, can be used as a basis for an archaeological analysis in a Foucauldian sense, and can uncover discourses regarding online privacy, risk and international politics.

Discourse, then, refers to the broader system of power-knowledge relations that regulate and produce social practices and identities. It encompasses not only language but also a range of practices, institutions and power relations that shape and govern our lives. Discourses are shaped by underlying structures of power, and they operate to define what is considered true, acceptable and normal within a given social context. Archaeology and discourse are connected in the sense that the archaeological method allows Foucault to analyse and understand the specific rules and conditions that govern discourses in a particular historical period. By examining the discursive formations, the underlying rules and concepts that organise knowledge production, Foucault seeks to uncover the epistemic limits, exclusions and power dynamics that shape a given discursive field.

Discursive Psychology

Discourse can also be analysed from other perspectives. In *discursive psychology* (Edwards & Potter, 1992), discourse is studied in the everyday practices of the language use of individuals. For example, when individuals talk to one another or answer questions in an interview setting, discourse psychologists focus on how rhetorical choices are made for different purposes of, for example, displaying specific aspects of one's identity as a discursive practice. Discourse psychologists are focused on the everyday uses of language as a signifier of discourse. They believe discourse is evident in our day-to-day lives, and that their role is to uncover it.

In particular, discursive psychology is interested in the human behind the discourse, which is why these individuals' positions within a discourse are an important part of the analysis. This is what is called *subject positions*, referring to how individuals position their identity in specific social situations, or how they are being positioned by others. This is key to understanding the psychological focus of this kind of discourse analysis, and the way it ultimately takes a stand against cognition as the basis for understanding identity. For example, Wetherell and Edley (2014) suggested that researchers interested in gender roles and masculinities should focus on the nuances of men's speech rather than their beliefs, norms and attitudes, in order to uncover the real-life conditions of masculinity. By focusing on the ways men talk, they were able to investigate affective, emotional, interactional and relational practices, rather than statements about their attitudes. 'When people show you who they are – believe them', as the great thinker Maya Angelou once said.

Discourse is, as such, embodied practices, both verbal and non-verbal. It is shown in active social settings and can be uncovered by exploring what is being said, how and why.

So, how does this all relate to the study of digital media and society? Well, in fact, discursive psychology, with its focus on subject positions, can be an invaluable tool for analysing how individuals position themselves and others within digital and social media contexts. Looking at highly expressive platforms such as, for example, TikTok, researchers can explore how users construct and negotiate their identities in relation to the norms and values that are prevalent within those online communities. As such, then, analysing the 'performances' of identity on such a platform can give knowledge both about the individuals and the underlying systems of meaning – discourses – that they are drawing on, operating within and perpetuating. Imagine, for example, a TikTok video where a vinyl record collector displays their ten favourite albums of all time. Through a discursive psychological lens, the focus would not solely be on the content of the list, but also on how this listing is helping the individual position themselves and others within the vinyl collectors' community, how they choose particular records and artists as a means to negotiate the norms and values of this specific subculture, and how they construct their identity in relation to it.

Discursive psychologists apply this 'anti-cognitivist' approach to identity (Billig, 2009), and stress the ways it is fluid and responsive to social conditions. Specifically, discursive psychology is interested in unpacking, critiquing and 'respectifying' (Button, 1991) studies not only of cognitive psychology but also of social and developmental psychology, as well as their methodologies (Edwards & Potter, 2001).

Because of this, rhetoric is central to studies in discursive psychology. By allowing rhetoric to become an important part of the analysis, discursive psychologists are able to stress the argumentative and persuasive nature of language use (Billig, 1987), and the 'argumentative texture of social life' (Wetherell, 1998: 394).

But, in a digital context, where do we find such conversations and argumentative textures? Maybe we could take Wetherell and Edley's study of masculinity as an inspirational starting point for an analysis of discussions on Reddit. Remember, we would not be interested in the attitudes that men claim to have, but rather in how masculinities are actively performed. So, in what type of subreddit would we be able to study this? One popular subreddit is related to true crime. When a homicide occurs, individuals turn to r/TrueCrime and start searching for posts on the specific case. What do we know? Are there pictures? Does anyone have any idea who the perpetrator was? Can anyone link their Facebook page? And ultimately: Can we crack this case?

Here we might want to focus on how individuals interact when trying to find out information in unison. We can focus on the ways some users are belittled for presenting faulty theories, wrong links or misinterpretations of the case. We can see which users' comments are upvoted or downvoted, and consider how this affects their visibility in the conversation and the hierarchy of users in the thread. All of these factors may speak to larger themes of how gender and masculinity presents itself in interactions, and also in digital contexts.

Discourse Theory

For Laclau and Mouffe (2014: 91), discourse is first and foremost understood as the practice of forming meaning through the 'structured totality resulting from an articulatory practice'. Discourse is, in other words, a linguistic representation of reality and the struggles of meaning that form it. Articulation is the actual act of creating, reshaping and negotiating the discourse (Winther Jørgensen & Phillips, 2011: 131–133), because a discourse is never stable; it constantly shifts and expands, withdraws and evolves. But it does seek stability.

According to Laclau and Mouffe (2014: 100), discourse is formed through artic-ulatory practices by partially fixating meaning around specific *nodal points*. A nodal point is a concept, word or construct that is, at least temporarily, given a relatively stable meaning. Some concepts never seem to be provided with definitive meaning, however hard one may try. Think of the concept of 'fake news'. It seems obvious that this means disinformation – defamatory, miscon-strued information disguised as news. But, depending on the context in which it is used, 'fake news' can correspond to many different discursive positions, and, as expressed by Farkas and Shou (2018), become a 'floating signifier'. The notion of floating signifier refers to those concepts that 'float' around, which different poles attempt to lock down into specific meanings (Laclau, 2005). In the research of Farkas and Shou, they reflect:

> Instilled with different meanings, 'fake news' becomes part of a much larger hegemonic struggle to define the shape, purpose and modalities of contemporary politics. It becomes a key moment in a political power struggle between hegemonic projects. In this way, we argue that 'fake news' has become a deeply political concept used to delegitimise political opponents and construct hegemony. (Farkas & Shou, 2018)

Within discourse theory, the context of a text is important for how we understand it, which is an idea derived from the poststructuralist tradition. Jacques Derrida, a key figure in poststructuralism, said *il n'y a pas de hors-texte* which is often trans-lated as 'there is nothing outside of the text', but means quite literally 'there is no outside-text'. What he meant by that is that you cannot understand the meaning of texts outside of the social structure and its power relations built into the cul-tural fabric and historical context of society. This is what Lacan calls the 'symbolic order' (Malpas & Wake, 2013: 80). Since language will possess the same social stratifications as does society at large, some social groups will be misrepresented (or not represented at all) within the language used. Lacan calls this 'the Other' of language, since language and discourse are created outside the individual and are forced upon us through interpellation, a term from Althusser, who describes the ways in which ideology simmers down through society to become part of the individual (Althusser, 1971).

With such a heavy focus on the discursive, it may seem that the material world is not as central to these types of theories. But Laclau and Mouffe never deny the realities of the material world; rather, it is intertwined with and interdependent on the discursive. Carpentier expanded on this point in the following manner:

> Laclau and Mouffe's position does not imply that the existence of the material is questioned [...], only that they deny that extra-discursive meaning exists, very much in line with Hall's interpretation, which rejects 'The idea that "discourse produces the objects of knowledge" and that

nothing which is meaningful exists *outside discourse* [...]' (Hall, 1997a: 44 – emphasis in original). In Hall's statement, the presence of the words 'nothing is meaningful' is crucial, as he (similar to Laclau and Mouffe) did not want to argue that 'nothing exists but discourse', which is a common misunderstanding when discussing discourse theory (and constructionism in general). Also, Butler (1993: 6) referred to this misunderstanding when she wrote: 'Critics making the presumption can be heard to say, "If anything is discourse, what about the body?" Discourse theory acknowledges the existence of the material (including the body) as structurally different from the discursive, but it also rejects the '[...] classical dichotomy between an objective field constituted outside of any discursive intervention, and a discourse consists of the pure expression of thought' (Laclau & Mouffe, 1985: 108). Discourse is not the same as the material, but still very necessary to make sense of it. (Carpentier, 2017: 19)

Social practices, according to Laclau and Mouffe, are always articulatory, which means that there never can be non-discursive practices. This might sound difficult to grasp, but let us give you one example. Even though you may not have watched the *Eurovision Song Contest*, meaning that you may not have shared an opinion about it ('the Finnish song sucked this year', 'the Polish vote was all over the place!'), or purposefully dragged it into conversations at the pub ('how can you possibly watch that crap, I could never'), you have probably been confused when you get back to university after the weekend and find everyone talking about it – this is still contributing to the discourse on the *Eurovision Song Contest*. Being nonchalant about a subject is also in itself a meaningful positioning in relation to it.

Discursive articulation can also take place in unexpected ways. While we may mostly think of 'political participation' in a traditional sense in the form of voting, registering as a member of a political party, campaigning, and so on, the idea of political participation can be extended into realms of less structured or obvious political action. For example, Tim Highfield explored the 'everyday politics' as performed online in his 2016 book *Social Media and Everyday Politics*, where he examined content posted on Twitter, Facebook, Instagram and other online platforms finding overlaps between the everyday and the political, where the silly and the serious overlapped, and where there was indeed a politics also to the banal and sometimes, seemingly, totally irrelevant conversations occurring online. In this book, he explores the role of sausages in the Australian elections, which to a non-Australian seems like a nonsensical relationship. The #democracysausage, however, was so recognisable in the Australian Twitter sphere during the 2016 election, that Twitter even chose to change its main emoji for the ongoing election under the hashtag of #ausvotes from a traditional ballot box (🗳) to a hot dog (🌭). In that way, the everydayness of the presence of hotdog stands outside of the polling stations all around Australia, was made part of the main collective understanding of this major political event on Twitter. The sausage, in this case, becomes a discursive component in the discussion of political participation – even though a sausage, in most other contexts is, in fact, just a sausage.

So how can we use Laclau and Mouffe's discourse theory in our own studies? Their concepts of articulation, floating signifiers, nodal points, and so on, can indeed be very useful in researching digital media and society. Carpentier (2010: 261) writes about 'discourse theoretical analysis' (or DTA) as a form of analysis that makes use of 'the conceptual toolbox' of discourse theory. In this case, the terminology of Laclau and Mouffe can function as 'sensitising concepts' that guide the analysis into specific conceptual frameworks, found within the theories. As Carpentier (2010: 261) writes, '[s]pecific to DTA is the use of the conceptual toolbox of DT, which provides the secondary sensitising concepts produced by the incorporation and re-configuration of other theoretical frameworks situated outside of DT'.

When it comes to using Laclau and Mouffe's approach in analysing digital media and society, one can focus on identifying central signifiers and how they are articulated within specific discourses on given platforms. For example, the concepts developed in discourse theory could help out in an analysis of discussions that occur around a certain hashtag on Instagram, because they provide a framework for understanding how different elements (e.g. images, texts, comments) are brought together and given meaning through the discursive practices of the users. The concept of articulation is useful in research like this as it identifies how the different threads of a discourse are interwoven and built up, and how different words, terms or symbols are chained together in order to construct a particular meaning. When it comes to the notion of floating signifiers, it could potentially be mobilised in analysing exchanges on Instagram by exploring how patterns of meaning-making around a particular phenomenon shift between being connected to different signifiers depending on the context of the discussion. For example, a hashtag that initially starts as a form of activism (#MeToo) could be adopted by commercial brands to market their products, leading to a transformation of the meaning originally attached to it.

Critical discourse analysis (CDA)

The purpose of critical discourse analysis (CDA) is to analyse 'opaque as well as transparent structural relationships of dominance, discrimination, power and control as manifested in language' (Wodak, 1995: 204). And this is why CDA is a great tool for starting to investigate discourses that surround us in 'critical' ways. The aim of CDA is to uncover the social relations of power present within texts both explicitly and implicitly (Van Dijk, 1993: 249). CDA scholar Ruth Wodak (1997) draws on Habermas' idea of language as being a medium of domination and social force, underlining the importance of staying critical of how history, power and ideology relate to language practices. CDA aims to study the:

> real, and often extended, instances of social interaction which take (partially) linguistic form. The critical approach is distinctive in its view of (a) the relationship between language and society, and (b) the relationship between analysis and the practices analysed. (Wodak, 1997: 173)

Norman Fairclough's critical discourse analysis divides discursive elements into three dimensions: 'text', 'discursive practice' and 'social practice'. This is a helpful tool for students in identifying the various parts and structures of discourse. The 'text' dimension is at the centre of this framework (see Figure 6.1). According to Fairclough (1992: 2), the textual dimension can encompass any form of communication. It could refer to any written or spoken product, such as Instagram posts, news articles, or flyers from an activist group.

Fairclough places discursive practice outside of the text (see Figure 6.1), meaning that the manifestations of discourse are connected to wider contexts of discourse. This allows us to understand these textual elements within a larger discursive practice. On the one hand, this level involves the actual production and consumption of texts, meaning that a text is always constructed in one context and consumed in another. Stuart Hall famously argued that while texts are encoded with meaning, their meanings are not uncritically decoded by readers. According to Hall, meaning is never fixed or determined, but rather the audience interprets texts based on their own frameworks of knowledge and perceptions, and they are not passive recipients of meaning.

When looking at digital media contexts, the analytical levels proposed by Fairclough (see Figure 6.1) can be applied to different platforms, social interactions and societal conditions. First, not all interaction on social media is textual, but rather, multimodal and diverse. As we will discuss further in Chapter 9, when we direct our attention to solely visual elements, the internet is largely visual. At times, text and images may be interconnected and require joint analysis rather than separate examination. Therefore, analysing various elements of the material at hand can be based on Fairclough's discourse analysis model.

Imagine you want to perform a discursive analysis of TikTok videos using the hashtag #BLM in June 2020. Here, we are able to repurpose Fairclough's three-level model of exploring the 'text', 'discursive practice' and 'social practice' as separate levels of the discourse (see Figure 6.1) while also including platform-specific modes of communication. On the first level, we are interested in 'what's there' – what we can see, how it is made, how this video has been interacted with, what hashtags are used, and so on. These tangible elements of the material should be analysed first in regards to the visual elements that are present (what is visible, how it is presented, what elements are incorporated), the technical features that have been used (stitch/duet functions, sounds, text-to-speech, etc.), the quantifiable measures available (number of likes, comments, shares, saves, etc.), and which hashtags have been referenced.

On a second level of analysis, where we focus on the discursive practices of the videos, we rather look at the interpretations and understandings of the videos rather than their physical aspects. Consider the content of each video, whether it showcases police brutality victims, BLM protests, reflections or jokes. Fairclough's approach urges us to examine how the material is produced and consumed. Texts are created within a specific context and consumed within another, making it crucial to analyse interactive elements like the comments sections. How are viewers responding to each video? Do the comments sections serve as a platform for political discourse? However, with more than 300 comments on each video, it can be challenging to analyse all the material thoroughly.

You need to scale back and make some cuts. Let's be realistic. Since TikTok's interface allows you to view the most liked comments at the top of the comments section, we can choose how many of these we will analyse. Maybe five? Ten? What do these comments reflect: are they supportive, critical, educational, and so on? What patterns can we see when it comes to the reception of these videos within the comments section?

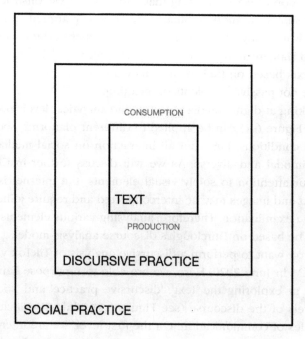

Figure 6.1 Fairclough's CDA model

The last step of analysis should be focused on the videos' 'social practice', where they become interpreted in relation to broader contexts. For instance, the Black Lives Matter movement is not restricted to the digital realm, and thus we must view the material within the broader societal context of that social movement, both on- and offline.

So, if we want to leverage CDA in researching digital media and society, there are several opportunities to do so. For example, one can use the methodology to analyse how social media platforms are being used as a tool for political mobilisation and activism, or to examine how user-generated content on these platforms constructs and reinforces social norms and beliefs. The contribution of CDA in doing such analyses is that it allows for a more nuanced understanding of how language, media and power intersect in shaping social reality, through focusing on the different levels of text and context that Fairclough's model highlights. Furthermore, CDA as applied to, for example, discussions in an online forum can help us understand how power dynamics play out in virtual spaces and how users position themselves within these power structures. The point of using CDA to try to get at such things is that it provides a critical lens that goes beyond surface-level analysis and can uncover the underlying power relations at play in the language use of the participants.

Doing Discourse Analysis

In carrying out a discourse analytical study of phenomena on digital media platforms there are, in sum, many different concepts and points of entry that can be used. As we have discussed in the preceding sections, one such way is to draw on the genealogical and archaeological metaphors of Foucault and approach what people say on digital media platforms as a type of discourse that constructs and reinforces power relations, constituting certain phenomena as 'true' or 'normal' while marginalising others. This, then, encourages us to adopt a critical and sceptical viewpoint towards what is being presented as 'common sense' or 'self-evident' and to try to scrutinise the underlying power structures that may create and be proliferated by the ways in which things are talked about.

Another way, then, would be to draw on the concept of subject positions from the field of discursive psychology. This means that we stay with a focus on underlying power structures, but now with a particular focus on how they make people position themselves, and be positioned by others, according to particular views of how the world functions and what roles should be filled in it. Doing research that focuses on subject positions, you can observe how people on digital media platforms align themselves with, or resist, particular discursive ways of understanding the world through how they construct their own and others' identities. Yet another way is to draw on Laclau and Mouffe's discourse theory, with concepts such as nodal points, floating signifiers, and articulation, which will still emphasise the role of power relations in shaping discourses, but in this case with a stronger focus on how certain concepts may become politicised through how users of various platforms articulate them in their discourse. Finally, the CDA perspective is about seeing texts in their discursive, and broader, context, for example in line with Fairclough's analytical model which emphasises the three levels of analysis: text, discursive practice and social practice.

Even with these conceptual pointers, however, it might be quite challenging to get going with analysing discourse. Our experience is that many students take an interest in the kinds of critical analysis that the discourse perspective offers, but its strongly theoretical side sometimes makes it difficult for them to apply it in practice. By comparison, the more structured approaches, such as thematic analysis, will seem less daunting, but may, on the other hand, not be set to capture the nuanced power relations that are at play in discursive practices. Therefore, once again, we should not hesitate to use combinations of approaches to suit our research question and study context. A quite common approach in qualitative text analysis is in fact to use some more neutrally mapping or explorative approach, for example qualitative content analysis or thematic analysis, as an initial step of text analysis, to then turn to a more critical framework, such as discourse analysis, for the subsequent stages of analysis, as this will make it possible to tease out the deeper levels of meaning.

Discourse analyst James Paul Gee explains that language always consists of certain *cues* and *clues* that guide us – regardless of whether we are researchers or everyday 'users' of the discourse in constructing our real-world situations through discursive practices. He calls these 'building tasks', which are the steps involved in constructing meaning through language. By engaging in these building tasks, we use language, and other meaning-making systems, to create and re-create our social reality. The tasks happen all at once, and among people that interact collectively. This may be in an actual interaction situation, such as between two people communicating in a YouTube comment thread or a discussion forum, but it may also be in more abstract ways such as when a reader of certain content enters – in their own mind – a process of interaction and negotiation with the author of the text, as well as with other texts that they know of, and with broader sociocultural knowledge that is brought into play in the reader's reception of the text. Discourse, therefore, according to Gee, can be seen simultaneously as a cognitive achievement, an interactional achievement and an intertextual achievement. That is, discourse happens in our minds, in our social situations, and between different texts and contexts of meaning-making. Gee (1999) defines six building tasks that can all be – regardless of which discourse analytical specialisation you take inspiration from more broadly – helpful in conducting discourse analysis in a systematic way. These tasks are:

1 *Semiotic building*: What specific knowledge, and which ways of knowing, are important in the analysed context?
2 *World building*: What is taken for 'real' and 'unreal' (accepted and not accepted as true; possible and impossible to do) in the analysed context?
3 *Activity building*: What activity or activities are going on in the analysed context, and of what specific actions are they composed?
4 *Socioculturally-situated identity and relationship building*: What identities and relationships are relevant to the analysed context, and with what attitudes, values, ways of feeling, knowing, believing, acting and interacting, are they related?
5 *Political building*: How are status and power, or any other social resources seen as valuable, constructed in the analysed context?
6 *Connection building*: How are the interactions that take place, explicitly or implicitly, connected to past or future events?

Gee explains that different elements in the discourse – choice of words, choice of grammar, choice of imagery, choice of emoji, choice of colour, choice of sound, and so on – contribute in different ways to carrying out these different tasks of meaning-making, and furthermore that many of the elements contribute to carrying out more than one task at the same time. Still, trying to analyse and deconstruct digital media content – a TikTok video, an Instagram image, a YouTube channel, a set of tweets, a subreddit, a Twitch stream – based on the six building tasks, can offer a systematic way of uncovering the underlying socio-cultural, historical and political factors that shape the construction of reality and social interactions in the context under analysis. Gee (1999: 86) points out that discourse operates through a chain where certain clues or cues in our language use 'help assemble or trigger specific situated meanings through which the six building tasks are accomplished', which then leads to the emergence of 'situated meanings' that 'activate certain cultural models', which in turn shape our understanding and construction of reality. Trying to analyse how the building tasks are carried out in the content you are analysing is thus a way of laying bare such 'cultural models'.

CONCLUSION

In this chapter, we have run through the basics of some different approaches to qualitative text analysis. It may seem daunting – which of these approaches will you ultimately end up using? In all honesty, we often decide this based on our gut feeling. If reading Foucault seems like a good call, do that. If thematic analysis seems to focus too much on the text, skip that. Hopefully, you will feel inclined towards some of these approaches, and keep reading. Because while this chapter can provide an overview of the methods available, there's more work to be done. Pick up the books from the library and get curious about them. We emphasised the role of curiosity in Chapter 3, and this is where it gets really important. In a sea of methodological approaches, you need to keep in mind the choices available to you, but also to pick and choose which of these you want to use. The overall idea we want to convey in this chapter is simply that text is an important unit of analysis, especially online. And by using these methods, you are able to uncover much more than the text itself – what does it represent on a higher analytical level? This is where you will be able to incorporate these methods in favourable ways moving forward.

7

COMPUTATIONAL TEXT ANALYSIS

Key Questions

- How have methods for computational text analysis developed, and how can they be used in digital media research?
- What is *distant reading*, and what is the motivation behind it?
- What is the relationship between *computational linguistics*, *natural language processing* and digital media research?
- Which different methods for text analysis exist, what kinds of knowledge can they bring out, and how can they be useful for scholars of digital media and society?

Key Concepts

distant reading * content analysis * corpus analysis * natural language processing * machine learning * topic modelling * word embedding * sentiment analysis

---

In recent years, new groups apart from computational linguists and computer scientists have become more and more interested in using computers for analysing text – for example, social scientists and media studies researchers. It was, however, linguists and computer scientists that started to develop these methods. This was because they saw a need for methods that could analyse large numbers of documents – generally, numbers large enough for it to be hard to read and make sense of for any reasonably sized group of human researchers. In this chapter, we will give you an overview of various methods and tools used in computational text analysis, such as computational linguistics, natural language processing (NLP), sentiment analysis and a couple of machine learning techniques.

After reading this chapter and becoming familiar with the techniques and what they can do, you will hopefully get a feeling for how you might be able to use them in your research. Our argument is that this is less about clearly distinguishing all the separate approaches from one another, and more about understanding their underlying principles. By doing so, you will know in which directions to look further when facing various future research challenges and be able to think more about the role of computational text analysis tools in your methodological bricolage.

A History of Computational Text Analysis

The internet and social media have given rise to new types of large-scale and text-based datasets, which has led to a growing interest among scholars in analysing patterns within them. Computational text analysis has become a rapidly expanding field with applications in various areas such as business and marketing, text editing software, and in online content recommendation systems. Additionally, it is an increasingly important area for research in the humanities and social sciences.

Generative AI is advancing rapidly with the development of models such as GPT (Generative Pre-trained Transformer), which can be used through clients such as ChatGPT. These types of generative AI programs allow users to ask any question they want and in seconds have fully-formed answers delivered to them in a format that resembles natural human language. This opens new avenues for research, as these models have a better understanding of language than previous technologies, making context-sensitive text classification and recognition more effective. But these types of language models may also threaten society and the media ecosystem, for example when used to impersonate others, by cheating on a test or creating false narratives.

The modern era of computational text analysis in media and communication studies started in the 1940s and 1950s when pioneers such as Norbert Wiener and Claude Shannon started out using computers for language analysis. Wiener developed a statistical approach to language analysis, which involved breaking down texts into smaller units and counting the frequency of certain words and phrases (Julià, 2001). Shannon also broke new ground by showing how language could be quantified and analysed mathematically (Shannon, 1948), paving the way for the development of natural language processing (NLP) and computational linguistics.

NLP was further developed in the 1960s and '70s through the creation of more advanced computer programs and algorithms, and during the 1980s with the addition of machine learning and neural networks. These technologies have allowed for more sophisticated language processing, including recognising patterns and making predictions based on large amounts of data (Spärck Jones, 1994). While NLP was rooted in a vision to facilitate communication between humans and computers by enabling computers to understand, interpret and generate human language, its tools are also powerfully used to analyse a wide range of text-based data, including social media posts and other digital sources of 'naturally occurring language online'. Examples of NLP techniques that may be useful in research on digital media and society include: sentiment analysis – which uses natural language processing to determine the emotional tone of written text; topic modelling – which identifies and categorises topics within text data; and what is called named entity recognition – which identifies and classifies named entities such as people, places and organisations in text data. An area related to NLP is that of computational linguistics. This area of study centres on the wider systematic and computational description and processing of language – such as speech recognition, machine translation, information retrieval and language modelling – while NLP refers to more specific applications of computational linguistics for processing and analysing texts.

While scholars in the areas described above tend to rely on these kinds of methods alone, as they have a particular interest in applying and developing the approaches as such, the use of computational text analysis that we advocate for in this book is a helpful component in the broader methodological bricolage used to analyse digital media and society. The methods described in this chapter will be the most powerful if used in mixed-methods combinations with other, more interpretive and qualitative approaches. Consider, for example, the possibility of enhancing the insights gained through online ethnography with text analysis approaches that can help you identify patterns and themes in much larger amounts of data. It could also be the other way around, such as when a pattern found through computational methods applied to huge text data can be enhanced by close reading parts of the same material through qualitative text analysis.

Before we move on with this chapter, we want to introduce you to two key concepts in computational text analysis: *documents* and *corpus*. First, there is the notion of *documents* which are the core units of the material you want to study. Documents can come in various forms, such as books, articles, emails, social media posts, and even entire websites. In digital media research, the documents we approach are most often social media posts, comment threads, forum posts, blog posts, and other units of textual content found online. Second, the collection of documents that our study works with is referred to as a *corpus*, which is simply a term used to describe a body of written or spoken language that has been gathered for analysis.

In sum, computational text analysis has come a long way since its inception in the mid-20th century. The techniques and approaches have evolved, and the field has expanded to cover more and more domains. But, again, while NLP and computational linguistics are crucial components of computational text analysis, it is important to use them in combination with qualitative and interpretive methods for a more comprehensive understanding of phenomena in digital media and society. One common use of computational text analysis in research on digital media and society is to carry out a content analysis of social media posts. This involves using software to extract and categorise the text of social media posts, allowing researchers to identify patterns and themes in the data (Schwartz & Ungar, 2015). Another commonly used method is sentiment analysis. This method has been used particularly on data from Twitter (Neri et al., 2012; Bhuta & Doshi, 2014; Sharma et al., 2019; Garg et al., 2020).

Conway et al. (2019) discuss using NLP in analysing social media for public health research, including mental health and substance abuse. As more people turn to social media to share their thoughts and experiences, Conway argues, they can learn more about these issues than ever before. By leveraging NLP in studying contexts such as these, researchers can unlock new insights into these complex problems and potentially even help develop more effective interventions to address them. Furthermore, Zagal et al. (2011) have proposed that NLP can be used in game studies research, such as for analysing the readability of game reviews and sentiment analysis of user-submitted reviews. More broadly, Louis (2016) discusses expanding NLP work to cover a wide range of social media content, including microblogs, social networks and online forums. The previously discussed insight that computational text analysis methods work the best in digital media research when combined with qualitative approaches, is underlined by Broniecki and Hanchar (2017), who discuss the potential of using NLP to systematise the analysis of qualitative data, such as interview data. In addition to these applications, NLP has been used to analyse political discourse and propaganda. By analysing political speeches, social media posts and news articles, researchers can understand how language influences public opinion and shapes political discourse (Martino et al., 2020; Chaudhari & Pawar, 2021).

DISTANT READING

When you start out doing computational text analysis, especially in the context of mixed methods, a good way of thinking about what the approach achieves is in terms of performing a *distant reading*. Distant reading refers to analysing large amounts of text data to identify patterns, trends and themes that may not be immediately apparent from qualitative close reading. This approach is particularly useful when one is working with datasets that are so large that a close reading would be impractical or impossible to manage. Imagine a whole dataset of one million tweets – how could you possibly be able to read through them all? But it is still important to note that distant reading should not, by any means, be seen as a replacement for close reading as such, but rather as an approach that can complement it. As shown in Chapter 6 on qualitative text analysis, close reading allows for a deeper analysis of individual texts, providing a more nuanced understanding of their language and meaning. Distant reading, however, allows for a broader analysis of a large corpus of texts, providing insights into their overall trends and patterns. The general idea behind distant reading is that, by 'reading' texts from a distance, we can see other things than by looking at the text up close. One way of seeing it is that close reading allows for reading between the lines, while distant reading allows for reading 'above' the lines to see texts in terms of their more general topology.

Simply put, this means that distant reading lets us see text data from a bird's eye view, allowing us to identify patterns and themes that close reading would not reveal. As described by the originator of the notion of distant reading, American literary scholar Franco Moretti, instead of seeing the texts as letters and symbols on a page, we can see them as 'graphs, maps, and trees'. Moretti (2005: 1) writes that the distance from the text should not be seen as an obstacle but as creating 'a specific form of knowledge: fewer elements, hence a sharper sense of their overall interconnection. Shapes, relations, structures. Forms. Models'. What he means is that by taking a step back, we can better understand the overall structure and connections between various elements within the text.

To put this concretely, we can turn to the following tweet by Donald Trump: 'Wow, so many Fake News stories today. No matter what I do or say, they will not write or speak truth. The Fake News Media is out of control!' (@realDonaldTrump, 2017-10-04). A close reading of this tweet would focus on the specific language and grammar used, perhaps analysing the connotations of 'fake news' or examining the context in which this particular tweet was posted, that is, on what stories Trump was referring to on that day. In other words, a close-up interpretive analysis of this kind would be able to uncover various information, nuances and meanings embedded within, or implied by, the tweet itself. If the close reading were extended to an increased number of tweets, we would gradually get more knowledge about these aspects based on a growing dataset. But, still, the limitation of the close reading approach is that it would not be able to reveal larger patterns or trends in Trump's use of the phrase 'fake news' over time or, for example, how it compares to his use of other phrases.

Figure 7.1 can be used as the starting point for a basic example of a distant reading, based on the frequency with which Trump used the term 'fake news' over time. It began with a tweet in December 2016, stating: 'Reports by @CNN that I will be working on The Apprentice during my Presidency, even part time, are ridiculous & untrue - FAKE NEWS!' – and thereafter fluctuated back and forth, but gradually increased. There were spikes around September 2019, around the first impeachment inquiry against Trump, and in April 2020 when Trump faced criticism for his handling of the COVID-19 pandemic, including his comments about injecting disinfectant as a possible treatment (Gittleson, 2021). 'Reading' this graph does not reveal any of the things that the close reading could show. For example, it does not tell us anything about the specific context around each use of the term. Furthermore, it does not analyse the language or grammar used in each tweet, nor does it say anything about the connotations or implied meanings of the term 'fake news'.

A distant reading, such as that achieved through Figure 7.1, gives us a different kind of knowledge. Namely, it allows us to identify patterns and trends across a much larger amount of data that would be much harder, if not impossible, to discern through close reading alone. For example, without knowing anything about what the tweets are even about, we can tell from the graph that nothing happens on its left side, while something drastically changes on its right side. Furthermore, we can inspect the right side of the figure closer, to see that there is a gradual increase and that some spikes stand out. Adding the knowledge about the timeline on the x-axis, and some contextual information about Trump's career,

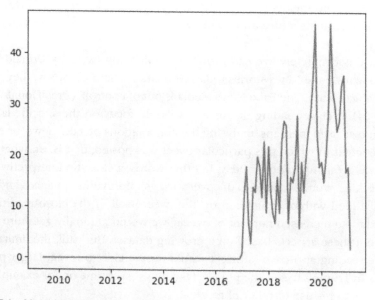

Figure 7.1 Monthly occurrences of 'fake news' or 'fakenews' in Trump's tweets

this reading – without ever looking closely at any individual tweet – says some interesting things.

These types of distant readings can also comprise of other forms of information, as can be seen in Figure 7.2. In this case, the concept of 'fake news' has been plotted as a central node in a network of related concepts. The interpretation of the figure is that those concepts that are connected by lines appear together in one and the same tweet – i.e. the same *document* – and that the more often they do so, the thicker the line in between them is drawn. Similar to Figure 7.1, Figure 7.2 is also a form of distant reading. 'Reading' this network graph, then, can provide us with a bird's-eye view of the relationships and connections between some of the key concepts in Trump's tweets, which we would not have the ability to discern in such a structured way from a close reading of the individual tweets. We see, for example, that 'fake news' is often mentioned by Trump, together with notions of 'media' and 'news media', which suggests that he is using the term to discredit mainstream media outlets. Furthermore, it can be noted that the concepts 'left' and 'radical left' are tied to 'fake news' as well as to one another, implying that Trump might be positioning the left as the originators of fake news. As a final example, we can see that 'media' is connected to 'corrupt' and 'democrats', which can be interpreted as Trump painting a picture of a corrupt and biased news industry that is working in favour of the Democratic Party.

Distant reading thus means approaching texts by 'finding numerical abstractions that can reveal qualities and patterns within those texts' (Liddle, 2012: 230).

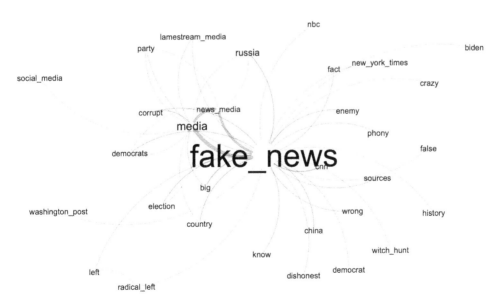

Figure 7.2   Terms co-occurring with 'fake news' or 'fakenews' in Trump's tweets

Returning to Moretti, he emphasises that the point of conducting distant reading is that it removes the focus from the particularities and details of individual documents. He writes:

> The trouble with close reading [...] is that it necessarily depends on an extremely small canon [...] You invest so much in individual texts only if you think that very few of them really matter. Otherwise, it doesn't make sense [...] What we really need is a little pact with the devil: we know how to read texts, now let's learn how not to read them. Distant reading: where distance [...] is a condition of knowledge: it allows you to focus on units that are much smaller or much larger than the text: devices, themes, tropes – or genres and systems. And if, between the very small and the very large, the text itself disappears, well, it is one of those cases when one can justifiably say, less is more. If we want to understand the system in its entirety, we must accept losing something. We always pay a price for theoretical knowledge: reality is infinitely rich; concepts are abstract, are poor. But precisely this 'poverty' makes it possible to handle them, and therefore to know. (Moretti, 2013: 48–49)

As we move on with this chapter, our introduction of a range of computational text analysis approaches is generally based on the underlying and central idea of distant reading, as described above. In a sense, maybe we are making a pact with the devil, as suggested by Moretti. But, at the heart of it, we want to provide you with the tools for distant reading which can be utilised to analyse large volumes of text data and uncover patterns you would not be able to map out with the help of close reading. Having said that, we also want to emphasise, again, that we don't believe that distant reading by any means should be seen as a replacement for close reading. Rather, it provides a complementary approach for analysing text data that can be usefully incorporated alongside other methods in the mixed-methods spirit of this book.

Doing Computational Text Analysis

The field of computational text analysis, especially since we are focusing now on its transdisciplinary use in researching digital media and society, rather than on the somewhat more clean-cut fields of computational linguistics and NLP, is very diverse. In practice, it encompasses a wide range of approaches, techniques and tools that researchers are using to analyse different forms and aspects of digital media and society, including social media and other forms of digital communication. This means that the best way to present these methods in a book such as this one is through providing a versatile toolkit from which you can pick and choose your methods and techniques based on the research task at hand. Each method has its own strengths and weaknesses, and depending on your research questions, data and context, some methods may be more suitable than others.

As we wrote about in Chapter 2, the guiding principle should be that of methodological pragmatism. As researchers, even though we all have our favourite methods, it is important to constantly remind ourselves of the importance of carefully selecting and adapting our methods to fit the specific research needs at hand, rather than blindly applying a single method or approach to everything that may come our way. This goes for research methods in general, as well as for combining the various computational text analysis techniques that are presented in this chapter. It is crucial to understand each technique's strengths and limitations and to select and adapt them according to the specific study in which you may want to use them.

Throughout the rest of this chapter, we will present six approaches to computational text analysis. In each section, we will discuss the background of the method, how it has been used in previous scholarship on digital media and society, and its strengths and limitations. We also provide a concrete example of applying the method in question by drawing on the same dataset used above, that is, the one consisting of tweets by Donald Trump. This dataset was retrieved from an online open-data repository,[1] and comprises all of Donald Trump's tweets (56,571 of them) dating back to 2009 until his first suspension from the platform in 2021. Our idea behind using this same dataset as a consistent point of reference for all examples in this chapter is that it allows for relatively direct comparisons between the different methods and their ways of working.

The first approach we will discuss is content analysis, which involves systematically categorising and quantifying the content of texts. Second, we focus on corpus analysis which does somewhat similar things as content analysis but draws on some specific techniques developed within the field of linguistics. Third, we introduce a couple of applications of natural language processing that are useful for identifying and analysing specific types of words and phrases within texts. Fourth and fifth, an introduction is provided to two popular machine learning methods for text analysis – topic modelling and word embedding. Finally, we will cover sentiment analysis which is a method for identifying and measuring the emotional tone of a text.

---

[1]Available in browsable form at www.thetrumparchive.com, and as raw data at www.kaggle.com/datasets/headsortails/trump-twitter-archive.

CONTENT ANALYSIS

Even though there are established forms of qualitative content analysis (Hsieh & Shannon, 2005; Elo & Kyngäs, 2008; Mayring, 2014), content analysis in media research is largely associated with its quantitative forms. Quantitative content analysis involves the systematic and objective counting of particular features within a media text, such as the number of times a particular word or image appears. This method is therefore often used to identify patterns and trends within media content, such as the representation of certain groups or themes.

While seemingly new and shiny, the approach has a long history and has been applied in different academic fields, including sociology and communication studies. Content analysis actually dates back to the late 1600s when the Church set out to scrutinise non-religious materials to determine whether they were to be considered dangerous or not. Since then, the method has evolved through studies of news reporting, political propaganda during the Second World War, children's literature, and more.

Quantitative content analysis has been the most clearly outlined by information scholar Klaus Krippendorff, whose doctoral thesis was titled 'An Examination of Content Analysis: A Proposal for a General Framework and an Information Calculus for Message Analytic Situations' (1967), where he stated that research was moving into a new phase of content analysis that would 'be dominated by the emergence of new computer techniques designed to analyze large quantities of text for various scientific and practical tasks' (Krippendorff, 1967: 31). He introduced a comprehensive approach to conducting quantitative content analysis, which involved defining the research questions and hypotheses, selecting the relevant texts, creating a coding scheme, and analysing the data using statistical methods.

Drawing on our example dataset, Figure 7.3 is a basic example of how content analysis can be used. The figure presents the top adjectives frequently used in Trump's tweets.[2]

As the figure shows, many of the adjectives used by Trump in his tweets are of quantitative and comparative type ('great', 'big', 'many', 'more', 'strong', 'new'). This could potentially be interpreted as a reflection of his emphasis on measurable achievements and a desire to establish himself as superior to others. Moreover, the common use of the adjective 'American' in his tweets could indicate a strong sense of nationalism and patriotism, which aligns with Trump's political ideology and overall rhetoric. The occurrence of the words 'true' and 'real' in the list of top adjectives, indicate a pattern of Trump asserting the validity and authenticity

---

[2]All analysis examples in this chapter are documented as Python code at https://github.com/simonlindgren/rdms-text. As for identifying which words are adjectives, see the section on Natural Language Processing, further ahead.

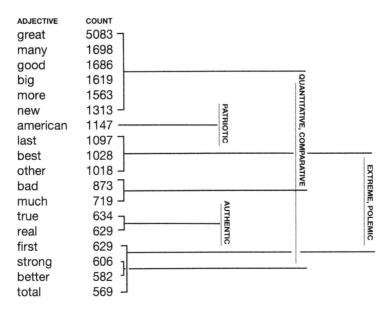

Figure 7.3 Top adjectives in Trump's tweets

of his own beliefs and ideas, while dismissing those that do not align with his worldview as fake or false. Finally, the use of adjectives that point to extremes, such as 'last', 'first', 'best' and 'total', suggests that Trump's tweets have a tendency to reflect a hyperbolic, sensationalist and exaggerative viewpoint. This example of content analysis highlights the possibility of using the method to study the potential ideological and rhetorical implications of Trump's use of adjectives in his tweets, which can shed light on his political message and communication.

The obvious strength of using different forms of quantitative content analysis is that it provides a systematic and fairly objective approach to analysing large amounts of text. While the choices you make in the different steps of applying the method will mean that there is always, as is the case with any research, a subjective element, the method still offers a level of consistency and reliability in the analysis as it is focused only on the content that is manifestly expressed. Content analysis is thus a suitable choice of method if you, for example, want to follow or map how certain patterns in digital media content relate to each other in terms of how often they appear. It is also helpful for looking at and comparing such patterns across different points in time, different user accounts, and so on. In practice, then, the analyses you might be able to conduct are likely to have a more complex, and less descriptive, design than the example in Figure 7.3. The downsides to quantitative content analysis include that the method does not account for context, tone or intent in the communication being analysed. Therefore, the approach is not suitable for capturing nuances or subtleties in language use.

Krippendorff's classic textbook on content analysis was first published in 1980 and was not specifically focused on the content analysis of internet data. In more recent editions of the book, however, Krippendorff (2019: 36–37) deals particularly with social media, and then illustrates how the method of content analysis can, and probably should, be put to more dynamic uses. For example, he contends that the short messages of social media 'make little sense in isolation, even as statistical aggregates'. He continues to explain that their 'networked quality', alongside the fact that online discourse tends to build on 'the emergence of community-specific vocabularies, abbreviations, emojis, and identifiable topics that develop in particular networks', means that content analysis as a research technique faces new challenges because of this. A straightforward counting of words and other meaningful units in texts – for example, hashtags, @-mentions, links to websites, and so on – can still be a quite interesting starting point for an analysis. In particular, when used in combination with one or several other approaches, either from within the computational text analysis toolkit or other methods explained in this book, content analysis can be a powerful method for gaining insights into patterns of communication and discourse in social media and other forms of textual data.

CORPUS ANALYSIS

As we previously explained, a corpus refers to the collection of documents that your research focuses on. And a document is, then, the unit of analysis, such as an Instagram caption or a Reddit post. A corpus is essentially a term for defining a compilation of texts that have been collected for analysis. The approach we refer to here as corpus analysis draws on methods used within the field of corpus linguistics (Sinclair, 2004). The main focus in corpus linguistics is placed on using large collections of machine-readable texts – corpora – in order to study various linguistic phenomena. These phenomena may relate to what linguistics scholars call syntax, that is, the structure of language, semantics (Katz, 2019), that is, the meaning of language, or pragmatics (Rühlemann, 2019), that is, the use of language in context.

The history of corpus linguistics goes back to the 1950s and '60s when advances in computing technology made it possible to analyse large amounts of language data in a systematic and efficient way. Initially, there was some controversy and disagreement surrounding the exploration of this approach. Notably, prominent scholar Noam Chomsky contended that the study of language should rely on introspection and intuition, as opposed to analysing extensive sets of language data. Conversely, proponents of the new techniques argued that corpus linguistics presented a more impartial, data-based method for analysing language and could offer valuable insights into its practical use in real-life settings (McEnery & Hardie, 2013).

English Corpus Lingustics in particular, saw significant growth in the 1980s and '90s with the creation of large-scale corpora such as the British National Corpus and the Brown Corpus. Corpus linguistics has, since then, grown in popularity within the broader areas of linguistic research, and it differs from other speciali-sations within that discipline because its focus is not specifically on examining any particular element of language. Instead, it is concerned with a specific set of techniques or methods for investigating language. Some scholars define corpus linguistics as a research field, and theory, in its own right, while others define it rather as a research method. In the context of this book, we focus on the latter.

Depending on who you might ask, many different methods could fall under the umbrella of corpus analysis. After all, any approach that looks at patterns in large collections of texts could, by some measures, be said to fulfil the definition criteria. This means that all approaches that we discuss in this chapter can, to some extent, be said to be tools for corpus analysis, actually.

As one example, corpus analysis engages with a method called *keyword analysis*. This approach builds on the idea of 'keywords' and their statistical definition in corpus linguistics through measures of keyness, which is a number for how important a particular word is to a particular corpus. The computation of keyness is based on the comparison of word frequencies in a 'target' corpus against a 'ref-erence' corpus. Essentially, this method determines whether a word appears more often in the target corpus than it does in the reference corpus, thereby indicat-ing its potential as a key term. Using this approach, we can analyse a corpus of Donald Trump's posted tweets to determine the keywords that he frequently uses. For example, by comparing the frequency of certain words in Trump's tweets against a reference corpus of general English language usage, we could poten-tially identify key terms that are particularly associated with his writing style. We used the open source corpus analysis software AntConc,[3] and compared Trump's tweets with a standard corpus of American English language, and found that words such as 'great', 'president', 'vote', 'America', 'country' and 'fake' had a high keyness score, meaning that such words appear unusually often in the Trump corpus in comparison to the American English corpus. By analysing the keyness of these and other terms, we can gain insights into the specific linguistic patterns and rhetorical strategies that Trump employs in his public communication.

You will probably realise that this is, in practice, quite similar to what could also be done within the framework of content analysis, as described above. In light of that, it is important to remember that, in this book, we explore a land-scape of mixed methods that have many overlapping features. It is crucial to

---

[3]www.laurenceanthony.net/software/antconc

recognise and to get comfortable with these overlaps and hybrid forms when working in the field of digital media and society. Our main idea in this book is that the best pedagogical approach is to present each method in its purest and most original form. As a reader, you can then identify similarities, differences and intersections, as well as conditions for fruitful combinations and mixtures of the methods. This type of thinking is an important step towards developing your own methodological toolbox.

Two approaches that are quite unique to corpus analysis, and that can be useful in researching digital media, are concordancing and collocation analysis (Sinclair, 1991). Figure 7.4 shows examples of such analyses: concordance analysis and collocation analysis.[4] Concordance analysis involves creating a list of all the occurrences of a particular word or phrase in a text corpus and presenting them in their original context, with preceding and succeeding text. The analytical point of

Concordance analysis

) so angry with Illegal Immigration. Great, and we should boycott	Fake News	CNN. Dealing with them is a total waste of time! ht
t.co/4yvPax9J3B Colin Powell was a pathetic interview today on	FAKE NEWS	CNN. In his time, he was weak & gave away everyt
a short period of time has been playing his biggest con of all on	FAKE NEWS	CNN. Michael D'Antonio, a broken down hack whc
on! NBC, my former home with the Apprentice, is now as bad as	Fake News ...	CNN. Sad! Andy McCarthy will be on @LouDobbs
can Public. There are many outlets that are far more trusted than	Fake News	CNN. Their slogan should be CNN, THE LEAST TR
it working OT to respond to last Sunday's tragedy. With all of the	Fake News	coming out of NBC and the Networks, at what poir
1oney up front in order to compensate for the false reporting and	Fake News	concerning our handling of the China Virus. Now th
1sk Force https://t.co/mLfPSV05Lj You will never hear this on the	Fake News	concerning the China Virus, but by comparison to i
t priding myself on my ability to write, it should be noted that the	FAKE NEWS	constantly likes to pore over my tweets looking for
t priding myself on my ability to write, it should be noted that the	Fake News	constantly likes to pour over my tweets looking for
it all together as to what an incredible year we had. Don't let the	fake news	convince you otherwise...and our insider Polls are
numbers. Our Country, unlike others, is doing great! Don't let the	Fake News	convince you otherwise. "If they don't get this Trad
sident Impeached, which is pretty low considering the volume of	Fake News	coverage, but pretty high considering the fact that
0z... I never asked Comey to stop investigating Flynn. Just more	FAKE NEWS	covering another Comey lie! Congratulations to @A
portant Humanitarian and Security Crisis" is a.... Big story. Hope	FAKE NEWS	covers it! https://t.co/NCtUYK6Eco RT @NWSColun
e really crashed. Very small audience. People are tired of hearing	Fake News	delivered with an anger that is not to be believed. S
aj9 Just as I said, Alabama was originally projected to be hit. The	Fake News	denies it! https://t.co/elJ7ROfm2p RT @NWSColun
an Countries are sadly getting clobbered by the China Virus. The	Fake News	does not like reporting this! Trump Announces Gro
given a big pay cut! MSDNC also did poorly. As I have long said,	Fake News	does not pay!!! It is very important for our Country'
other all time high on Friday. 5.3 trillion dollars up since Election.	Fake News	doesn't spent much time on this! People get what
g and playing "fingers" with his mask, all over the place, and the	FAKE NEWS	doesn't wa... RT @ACTBrigitte: I hear leftists sayin
g and playing "fingers" with his mask, all over the place, and the	Fake News	doesn't want to even think about discussing it. "Jo
destroying evidence should be a huge story but whatever... The	Fake News	doesn't show real polls. Lamestream Media is tota
lted States if Joe Biden ever became President. Our Coun... The	fake news	doesn't want to report these numbers. The @latime
while the number of deaths (mortality rate), goes way down. The	Fake News	doesn't like telling you that! Great going Natalie! ht
luding nations which were thought to have done a great job. The	Fake News	doesn't report this. USA will be stronger than ever
int continues! How stupid and unfair to our Country....And so the	Fake News	doesn't waste my time with dumb questions, NO,..

Collocation analysis

WORD	MOST COMMON PRECEDING	MOST COMMON SUCCEEDING
Hillary	crooked →	→ Clinton
Bernie	crazy →	→ Sanders
Joe	sleepy →	→ Biden
virus	China →	→ cases
fake news	the →	→ media
Russia	with →	→ hoax

Figure 7.4 Concordance analysis of 'fake news', and collocation analysis of a selected set of names and terms in Trump's tweets

---

[4]Once again, we used the free software AntConc to conduct these example analyses. See, for example, Anthony (2019) and Froehlich (2015).

showing the words in context is to allow for a deeper understanding of how the word or phrase is being used and what its 'connotations' may be. The notion of connotations comes from the field of semiotics – the study of signs and symbols – which we will return to in Chapter 9 on visual analysis. Connotations are, then, defined as 'the mechanism by which signs may seem to signify one thing but are loaded with multiple meanings' (Chandler, 2022: 213). In other words, it refers to the cultural and social associations that a word or symbol carries beyond its literal, dictionary definition. These meanings can be derived, for example, through concordancing as it allows for a close analysis of how a word or phrase is used in different contexts and the various connotations it thus may carry. In Figure 7.4, we find the tweets where Trump says 'fake news' listed in a way where we are set to analyse the context in which he uses that word. Looking closer at this type of list can reveal many different types of patterns, and also lead to the formulation of further research questions that might lead us to engage other parts of the data and of our methodological toolkit. For now, however, we can note that Trump tends to often speak of fake news with a definite article attached to it, as in '*the* fake news', where he indicates that these so-called fake news media are plotting against Trump, and that CNN is painted as one of his main enemies.

Collocation analysis, or 'word co-occurrence analysis' (Sinclair, 1991: 109) on the other hand, involves identifying words that tend to appear together frequently in a given text corpus. This can reveal patterns of meaning and usage within the language. For example, the collocation analysis of Trump's tweets that is presented in Figure 7.4 is focused on which words tend to come before or after some selected key terms. When tweeting about his political opponents, Trump often speaks not only of 'Hillary *Clinton*', 'Bernie *Sanders*' and 'Joe *Biden*', but also about '*Crooked* Hillary', '*Crazy* Bernie', and '*Sleepy* Joe'. Here, the corpus analysis helps show the tirelessness of Trump's well-known technique of using derogatory nicknames to deride his opponents, and thereby setting up 'language-based antagonist barriers' that hinder democratic dialogue (Anggraini et al., 2021: 60). Furthermore, during the COVID-19 pandemic, Trump tweeted not only about 'virus *cases*', but also persistently spoke of the virus as the '*China* virus', with the potential consequence that such language promoted anti-Asian discrimination by contributing to the racialisation of a public health crisis.

In sum, then, the advantages of drawing on corpus analysis in research on digital media and society, is that it makes it possible to see words, and other meaningful units, in terms of their role, function or position within a larger body of text. The corpus used here, once again, is that of Trump's tweets, but these same corpus analysis techniques can of course also be applied to other types of digital media, such as blog posts, news articles, comment threads and forum posts. Furthermore, as with all approaches discussed in this chapter, the larger the corpus, the more comprehensive and representative the analysis is likely to be.

NATURAL LANGUAGE PROCESSING

As we discussed in the introductory parts of this chapter, natural language processing (NLP) is a very broad concept. Just like the notion of corpus analysis, it may, in many respects, be used to refer to most of the different approaches that we are presenting here. In brief, NLP, as a concept, is linked to the period when computational linguistics went through a significant transformation towards being more focused on data and quantitative analysis, which took place around the early 1990s. While the area of computational linguistics is defined as being 'concerned with understanding written and spoken language from a computational perspective, and building artifacts that usefully process and produce language' (Schubert, 2020), NLP is 'its engineering domain' (Clark et al., 2010: 1). NLP combines linguistics, computer science and artificial intelligence to make computers understand, interpret and generate human language. With that definition, it is clear that many of the methods that we are dealing with here are examples of NLP. But while methods such as sentiment analysis, word embedding and topic modelling – all being NLP techniques – have become used as clearly delineated singular methods in their own right in digital media research, there are some more generic and multi-purpose NLP tools that can be useful in support of several of the other methods we are discussing in this book. Two of the generic NLP tools that can be useful are part-of-speech (POS) tagging and named entity recognition (NER).

POS-tagging is about assigning grammatical tags to each word in a sentence based on its role in the sentence structure. This means putting labels, such as noun, verb, adjective, adverb, pronoun, preposition, conjunction and interjection, on each word to indicate its part of speech. For language scholars, this is obviously useful because it allows them to better understand the syntax and semantics of a sentence. In digital media research, such as if we are applying POS-tagging to social media content, it can also be helpful as it enables us to extract insights about the language usage and communication patterns of individual users and communities. For example, Gimpel et al. (2010) developed a POS-tagger that was specifically designed for Twitter data, explaining that their approach was particularly suited for dealing with the changing linguistic conventions (emoji, abbreviations, slang, etc.) that are constantly emerging as part of social media discourse. In another contribution to the field, Ghosh et al. (2016) also developed the use of POS-taggers for social media texts by introducing the WebTrain corpus for use in the retraining of taggers.

In the case of the corpus of tweets posted by Donald Trump, POS-tagging could be fruitfully used as a means to identify certain patterns in how he uses language when posting. And this was exactly what we did earlier in the content analysis example. While the main point of that example was that content analysis counts important terms in a text, we did also focus specifically on adjectives, and when crafting that example we used the POS-tagger in the Natural Language Toolkit for Python (Bird et al., 2009).[5]

So, you have already seen then how it could be analytically useful to look, for example, at the frequent use of adjectives to emphasise other words or concepts. POS-tagging might also help in mapping out Trump's tendency to use short, simple sentences to convey his messages, or his frequent use of pronouns such as 'I' and 'you' to personalise the statements made. Maybe, however, POS-tagging in social and cultural research is the most powerful when used as an intermediary step in more elaborate methodological strategies. For example, if we can identify all the verbs used in a comment thread on, let's say, TikTok, we will be able to discern – through the verbs' roles in describing activity – the prevalent modes of acting that are described, encouraged or discussed by the participants. Just as some are inspiration and food for thought, some of the most common verbs in Trump's tweets are 'want', 'need' and 'know'. What do you think the use of these specific words might imply?

NER, as in *named entity recognition*, is a similar approach, but one that goes beyond the mere parts-of-speech to tag a broader variety of 'entities' that are mentioned in a given body of text. In the field of NLP, NER is a useful way of automatically identifying and labelling names of individuals, locations, organizations, corporations, nationalities, points in time, events, and other relevant information that may be mentioned in the content that is analysed. The most basic NER approaches are dictionary-based, which means that they rely on pre-built lists of words and phrases that are associated with specific entities. Second, there are rule-based approaches, in which patterns and rules are set up to identify specific entities, based on their context and relationships with other words and phrases in the text. The most advanced version of NER, finally, is based on machine learning, and demands an initial step where a model is trained on pre-tagged documents. Using machine learning for NER can improve the accuracy and flexibility of the method. In the next step, the model is used to identify and label entities in new, untagged documents.

NER was developed in the research field of information extraction as a technique that 'basically involves identifying the names of all the people, organizations, and geographic locations in a text' (Grishman & Sundheim, 1996: 467). Subsequent iterations of the technique also help identify the names of other entities such as, for example, nationalities, infrastructural elements, events, works of art, and so on. One of the most commonly used NLP libraries for the Python programming language, spaCy, uses machine learning and tags a broad set of entities, as shown in Figure 7.5.

---

[5]This step is also documented in detail at https://github.com/simonlindgren/rdms-text.

TYPE	DESCRIPTION
PERSON	People, including fictional.
NORP	Nationalities or religious or political groups.
FAC	Buildings, airports, highways, bridges, etc.
ORG	Companies, agencies, institutions, etc.
GPE	Countries, cities, states.
LOC	Non-GPE locations, mountain ranges, bodies of water.
PRODUCT	Objects, vehicles, foods, etc. (Not services.)
EVENT	Named hurricanes, battles, wars, sports events, etc.
WORK_OF_ART	Titles of books, songs, etc.
LAW	Named documents made into laws.
LANGUAGE	Any named language.
DATE	Absolute or relative dates or periods.
TIME	Times smaller than a day.
PERCENT	Percentage, including "%".
MONEY	Monetary values, including unit.
QUANTITY	Measurements, as of weight or distance.
ORDINAL	"First" , "second", etc.
CARDINAL	Numerals that do not fall under another type.

Figure 7.5   NER types in spaCy (Honnibal & Montani, 2017)

While NER, together with many of the other approaches that we discuss in this chapter, is often used for applied, so-called downstream, tasks to provide functionality in search engines, content recommendations and customer support, it can be used in media research to analyse patterns and trends in the mentions of certain entities across a corpus of texts. The results of such analyses may be of some interest in their own right, but also as a means to inform broader research questions, and to be incorporated in more complex methodological designs, relating to social and cultural phenomena in digital society. Figure 7.6 illustrates how NER can be used in the analysis of Trump's tweets. The top part of the figure shows how entities are recognized by the Python library spaCy (Honnibal & Montani, 2017) in content from two of the tweets in the dataset. In extract (a), we see a mention of Trump's political opponent Joe Biden being recognised as a 'person', the wordings '47 years' and 'half a century' being tagged as 'date', and 'American' as a nationality. This example is illustrative of a very straightforward application of NER, to pick out components in texts.

In extract (b), however, we see how both 'the China Virus' and 'the Fake News' have been recognised as 'ORG' by spaCy; while 'the China Virus' is certainly not an organisation, and 'the Fake News', while being a way for Trump to discredit a number of news outlets, is not by any means an organisation in itself, but rather a collective term. If we read closer in Figure 7.5, however, we will see that the ORG entity may also include things such as 'institutions', and it is clear from practical use of the tool that this works in a very broad sense. In sociology, an 'institution' is defined as 'the fixing of stereotyped social interactions' (Ritzer, 2007: 2344). Seeing how the NER operates on the tweets, tagging 'the China Virus' and 'the Fake News' as ORGs, the interpretation is that the ORG category can be seen as detecting a range of fairly stable entities that play roles in the world of Trump – things

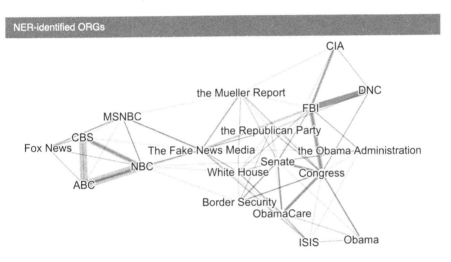

Figure 7.6 NER examples based on Trump's tweets

that he opposes, critiques, supports or otherwise plays off. So, even though these two entities are definitely not organisations, and only institutions by a very broad definition, they are certainly entities that are valuable to detect in order to map out the universe of Trump's tweets. The lower part of Figure 7.6 shows a network of such entities that Trump tends to speak about in his tweets. In other words, this is an example where NER is used as input for further analysis, using other methods, such as, in this case, network analysis (see Chapter 8).

We can see, for example, that the notion of 'the Fake News Media' holds an important position in the language that Trump uses when tweeting, and that his talk of that entity is connected to a set of media organisations. Furthermore, a subset of his discourse revolves around national security, 'the Mueller Report', and Obama. In conclusion, when it comes to using POS-tagging and NER in relation to researching digital media and society, there is no doubt that these tools can contribute to improving our understanding of the ways in which language is used to make and convey meaning, as well as shape social interactions online. But, once again, while these methods may provide some quite interesting results on their own, they are most effective when used in combination with other forms of qualitative and quantitative analysis.

TOPIC MODELLING AND WORD EMBEDDING

The approaches of topic modelling and word embedding are two machine learning methods that have gained a lot of popularity in digital media research in recent years. *Topic modelling* is commonly used for identifying the main topics or themes that exist in a corpus, without any close reading of the texts. Similar to a collocation analysis, described previously in this chapter, it involves analysing the words and phrases found in the corpus and grouping them together based on their co-occurrence. The output of topic modelling, then, is that it presents the researcher with a set of clusters or groups of words or phrases – these are the 'topics' – through which the corpus can be described (Blei, 2012; Graham et al., 2012).

Word embedding is a similar approach, but it is based on a different mathematical logic. Word embedding is more concerned with understanding the semantic relationships between individual words and phrases in terms of how 'similar' they are to each other based on their co-occurrence patterns (Mikolov et al., 2013; Pennington et al., 2014). Both of these methods can be used to find words or phrases that tend to appear together in the corpus, which, by extension, means that various forms of clustering can be applied to get to know more about the topology of the text. The fact that these approaches use machine learning means that they are able to automatically and, so to say, 'intelligently' process large amounts of text data, allows researchers to derive insights and patterns that are not likely to be immediately apparent through manual analysis. Without any supervision from the researcher, in terms of what the content and context of the analysed corpus are, the models will be developed through processing the text, and learning from it so that they can then use what they have learned to identify topics, themes and relationships within that data.

Compared to approaches that demand more from the researcher in terms of knowing things about the data beforehand, machine learning approaches such as these will analyse the corpus from scratch and present the researcher with an output for interpretation. Very importantly, however, this actual interpretation will definitely demand that the researcher has knowledge about the content and context because, otherwise, the purely mathematical output will not lead anywhere in terms of analysing digital media in a social and cultural context. So, while these methods can be very powerful and efficient, and sometimes produce quite impressive results that give a feeling that the models have indeed read and 'understood' the content, the actual understanding always comes from a 'theoretically sensitised' researcher (Lindgren, 2020). Therefore, it is always crucial, even when using automatic and unsupervised approaches such as these, to have a deep understanding of the subject matter and cultural context surrounding the digital media you are studying. Interpreting the results is, in many ways, like 'reading tea leaves' (Chang et al., 2009), meaning that the patterns generated by the machine learning models must always be carefully examined and interpreted in light of the researcher's theoretical framework and previous knowledge about the area that is studied.

Figure 7.7 shows the resulting topics from applying LDA – Latent Dirichlet Allocation, a popular algorithm for topic modelling – to the full set of Donald Trump's tweets. The model was trained using the Gensim programming library for Python, and visualised using the tool pyLDAvis.[6] LDA demands that the number of topics is decided beforehand, and in this case we created a model with ten topics. This means that the algorithm will work to identify ten distinct patterns or themes within the given dataset, based on the frequency of words used and their co-occurrences.

PyLDAvis lays out the identified topics and their interrelationships in a visualisation that is based on a so-called principal component analysis. Furthermore, MDS, meaning Multidimensional Scaling, is the approach used for calculating the distances between the topics. The interpretation of the visual image is that topics that are overlapping or close to each other in the image are similar, while those that are far away are more dissimilar.

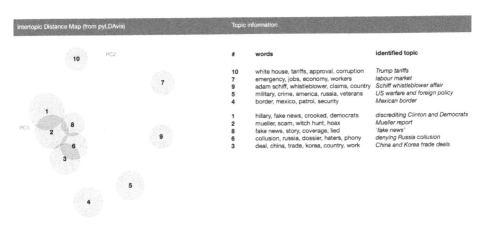

Figure 7.7 LDA topic model trained on Trump's tweets

---

[6]The process is documented at https://github.com/simonlindgren/rdms-text.

We can see in Figure 7.7 that topics 10, 7, 9, 5 and 4 are relatively distinct, while the other five topics are overlapping. In a real-life research scenario, this might urge us to re-evaluate our approach and consider reducing the number of topics to ensure that each topic is well-defined and meaningful. In this case, for example, it might have been interesting to try to train a model with six topics to see if the clustering improves. For the sake of our basic illustration here, however, we will stick with the ten topics. The output of LDA is a list of topics, represented by a list of words (ranked by falling relevance) that are important in defining the topic at hand. In Figure 7.7, we list some of the top key terms for each identified topic. In the column 'identified topic', our qualitative assessment of what the topics represent is presented, based on an analysis of the top keywords, together with our pre-existing knowledge about the political context around Trump and his presidency.

While one of the key shortcomings of LDA is that the researcher must specify the number of topics beforehand, there also exist other topic modelling techniques that do not require this step. One example is HDP (Teh et al., 2004). In this book, however, even though we used LDA for our example, the main point is to introduce the method of topic modelling as such, even though it can be conducted in several different ways that vary in terms of the assumptions and parameters that they are based on. A topic model then, at the most basic level, is used to identify the underlying themes or topics within a collection of documents to be able to say something about the patterns of content in the corpus as a whole. This, very roughly, means that topic models can be used as a form of automatic thematic analysis to find commonalities and differences within a dataset.

Additionally, topic models can be very powerful as generators of new metadata about the documents in your corpus. Once you have trained a model, you will be able to query it to see which 'documents' are the strongest linked to any given topic. In the case of Trump's tweets, if we group the tweets by the month during which they were posted, and create one document per month, we would be able to see which topic out of the ten shown in Figure 7.7 is the most strongly connected to any given month in the dataset. Based on such knowledge, we could then plot the occurrence of any given topic over time. Similarly, if we instead had a corpus consisting of tweets posted by several different users, the topic model would mean quite different things if we had used one tweet per document, as compared to if we had created one document per user, containing all tweets of that user. In the first scenario, we would be able to say things such as which tweet matches the most strongly with a given topic. In the latter scenario, however, we would get knowledge about the potentially more interesting question of which user is the most likely to express a certain topic.

As mentioned earlier, the method of *word embedding* takes a somewhat different approach than topic models, by focusing on the meaning and context of individual words rather than on the broader themes in a text. The most well-known word embedding model, word2vec, will assign numerical values to each word in a text based on its proximity to other words. Based on this, it is further possible to do different kinds of analyses, such as identifying words that are commonly used together or understanding the semantic relationships between words. The most often-used example of how word2vec can highlight such semantic relationships is the famous example of the relationship between 'king' and 'queen'. In a word embedding model, trained on common English language use, we are likely to see that the word vectors (i.e., their numerical representations) for 'king' and 'queen' are very similar to one another. This makes sense because these two words are often used together in many different contexts. Even more interesting, however, is the fact that the numerical representations, so-called vectors, can be used to do mathematical operations on the pairs of words. For example, if we subtract the vector for 'man' from the vector for 'king', and then add the vector for 'woman', we will end up with a vector that is very close to the vector for 'queen'. This means that word2vec has identified a mathematical relationship between these four words: specifically, it has recognised that 'queen' is related to 'king' in much the same way that 'woman' is related to 'man'. In the case of Trump's tweets, the same approach can be used to bring out such relationships that are specific to his use of language, and that are not as self-evident as that of the king and queen example. The information in Figure 7.8 is based on a word2vec model that was trained on the corpus of Trump's tweets.[7] As can be seen in the figure, the most similar words to the word 'Clinton' (referring to Trump's main opponent in the 2016 election) refer to Clinton being 'crooked', and to the scandal surrounding leaked emails, to Russia's alleged involvement in the latter, and so on. Furthermore, the discourse surrounding the term 'flotus' ('the First Lady of the United States', Trump's wife) indicates in what capacities she enters the public life of the president ('tour', 'visiting', 'gala', 'excited'). Finally, Trump's talk of the 'media' is closely related to his antagonism towards the 'mainstream' or 'lamestream' media.

Once we understand this logic of semantic relationships, we can query our trained embedding model in a wide variety of ways to uncover the 'rules' of the discourse that we are analysing. For example, we can see which words a

---

Word2vec: Most similar

clinton: *crooked; emails; investigation; collusion; russian; campaign*

flotus: *arrived; visiting; afternoon; tour; excited; gala*

media: *mainstream; lamestream; dishonest; reporting; corrupt*

Figure 7.8 Most similar words to a select set of words in Trump's tweets, based on a word2vec model trained on the dataset

---

[7]The exact steps, which used the Gensim library in Python, are documented at https://github.com/simonlindgren/rdms-text.

given author or speaker often uses together, or which words are discursively constructed as being diametrically different from one another. Furthermore, by simply accessing the similarity scores for certain words, we will be able to construct visualisations or design further analyses of the language that is analysed. Analysing general-domain corpora is only likely to bring out general ways of speaking, such as linking 'woman' to 'queen', but using the same approach on specific and vernacular ways of construing the world through language use, will reveal much more nuanced and culturally specific patterns of meaning-making. Analysing Trump's tweets can be understood as a way of analysing the language of the US alt-right, and the ways in which they construct and communicate their worldview. For example, for Trump, the similarity (0.0 – 1.0) is 0.98 for 'leftist' and 'idiot', while the similarity between those two words is only 0.19 in a model trained on Google News. And, in the Trump tweets 'China' has a 0.70 similarity with 'plague', with the corresponding number in the news model being 0.09.[8]

SENTIMENT ANALYSIS

The last of the computational methods for text analysis that we will discuss in this chapter is sentiment analysis. Sentiment analysis, sometimes referred to as opinion mining, involves using dictionaries, natural language processing and machine learning techniques to identify and extract emotion or affect from textual data (Sharma et al., 2019; Garg et al., 2020). At its core, sentiment analysis is a computational method for analysing documents to determine the sentiment behind them. Because of this, the method is often used by businesses to monitor the public opinion on their brand or products, as well as by political campaigns to measure the public's reaction towards candidates and current issues of political debate or contention.

The key idea behind sentiment analysis can be illustrated through the AFINN lexicon, which is a list of words with assigned values ranging from −5, negative, to +5, positive (Nielsen, 2011a, 2011b). This lexicon was created by data scientist Finn Årup Nielsen, with the aim of developing a simple and effective way to measure sentiment in social media data. The lexicon is based on the assumption that words have an inherent emotional value and that the overall sentiment of a text can be determined by summing up the values of the words within it. Some examples of words with a negative sentiment, according to AFINN, are 'boring' (−3), 'dirty' (−2) and 'bastard' (−5), while examples of positive sentiment words include 'amazing' (4), 'lol' (3) and 'thrilled' (5). The following is an example of a Trump tweet that scored −5 with AFINN:

---

[8]The pre-trained Google News model used is provided by Google and can be found in multiple places online, for example at https://github.com/mmihaltz/word2vec-GoogleNews-vectors.

There is TREMENDOUS Lawlessness in America's Liberal Cities. Would be so easy to stop but they have a clouded vision of what should be done. They are indoctrinated with a philosophy which will never work, a philosophy which would destroy America. Portland would be the norm!

While this following tweet scored +5:

China has been working very hard to contain the Coronavirus. The United States greatly appreciates their efforts and transparency. It will all work out well. In particular, on behalf of the American People, I want to thank President Xi!

The obvious use of approaches such as these is to get a general feel for the tone and temperature of textual content, especially for the sake of comparing different texts or tracking changes over time, differences between different groups of users, and so on. Might it, for example, be the case that the tone of Trump's tweets became more negative or positive as his presidency progressed, or during any particular period of time when certain events took place?

The main shortcoming of sentiment analyses that are conducted based on dictionaries, such as the AFINN lexicon, is that they rely fully on their pre-defined categories and may therefore not be able to capture the nuances of how the language is used. For example, a sentence like 'I'm not happy about this, but I understand why it had to be done' may be classified as neutral or even positive by a sentiment analysis tool that would only be looking for words like 'happy' and 'understand', while a human researcher would no doubt be able to pick up on the underlying negative sentiment. Beyond that, there is also the issue of irony and humour by which the sentiment analysis tool may completely misinterpret the intended meaning of a sentence. Current tools, however, generally draw on lexicons in combination with more advanced algorithms and also machine learning to handle things such as negations (Kiritchenko et al., 2014) and sarcasm (Du et al., 2022). We used the openly available tool Valence Aware Dictionary and sEntiment Reasoner (VADER), which is one such tool that takes into account the complexities of language by combining the lexical features with a set of parameters (rules) that capture different 'grammatical and syntactical conventions that humans use when expressing or emphasizing sentiment intensity' (Hutto & Gilbert, 2014: 216). Furthermore, VADER was also developed particularly for social media texts.

We carried out an analysis of Trump's tweets with VADER, and were able to show that the majority of his tweets had a positive sentiment. The line in Figure 7.9 shows the weekly average 'compound' score, which is 'a single unidimensional measure of sentiment for a given sentence'.[9]

---

[9]See https://vadersentiment.readthedocs.io/en/latest/pages/about_the_scoring.html.

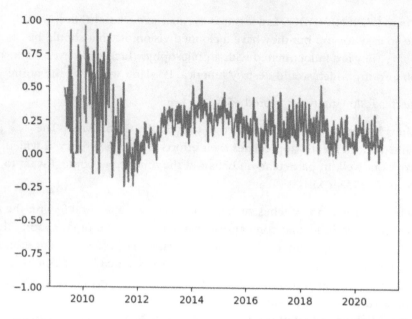

Figure 7.9 Weekly average compound sentiment scores (–1.00 negative to 1.00 positive) for Trump's tweets based on VADER

It may not be surprising that the tone in the tweets is generally more positive than negative, as building political opinion and gathering followers is generally about presenting a positive outlook and messaging that resonates with the audience. So, while some of Trump's tweets, maybe the most famous ones, tend to be aggressive, this sentiment analysis reveals the overall pattern that the tone is still generally positive at the aggregated level. In the earliest part of the study period, the tone was markedly more positive, which may partly be due to the fact that Trump posted less frequently in those early years, with only 56 tweets in 2009, 142 in 2010, 773 in 2011, but with yearly counts rising to the thousands thereafter. If we assume that the posts around that time were more generic, and about his reality TV and real estate ventures, it is also possible that they were not as controversial or politically charged as some of his later tweets. This could then explain the more positive sentiment scores around those years. In the years following the 2015 announcement of his candidacy for the 2016 election, the overall tone of Trump's tweets gradually became more negative, which might indicate that he then started to tweet about more contentious issues and topics. In the years following the 2016 election win, the tone turned slightly more positive, to turn slightly more negative again around the subsequent election in 2020.

In relation to these quite general examples, it is also worth pointing out that, just as we discussed in relation to topic modelling, sentiment analysis scores can be extra powerful in an analysis if they are used not as end results in themselves, but rather as metadata. For example, sentiment analysis scores can be combined with other data such as location, or the topic of the tweet, in order to get more dynamic insights into online reactions to certain issues or events. Also, in datasets where many different users are represented, it may be of interest to see which sentiments are connected to different individuals or groups.

Additionally, while the tool that we have explored here only maps sentiment in terms of positive and negative, there are other sentiment analysis tools that you may want to explore. One such is LIWC, which goes beyond the mere labelling of plus or minus, to also include more nuanced emotional categories such as anxiety, anger and sadness (Tausczik & Pennebaker, 2010).

CONCLUSION

Computational text analysis involves a quite complex, and constantly emerging, set of methods that can be used when researching digital media and society. With this chapter, however, we have offered an introduction to some of the most commonly used techniques and tools in this field. Hopefully, somewhere among and across these, you will be able to find a starting point for your own research project. Always remind yourself that the most interesting results are likely to be found through combining and layering different methods, rather than relying on just one approach. This goes both for combinations within the computational text analysis methods, and for integrating them with other research methods, such as those that we introduce in other parts of this book.

8

SOCIAL NETWORK ANALYSIS

Key Questions

- What are the general principles of *social network analysis*, and how can the method be applied when researching digital media and society?
- What are *edges*, *nodes* and *graphs*, and how do they relate to each other?
- How can the *topology* of networks be analysed, with which metrics, and how are they useful?
- What are some key considerations to make when *visualising networks*, and how can the visualisations be interpreted?

Key Concepts

graphs * nodes * edges * directed and undirected graphs * weighted and unweighted graphs * network topology * centralised * decentralised and distributed networks * network diameter * centralisation * clustering * communities * betweenness * network layout

This chapter introduces network analysis as a method for researching digital media and society. While 'network analysis' is an approach that can be used in a wide range of scientific fields, such as for studying transportation systems or ecological structures, in this chapter we focus specifically on the application of network analysis to the study of digital media and society. This means that the method that we are interested in broadly belongs in the area of what is called *social network analysis* (SNA). In SNA, individuals or groups are seen as entities, and the analysis is about looking at different types of relationships or connections between those entities, in order to be able to say something about the structure and dynamics of the network as a whole, as well as about the characteristics of the different entities (Wasserman & Faust, 1994).

SNA is based on the idea that interactions between different entities – which might be humans, organisations or even machines – can be represented by their connections in a network structure. As we will explain later, these entities are called *nodes*, and the connections between them are referred to as *edges*. It may not be entirely intuitive to use the term 'edges' for the lines or connections in the network, but this name comes from the terminology used in graph theory, which is the mathematical framework behind SNA. Sometimes – for example in the field of geometry – the concept of 'vertices' is used instead of 'nodes', but they both refer to the same thing: the social entities that are being studied in the network. Nodes are connected by edges to form a 'graph', which is the mathematical term for what we call a network in SNA. So, in sum: networks consist of nodes and the edges that connect them.

The origins and basic premises of graph theory are often explained through the classic story of *the seven bridges of Königsberg* (Scott & Carrington, 2011: 4; Tsvetovat & Kouznetsov, 2011: 23–25). Königsberg was a city in Prussia (now Kaliningrad, Russia) that was situated on both sides of the Pregel River and included two islands connected to each other and the mainland by seven bridges. The city was home to both philosopher Immanuel Kant (1724–1804) and mathematician Leonhard Euler (1707–1783). Kant used to take regular long walks around the city but was annoyed by the fact that he had to cross the same bridge twice: when leaving his home and upon returning. Kant presented the dilemma to his friend Euler over dinner, which led to Euler formulating the problem as a graph (as in Figure 8.1).

In that graph, the nodes represented the islands, and the two mainland riverbanks, and the edges were the seven bridges. Seeing the problem in terms of such a graph made it possible for Euler to pose it in network terms: Is it possible to move across the graph without repeating any edges, and then return to the starting node? Based on this, Euler could prove that this is certainly not

Figure 8.1 The seven bridges of Königsberg

possible. This kind of thinking, in terms of network structure and connections, can be translated into innumerable areas of research. In the case of researching digital media and society, drawing on graphs can help ask and respond to questions about the connections and relationships between different actors, such as individuals, groups and platforms. For example, the network perspective can be useful in analysing communication patterns and power relationships within online communities, as it allows researchers to identify key actors and understand how information flows between them: Which 'bridges' are we forced to cross, in order to reach certain 'islands'? Or, rather, which important actors in the communicative network must the information pass by in order to reach certain receivers or audiences?

Network analysis can help respond to a wide range of questions that relate to the characteristics of certain platforms or communicative settings, for example TikTok can be analysed in terms of its network structure to understand how content creators and viewers are connected, and how information flows within the platform. Similarly, YouTube can be analysed to identify the most influential content creators and how they interact with their audience. Furthermore, network analysis applied to a Facebook group or a forum discussion can bring out the social dynamics at play, such as who the most active members are and how they interact with each other, as well as identify any tightly-knit subgroups that may exist within the broader setting. Researching memes and other viral phenomena online, one may also draw upon network analysis to gain insights into how they spread and go viral, including the individuals and communities that are the key players in driving their circulation and popularity.

We could, for instance, envision an SNA study of Reddit, where the nodes would represent individual users, the edges would represent their interactions through edges defined by comments and upvotes, and the resulting network would show how the users are connected to each other through their interactions. The network could also be analysed further to reveal power structures or the presence of sub-communities within the larger Reddit community that was analysed. Similarly, SNA can be used when analysing memes on TikTok. In such a study, one could identify the nodes as individual TikTok users who have created or shared a particular meme, and the edges would represent the flow of the meme by way of shares and remixes. In today's digital world, media users are often connected to many different social networks at the same time, for example to Facebook groups, X (formerly Twitter) communities, Instagram followings, and news site audiences.

So, while social networks in themselves are as old as human societies, today's digital context allows for the study of interconnected online communities in a way that was not possible before. In this chapter, we introduce the background of SNA, some of its core concepts and their uses, as well as taking you through a hands-on tutorial on how to conduct an analysis.

ANALYSING SOCIAL STRUCTURE

The history of SNA as a method begins with classic sociological theory, where some scholars conceived of society as a kind of organism, rather than as a jumble of disconnected parts. Émile Durkheim wrote in *The Rules of Sociological Method* (1895) about how society consists of a set of interdependent parts, and that this interdependency will impose structure upon the behaviours of individuals, groups and institutions. In other words, it was Durkheim's belief that the relationships between individuals and groups in society were not random, but rather formed complex networks of connections with the potential to influence social actions and identities. Such ideas are the starting point for thinking in terms of social networks. SNA pioneer Linton Freeman (2004), when outlining the history of the field, cites a striking passage from a 1968 article by sociologist Allen Barton. In that article, Barton writes that social research has a tendency to look at individuals without considering their social contexts, and without considering the fact that individuals always interact with other individuals. Therefore, Allen argues, such survey research 'is a sociological meatgrinder':

> It is a little like a biologist putting his experimental animals through
> a hamburger machine and looking at every hundredth cell through a
> microscope; anatomy and physiology get lost, structure and function
> disappear, and one is left with cell biology […] If our aim is to
> understand people's behavior rather than simply to record it, we want to
> know about primary groups, neighborhoods, organizations, social circles,
> and communities; about interaction, communication, role expectations,
> and social control. (Barton, 1968: 1)

Freeman's point in revisiting this argument is that the meatgrinder tendency still exists in 21st-century social research, which is why we still need SNA. Our research will be much better at taking account of contexts and relations if we start from a *structural perspective*. The field of SNA has promoted this view for quite some time. Freeman (1996) shows that there were several precursors to the field of publishing studies already during the 1920s and '30s. According to Berkowitz (1982: 1), it was during the 1950s and early '60s that social scientists more broadly began adopting some of the fundamental concepts of graph theory to explain the connections and interactions among individuals, families, businesses, governments and other elements of social structures. Important foundations were laid at Harvard University in the 1960s and '70s through the work of sociologist

Harrison White and his research group (see, for example, White, 1992). Aligning with the view expressed by Allen above, White would also be very much against the meatgrinder approach to social research. It was crucial to White's perspective that sociology move away from individualistic forms of analysis and instead focus on social relations and contextual patterns to study 'regularities in the patterns of relations among concrete entities' (White et al., 1976: 733). Since White's time, SNA has become a widely recognised approach to studying social phenomena, which has naturally also found its way into digital media research.

The SNA approach is at its core based on the idea that social connections play a significant role in determining social life, its patterns and its outcomes. Therefore, researchers in this field aim to identify diverse types of linkages and explore the factors that lead to connections being formed, and what effects they may have. Freeman (2004: 3) suggests that the contemporary SNA field shares four core characteristics across its various sub-specialisations:

1 Social network analysis is motivated by a structural intuition based on ties linking social actors.
2 It is grounded in systematic empirical data.
3 It draws heavily on visualisations.
4 It relies on the use of mathematical and/or computational models.

While these core characteristics are fundamental to SNA, it is still important to note that it is not a fully coherent field of research. Rather, it is a collection of methods and theories arguing that the behaviours of individuals, groups and organisations are shaped by their social connections and the different networks that they are part of. In the context of digital media research, the SNA perspective becomes even more relevant and useful. This is because online communication and interaction functions according to a network logic, as digital platforms provide users with the opportunity of connecting with others in ever-new ways. SNA, then, offers a framework for conceptualising, analysing and understanding how these different types of connections come into expression and what potential consequences they may have. This might be, for example, in analysing online political activism using hashtags, or studying how social media influencers build and maintain their networks of followers. As SNA provides us with tools to map out the relationships between individuals and groups throughout networks in digital media, we can design research that gives insights into how information flows and how communities, publics and counterpublics form around specific topics or issues.

According to sociologist Manuel Castells (1996), we live today in a *network society*. This concept refers to how our societies, institutions and relationships are predominantly being structured by digital networks. Castells further argues that these networks have become the central characteristic of our modern-day social and economic systems, which has led to significant changes in the ways in which we interact, communicate, produce and consume. In this networked world, we are constantly connected and information flows incessantly and rapidly. And, clearly, the rise of social media and other online platforms has further accelerated the pace of communication and the spread of messages.

In a similar vein, internet researchers have written widely around the concept of *networked publics* (Ito, 2008). This refers to how online platforms and social media have created new spaces for public discourse and engagement, where individuals can connect with each other and form communities based on shared interests, identities and values. In today's world, we are more connected than ever before (Barabási, 2002; Christakis & Fowler, 2009). According to internet researchers Lee Rainie and Barry Wellman (2012), this is due to the emergence of *networked individualism*. Basically, people increasingly connect with each other through personal networks that are more fluid, far-reaching and varied than in previous historical eras. This means that we are no longer limited by physical proximity when it comes to building social relationships. Instead, today's social connections rely heavily on digital communication. From the perspective of SNA, these social changes allow for new possibilities, as well as a new need, for analysing and understanding patterns of connections and interactions.

FROM EDGES TO NETWORKS

When carrying out SNA, the starting point and minimum requirement is that we have what is called an *edgelist* – a list of edges. From the perspective of social theory, this means that the basis for being able to do SNA is what classic sociologist Georg Simmel called the *dyad*. Being the first sociologist to develop theoretical ideas around social network dynamics, Simmel compared 'dyads' (constellations of two individuals) and 'triads' (constellations of three people). The key point that he put forth was that dyads were very different if compared to larger-sized social groups. This was because dyads can be characterised by more intense emotions, and of an elevated degree of fragility. Triads, by contrast, are emotionally balanced to a higher degree, and they can persist as groups even if one of the members is replaced. This elementary comparison of dyads and triads helped Simmel show how social structure, as we discussed earlier, is important in and of itself, independently of the specific individuals that form part of the groups. He explained:

> Where three elements, A, B, C, constitute a group, there is, in addition
> to the direct relationship between A and B, for instance, their indirect

one, which is derived from their common relation to C. The fact that two elements are each connected not only by a straight line – the shortest – but also by a broken line, as it were, is an enrichment from a formal-sociological standpoint. Points that cannot be contacted by the straight line are connected by the third element, which offers a different side to each of the other two [...] Yet the indirect relation does not only strengthen the direct one. It may also disturb it. (Simmel, 1950: 135)

A dyad, then, refers to a micro-network that consists of two social actors, for example A and B. As you will remember from earlier, edges are the connections between nodes in the network. As shown in Figure 8.2, in order to draw the network on the right, we need the edgelist on the left as its input information: A is connected to B; A is connected to C; B is connected to C; and C is connected to D. This information is the edgelist, and it consists of four dyads. As we super-impose all of these dyadic relationships on each other, however, we end up not with a triad, but actually with a network of four. From Simmel's perspective, this increases the complexity immensely, and if adding further nodes and edges, the intricacy of the network grows exponentially. In the case of digital media analysis, drawing on platforms like X (formerly Twitter), TikTok, Instagram or Reddit, we may often deal with edgelists that are thousands or even millions of rows long, thereby creating networks that are extremely complex, and for which computational approaches to SNA – such as that discussed further on in this chapter – are essential.

In conducting empirical SNA in the context of digital media, the nodes (A, B, C and D) may represent a broad variety of things depending on how you have designed your study. Also, your theoretical assumptions and study design will always be crucial for what is defined, in the given context that you are analysing,

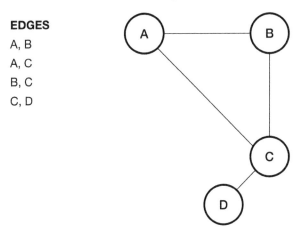

Figure 8.2 An edgelist

as constituting a dyadic connection between two actors. Is it the fact that they are sending DMs to each other, that they are Facebook 'friends', that they follow each other on TikTok, that they chatted in the same Twitch stream, or that they have both commented on the same Instagram post? In an X (formerly Twitter) example, one could decide, for example, that when any user directs a tweet – through mentioning a @username – to another user, this constitutes an edge between the two.

If the edges are based on hyperlink information – about which website links to which other websites – the nodes are clearly the websites. If, on the other hand, the edges are based on which X users are retweeting other X users, the nodes are the user accounts. Yet another example would be analysing a social network within an online gaming community, where the nodes could represent individual players and the edges could represent interactions such as sending messages, trading items or playing together in a virtual world. These are all examples of graphs – remember that 'graphs' is a synonym of 'networks' for our purposes – that are *unipartite* or 'one-mode' networks (Nooy et al., 2005: 103)

That a graph is unipartite means that all of its nodes are the same type of entity, such as websites, X users or players in a gaming community. In the examples above, then, we would not be looking at connections between, for example, users and the websites that they link to – which would involve nodes of two types: user accounts and websites. In such cases, we are dealing with *bipartite*, or 'two-mode', networks, which are a kind of network where the included nodes belong to two different types of entities. In the context of social media, bipartite networks can be networks of users and content items, where edges connect user nodes to nodes representing the content items they have interacted with. Beyond that, one can also work with *multipartite* networks where the nodes are of multiple different kinds (Cai et al., 2020). It is generally assumed in bipartite and multipartite graphs that all edges are connecting nodes of different types. In a bipartite graph containing users and linked websites, we would then work with edges that have a user at one end and a website at the other. We could also think of a variation of this, where the graph includes such connections, but where there may also be edges that hold information about connections between two users, or between two websites. This might be seen as the graph being partially bipartite, or possibly that we would be better served by unipartite thinking once again, where we might conceive of the users and the websites in fact belonging to the same category, as they may both be 'online entities', or something like that. In the end, how we define the network relationships that we want to analyse comes down to what we want to focus the analysis on, and what we want it to achieve.

Another property of graphs has to do with whether they are *directed* or *undirected*. In directed graphs, we assume or know that the relationships (the edges, that is) between nodes indicate a certain orientation, so that there is a difference between the node that is the source of the relationship and the node that is its target. If you look back at Figure 8.2, you will see that the network is drawn as undirected. But the edgelist on the left-hand side of that figure could also have held information about directed relationships, such as that, for example, A and B were not only connected somehow, but in fact that A was also *sending* a message *to* B. With that logic applied to all of Figure 8.2, we would know that A sends to B, A sends to C, B sends to C, and C sends to D. Note that the edgelist would still look the same, with the only difference being that we have more, or other, information about what the pairwise combinations represent. In the visualisation on the right-hand side of Figure 8.2, we would then mark the lines between the nodes with arrowheads to indicate the direction. And if, let's say, the edgelist had also included the line of 'D, C', the connection between those two nodes would be drawn with arrows in both directions.

In terms of real-life examples, we could, for instance, in a network of Instagram users and the websites that they share links to, assume that the relationship between a user and a website is directed, as the user can be conceived of as the source and the website as the destination. In the case of messages being exchanged within a gaming community, the relationship between players may also be directed, as one player may be the person initiating the conversation or the game play while the other responds in various ways. Retweets, or other forms of tagging, quoting and liking, are a bit more complex and take some theoretical consideration. While it may be reasonable to assume that such relationships are directed, it is not completely obvious what the direction is. For example, if a user, A, retweets a tweet that was posted by another user, B, it may seem fitting to say that the edge direction goes from A to B, because A is performing the act of retweeting upon content produced by B. If the retweet is of the type where A is quoting the post by B while also adding their own content to it – for example, addressing a question about the content to B – this appears even more so. Another way of seeing this relationship, however, is in terms of A's retweet of B possibly having been caused by the content of B having influenced A to share it further through the act of retweeting. This example shows that if we are designing our network analysis to study influence, we might be better off seeing the directionality as one from B to A, but if our focus is instead on some other process, such as who endorses who, it might be from A to B.

In undirected graphs, however, the edges do not have any specific orientation. Examples of undirected graphs are networks based on different forms of co-occurrence. This can be social networks where the edges represent friendships or connections between individuals, or it can be a network of words where the edges represent how frequently two words appear together in a text. In other words, the relationship on a platform such as TikTok between a user and their followers is directed, as the follower is following the user who is being followed. The relationship between the followers of one and the same influencer, however, is undirected, as they all co-occur in the influencer's list of followers. They are connected by an edge that represents their shared property of following the influencer. Other examples of undirected networks in digital media may be those that represent users that co-participate in certain discussion threads on a forum such as Reddit. For example, if multiple users comment on a particular post or thread, they are connected by an edge in an undirected graph that represents their co-participation in that discussion.

The case of discussion forums is particularly illustrative of the multitude of possibilities that are available when it comes to defining the edges. One could, for example, simply decide that all participants that have posted within one and the same thread are seen as being in dyadic relationships with all others that have posted, as they have all somehow formed a connection (even if indirect) with each other by being part of the same forum thread. This would mean that if users A, B, C and D have all posted in the thread, the edgelist would consist of all possible pairwise constellations among the four. One alternative approach to this would be to consider participants as having a dyadic connection only with the user who made the first post in the thread so that – if A is the initiator – A connects to B, A connects to C, A connects to D, and so on. Yet an alternative approach would be to decide that each participant has formed a one-on-one connection with the participant who posted an entry immediately before theirs in the thread, so that if users took turns posting in the order of A, B, C, A, C, B, D, there would be the edges A-B, B-C, C-A, A-C, and so on. Another, more dynamic, approach could involve identifying the relationship between participants based on whether they explicitly mention one another in their posts.

Furthermore, the nodes that are connected by the edges in an edgelist can also be words and concepts that are co-occurring (Kostoff, 1993; Lindgren, 2016). With such an approach, we are basically then devising the method of SNA for various forms of 'network text analysis' (Carley, 1997). In analysing social media posts, variations of co-occurrence analysis can be used in fruitful ways for analysing co-mentions of @usernames or #hashtags in posts to produce edgelists of pairs of such names, tags, or other entities within social media posts. For example, if a tweet would include all three hashtags #blacklivesmatter, #metoo, and #fridaysforfuture, this could form the basis for an edgelist of all possible pairs within that group of three. Moving through a larger number of tweets, adding to that edgelist information on all possible pairs of tags within each tweet could then be the start of a network analysis of hashtag co-occurrences that would reflect how the users tend to use certain hashtags together with each other according to certain patterns (Dahlberg-Grundberg & Lindgren, 2015; Eriksson Krutrök & Lindgren, 2018).

Overall, then, while we need a list of edges to get going with any network analysis (cf. Figure 8.2), the construction of the pairs that make up the list is driven by a range of theoretical assumptions, and we can be sure that the choices made will strongly shape the patterns that we map out and analyse in the end. In pre-digital versions of SNA, pairs could be identified by asking people in a workplace to suggest which of their colleagues they would be more likely to socialise with, then using the responses to analyse who was connected to whom. This approach is mostly associated with the field of *sociometry*, which is about trying 'to lay bare the fundamental structures within a society by disclosing the affinities, attractions and repulsions, operating between persons and persons and between persons and objects' (Moreno, 1937: 208).

The originator of the approach, psychiatrist Jacob L. Moreno, explained:

> Sociometric measurement started with things like this: how much
> 'time' does an actor A spend with another actor B? He may spend
> half as much time with another actor C and three times as much time
> with another actor D. Or, what is the 'spatial distance,' near or far,
> in inches, feet or meters, between actors A, B, C and D in the course
> of the same situation and what effect have nearness or distance
> upon behavior and acting? Or, how frequently do two actors appear
> simultaneously in a scene and how frequently do they exit together?
> (Moreno, 1953: xxxv)

Before you can get going with SNA, you need to retrieve or register this kind of data. This may mean downloading a ready-made edgelist from online open data repositories, or creating one yourself. If you are creating the list of edges by yourself, this might mean gathering entire new data that include the information about social connections that you need, or it could entail processing already existing data so that they meet the requirements of an edgelist. An example of the latter would be to use a dataset of full-text social media posts, and then process each post looking for mentions of usernames, and then registering edges between the author of the post and any user mentioned, throughout the entire dataset. In the end, then, we want something like this:

User A mentions User B
User A mentions User C
User B mentions User C
User D mentions User E
User C mentions User B

When analysing social networks in the digital world, the lists are typically longer and the graphs much more intricate. However, for the sake of illustration, the above would result in a smaller network. The most impactful analyses occur, however, when examining networks that are complex enough to require deeper analysis that goes beyond simply reading the edgelist.

If we were to input our edgelist above into SNA software, it would know to create a graph which included the nodes A, B, C, D, and E. It would also know to create edges between A and B, A and C, B and C, and D and E.

The handling of the last edge ('User C mentions User B') would depend, as we discussed above, on whether the network was defined as directed or undirected. In the case of a directed network such as this one (based on mentions), the software would draw a connection between C and B, in addition to the one between B and C, as the two edges differ by their direction. If the network was undirected, however (as in 'User C occurs together with User B'), the last line of the edgelist (C and B) would be identical to that in the third line (B and C).

To understand how that line would be considered, there is another property of graphs that we need to know about, namely that they can be described as either *weighted* or *unweighted*. In an unweighted graph, the focus is on the mere existence of the edge between B and C, no matter how many times it is manifested in the edgelist. So in that case, the last line in our example edgelist above would not add anything new to the network (as we already have the information in line three, and because the network is now to be considered undirected). In a weighted undirected graph, however, the software would use the information in the last line (C to B) to increase the weight of the edge between B and C to a value of 2. This is because that connection already has a weight of 1 because of the information in line three. All other edges have a weight of 1.

Once we have the edgelist ready we are ready to conduct the SNA. And, while we have focused strongly on the edgelist format here, it may be good to be aware that there are also other ways of representing the same information, such as through so-called adjacency lists (Tsvetovat & Kouznetsov, 2011: 22) or matrix representations (Wasserman & Faust, 1994: 150–164). The edgelist may also be complemented with a list of nodes, consisting of one line for each node in the graph (A, B, C, D, E in the above example) with additional metadata. For example, we may know that Users A and C are political leaders, and that Users B, D, and E are activists. Similarly, the edgelist may include other information besides the pair and potentially the weight, such as for example information about different types of connections. One edge may be a mention, another may be a comment, and so on.

With the basic edge and node data in order, which as a minimum is a list of pairs in the form of a basic edgelist, the actual analysis can begin. This means using SNA software to read the edge and node data, and to move on to steps such as analysing network metrics and creating network visualisations.

NETWORK DATASETS FOR GEPHI

For the SNA analysis examples in this chapter we will rely on *Gephi* which is a widely used open source, free, software for network analysis and visualisation. It is the de-facto standard in the field of digital media SNA, and offers a user-friendly interface that allows users to easily import, manipulate, and visualise network data. There exist other alternatives out there, some paid and some free, some online and some standalone, such as Cytoscape (Shannon et al., 2003), Polinode (Pitts, 2016), NodeXL (Hansen et al., 2010), as well as combinations of coding-based options such as NetworkX (Hagberg et al., 2008) or igraph (Csardi & Nepusz, 2006) with various visualisation libraries for programming languages such as Python and R. Gephi has however become a widely used standard, if not in all forms of network science, definitely in the field of researching digital media and society through SNA. Gephi is freely accessible at gephi.org, and boasts a vibrant user community, as well as a long list of plugins and expansions. It was initially developed by Mathieu Bastian, Sebastien Heymann, and Mathieu Jacomy (2009), and has since been maintained by a team of developers. For the purpose of this book we use Gephi for two main reasons: First, because its workflow is an example as good as any of how SNA works, from importing data, through analysis, and ending up with visualisation. Second, because being familiar with Gephi in particular is a good skill to have when embarking on a research career in researching digital media and society.

But in order to start off our analysis, we – once again, and sorry if we are repeating ourselves too much – need that much coveted edgelist (remember Figure 8.2). To make our examples a bit more dynamic, we will work in the following with two different datasets, so as to enable some elements of comparison, and to make it possible to give somewhat more varied examples. The first dataset we will use is a version of an openly available dataset consisting of co-occurrences among characters in the three original Star Wars movies taken together: *A New Hope* (1977), *The Empire Strikes Back* (1980), and *Return of the Jedi* (1983). This network is based on the datasets provided by Evelina Gabasova (2016), where the links between characters are defined by the number of times that the characters speak within the same scene. For two non-English speaking key characters, R2-D2 and Chewbacca, they are counted as speaking if they are mentioned within the scene. This network, which we will call 'the Star Wars network' should be considered to be undirected and weighted. It is undirected because the co-occurrence of characters in a scene is seen as a symmetric relationship, and it is weighted because the number of co-occurrences between every two characters is taken into account.

The second dataset that we will use represents co-occurrences between hashtags in a sample of tweets about climate change that was collected during

2020. In this network, the links between hashtags are defined by the fact that the two tags have been used together in tweets simply more than zero times, regardless of how many times. This network, that we will refer to as 'the climate hashtag network', should be considered to be unweighted and undirected. It is undirected because the co-occurrence of hashtags in a tweet is also seen as a symmetric relationship – hashtags are not interacting with each other in any specific direction, unless we would account for, for example, the order in which they follow upon each other (which we do not) – and it is unweighted because in this case, we are not taking into account the frequency of co-occurrences between every two hashtags.

While the hashtag network shows a very direct application of SNA in researching digital media and society, you will need to use your imagination in the case of the Star Wars network. The latter is used, not the least for the reason that we otherwise would run into ethical issues of anonymisation and so on (see Chapter 4), as a generic illustration of a network analysis of relational patterns between social actors. As we have emphasised earlier, however, the same analytical steps could be followed for analysing interaction between users or groups in the context of digital media communication. We have made both datasets available in an online repository from which you can download them.[1] In that repository, you will also find pointers to tutorials that provide instructions on the hands-on steps required in Gephi to carry out such operations that we will write about. Because, in the text that follows, we will not guide you through all the interface level pointing and clicking that is required, as that would make the text too technical. We will simply speak about 'calculate this metric', or 'visualise the network in such and such way', and we encourage you to look into the available tutorials to find out exactly how.

ANALYSING NETWORK TOPOLOGY

The first way of analysing graphs is to focus on the overall structure of the network. By looking at what characteristics the network has as a whole, one can get knowledge about how it functions, and what its potential strengths and weaknesses are. Back in the early 1960s, around the time when the early versions of what was to become the internet were developed, the engineer Paul Baran, proposed an idea for how to design a resilient communication system that was able to withstand attacks from the outside. His concept was that of 'packet-switching' technology, which, in short, creates a network that is 'independent of command and control centers, so that message units would find their own routes along the

---

[1] The datasets are available at https://github.com/simonlindgren/rdms-networks.

network, being reassembled in coherent meaning at any point in the network' (Castells, 1996: 45). Baran presented the design in a research paper, in which he distinguishes networks that are *centralised*, *decentralised* and *distributed*.

As the renditions in Figure 8.3 show, centralised networks have a structure which is characterised by a central node, or hub, that connects to all other nodes in the network. And while Baran's example was that of communication networks at the infrastructural level, this network shape can also be helpful in analysing the patterns of relationships that emerge on today's digital media communication platforms. In a discussion forum or other online context, where all interactions are centred around one super-important user, clearly the communication breaks down if that individual leaves the network. There are no, or very few, connections between the remaining users meaning that the network is extremely vulnerable and easily disrupted. The logic goes for anything from a small group of friends, to a large online political mobilisation. In both cases, if the network relies too strongly on one single hub, the communication system is vulnerable.

In decentralised networks, the reliance on a single node is balanced out some-what as there are multiple nodes that hold key positions. This means that if one of these is removed, a significant part of the network becomes fragmented, but still the majority of the activity can continue around the remaining hubs. Finally, in Baran's ideal image of a distributed network everyone is connected to basi-cally everyone else, resulting in a resilient and organic structure of communica-tion. Through such networks, Yochai Benkler and colleagues (2018: 343) argue, networks of activists can 'raise a campaign in a truly decentralised, peer-driven

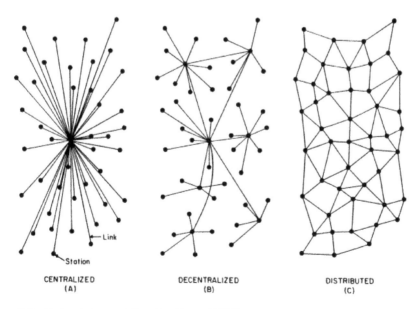

CENTRALIZED
(A)

DECENTRALIZED
(B)

DISTRIBUTED
(C)

Figure 8.3 Network types defined by Baran (1962)

way'. In relation to the theoretical and unambiguous ideal models of Baran, we can consider the real-life examples in Figure 8.4.

The four network visualisations that are shown in Figure 8.4 are based on an analysis of four different Facebook pages that we developed when teaching a course some years back. We collected data from each page, and used Gephi to analyse and visualise which kinds of network structures that they showed. The nodes in this case represent the individual users in each network, while the edges represent how they engage with each other. In terms of the edges, we treated a range of engagement types as connections, so that liking, sharing and commenting were all treated equally as forms of connections in the network. Our choice of which Facebook groups to analyse was strategic, and aimed to capture different types of network structures that can be found online. The first one was based on the page of the Swedish branch of the McDonald's corporation. As can be seen in the figure, this network displays a highly centralised structure, where one user – the corporate account itself – is the main actor and is the centre of

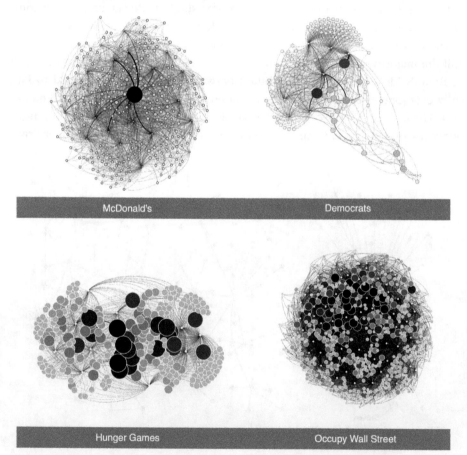

Figure 8.4 Four network visualisations based on interactions in Facebook groups

the communication and interaction. The second network that we looked at was the Facebook page of the US Democratic Party. As you will be able to see in the figure, this network is clearly decentralised, with a group of participants – rather than one single participant as in the McDonald's case – communicating significantly more than other users.

Comparing Figure 8.4 to Figure 8.3 it is apparent that the McDonald's network is an almost perfect example of a centralised network, as visualised by Baran, while the Democrats network is a quite good match with the image of a decentralised network. The centralised McDonald's network is dominated by a central capitalist actor surrounded by low engagement from a disjointed network, while the decentralised network of the Democrats page also features low-engaged participants, but in this case clustering around a couple of opinion leaders. In the bottom right corner of Figure 8.4, we can see the network visualisation for the Facebook page of Occupy Wall Street, an anti-capitalist and pro-democratic activist movement that was active globally around the time of the analysis (Fuchs, 2014). The resulting network aligns with the image of a distributed network, where no individual actor holds significantly more power than anyone else, meaning that the pattern quite clearly shows the image of a grassroots uprising that functions according to a distributed logic that digital activism scholars Bennett and Segerberg refer to as a 'connective action' model (Bennett & Segerberg, 2012). In short, the theory states that such forms of action are characterised by a large number of loosely connected individuals, who employ digital media technologies to communicate and coordinate their efforts towards social and political change without the need for hierarchical organisational structures.

Finally, in the bottom-left corner of Figure 8.4, the network based on a Facebook page for fans of the *Hunger Games* book series is shown, and it presents an interesting hybrid between decentralisation and distribution. This network can be seen as exhibiting both decentralised and distributed characteristics and is an illustration of the fact that, in empirical reality, we are most likely to observe network structures that are not pure representations of the ideal types put forward by network theorists, but rather different hybrid forms that are shaped by the specific context in which they emerge. It is also worth noting that the network visualisations in Figure 8.4 are all filtered so that only the strongest connections (edges) are shown, in order to make the images readable. We must also keep in mind that the four cases were strategically chosen as we had the expectation that they would indeed exhibit different network structures along the lines that we finally found, and that this sample is not likely to be representative of either Facebook pages or other digital media communication settings in general. The examples however illustrate the potential of analysing the structure of communication networks online. As a contrast, Figure 8.5 shows the structure of the Star Wars network and the hashtag network.

The Star Wars network, which contains relatively few nodes (representing the key characters in the films) has a structure not unlike the Democrats one in Figure 8.4, and the decentralised one in Figure 8.3. There are a small number of characters – Luke Skywalker, Darth Vader, Princess Leia, C3PO, and Han Solo – around which the communication is organised and in relation to which a larger number of lower-engagement nodes are positioned. The climate hashtag network, on the other hand, is quite dense and displays what is sometimes referred to as a 'hairball' structure. This structure poses certain challenges in terms of analysis and understanding, as it does not have a clear and organised structure and because most nodes are connected to most other nodes. The pattern is, on the one hand, quite similar to that in the Occupy Wall Street network in Figure 8.4, where we interpreted this beehive-like structure as the image of a democratic and massive grassroots uprising. In the case of the hashtag network however, the nodes are not representing people that interconnect broadly and horizontally, but hashtags being used very often together. In this case, we would need further research, and further interpretive work in order to untangle the hairball to understand if anything that is analytically interesting may lie within it.

In the examples above, we have focused on visually inspecting the *topology* of the networks. This means that we have analysed the structure of the networks, looking at how nodes and edges are connected to each other. Visual inspection of network topology provides important insights into the organisation and behaviour of complex systems. There are however also certain network metrics that can be calculated for analysing the networks as a whole. One such relates to *cohesion*, which refers to the connectedness of the entire network. SNA scholar Borgatti and colleagues (2013) write about this that:

> There is a Spanish word – enredado – that expresses it nicely. It means
> tangled up, like a big clump of electrical wires or fish caught in a trawler's

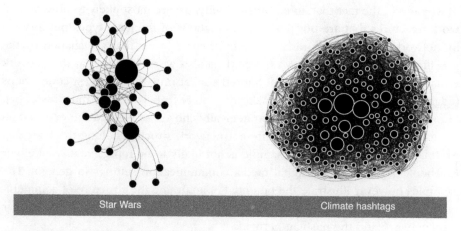

Star Wars Climate hashtags

Figure 8.5 Visualisations of the Star Wars and climate hashtags networks

net. It is particularly appropriate because the word is based on the word for network, which is red. However, it is important to note that, depending on the nature of ties in the network, the term 'cohesion' may not necessarily correspond to sociological cohesion. For example, if the network consists of 'who hates whom' ties, greater network cohesion would actually imply less sociological cohesion. (Borgatti et al., 2013: 150)

A common and useful measure of network cohesion is *density*, which is 'the number of ties in the network, expressed as a proportion of the number possible' (Borgatti et al., 2013: 150). In other words, density represents the share of all possible connections between nodes in the network (if all nodes were connected to each other) which exist as actual connections in the present network. This means that a higher density indicates a more connected and cohesive network, so that a value of 1.0 means that all possible connections exist also in reality. On the contrary, lower density implies weak connections and less interaction between nodes in a given network, so that, for example a value of 0.2 means that a fifth of all possible connections exist in reality. Therefore, density is an important measure which can be used to determine how tightly knit networks are when it comes to their overall structure.

With the Star Wars and climate hashtag networks loaded into Gephi, we can calculate their respective densities. The density of the Star Wars network is 0.169, and the density of the hashtag network is 0.0223. These density scores, first of all, suggest that the Star Wars network is more cohesive and interconnected than the climate hashtag network. Due to the significant differences between a network that reflects interactions between characters in a story, and a network that reflects the use of specific hashtags, it is not surprising that their densities diverge. Furthermore, the difference in density can also be influenced by a number of factors such as, for example, the size of each network or the criteria that were used for connecting nodes. In actual research practice, the uses and interpretations of these scores will be highly dependent on the context, the particular dataset used, and the research questions that are being asked. So, for the hashtag network where the nodes are the hashtags themselves, a lower density does not necessarily mean that the network is weaker or less meaningful than networks with higher densities. It does, however, say that there is a 2.2% probability (density 0.0223) that any hashtag in the network is used together with any other hashtag.

But density scores are the most useful when they are used to compare networks that are roughly of the same type and size, in order to determine their relative cohesiveness or connectedness. For example, analysing the three Star Wars films separately, *A New Hope* has a density of 0.286, *The Empire Strikes Back* has one of 0.262, while *Return of the Jedi* has a density of 0.289. These differences are small but could possibly to some degree indicate that the first and third films in the original trilogy are slightly more interconnected than the second one in terms of the interactions between characters. More interestingly, however, is that if one loads one of the included sample networks into Gephi – namely the one based on co-appearances of characters in Victor Hugo's novel *Les Misérables* – a density of 0.087 is obtained, which is dramatically lower than in the Star Wars films, indicating that the network of characters in *Les Misérables* is much less interconnected than those in the three Star Wars films. Now, translate this insight into the area of researching digital media and society. We could imagine, for example, that the Star Wars dataset was representing interactions among online activists in a campaign to discredit a political candidate, while the *Les Misérables* dataset would represent interactions within a counter-movement in support of that candidate. In this case, the density scores would have provided us with interesting and crucial knowledge about the relative cohesiveness – and thus potentially the power to mobilise – of the two activist groups.

Some other network-level metrics that can be valuable to explore for getting further insight into network topology are network diameter, centralisation, and clustering coefficient.[2] The metric of *network diameter* refers to the maximum distance between any pair of nodes in a network. In analysing communication and interaction patterns in the context of digital media, the measure can be useful to get knowledge about the extent to which information or influence can spread and propagate efficiently throughout a network. In other words, the diameter of a network can be part of an assessment of how fast or slow a message can travel through that network. Basically, in the case of the hashtag network, it would respond to which two hashtags are the furthest removed from each other in practical use, and in the Star Wars case, it may show which characters are the most disconnected in terms of their interactions. If you try calculating the network diameters in Gephi, you will find that the climate hashtag network has a much shorter diameter than the Star Wars and Les Misérables networks. While these networks are not directly comparable, it still shows that it is more likely that any two climate hashtags are connected through a shorter path than any two characters in the Star Wars and Les Misérables networks. Furthermore, you could find that the paths are shorter in *A New Hope* than in the two following films, which might potentially be interpreted as a reflection of the plot structure in that particular film, in terms of the connections between key characters being more tightly interwoven in the beginning of the saga.

---

[2]Both network diameter and clustering coefficient can be easily calculated in Gephi. For the clustering coefficient, note that a plugin must be downloaded. It may be confusing that there exists a metric of the same name already with Gephi's basic installation, but that one is for a different use (for so-called dynamic networks). As for the centralisation score discussed below (Freeman centralisation), a method for calculating it is available in the previously cited repository at https://github.com/simonlindgren/rdms-networks.

We could, similarly, go on experimenting with the metric of *centralisation* in these networks, which gives knowledge about the extent to which a few nodes are particularly important in holding the network together. One way of getting knowledge about the centralisation of a network is to calculate the Freeman centralisation score (Freeman, 1978). This score will vary between 0.0 and 1.0, where 0.0 indicates that the network is completely decentralised in the sense that all nodes are equally important and that there is no concentration of importance or power to any particular node. A score of 1.0 on the other hand indicates that the network is completely centralised, meaning that there is a single node that holds all the power and importance in the network. Looking back at Figure 8.4, you can probably guess which one out of those networks would have the highest centralisation score.

Yet another, out of the many possible ways to explore networks at the level of the whole graph, is to calculate the *clustering coefficient*, which is a measure of to what extent the different nodes in a network have a tendency to form groups by clustering together. This metric basically 'measures the proportion of your friends that are also friends with each other' (Tsvetovat & Kouznetsov, 2011: 66). In SNA, this coefficient is therefore useful if we want to know more about whether cohesive subgroups are present in the network that we are analysing. For example, in the Star Wars network, if the clustering coefficient is calculated in Gephi (using its 'Triangle Method') one will find a slightly increasing clustering coefficient from the first, via the second, and to the third film in the trilogy. While these networks might not be fully comparable in practice, we can still see that as an illustration of how the clustering coefficient can be used in digital media research to show, such as in this case, that the Star Wars trilogy is becoming increasingly cohesive over time, with more characters forming close-knit groups. Translated into the field of digital media research, the clustering coefficient could be used for analysing how different social groupings online differ in terms of their level of cohesion and interconnectedness.

NETWORK VISUALISATION

By moving on past the overall network level, to calculate some other metrics at the node and subcommunity level we can get some more information about the networks and its parts, which can also be used as formatting parameters when creating visualisations. Figure 8.6 below shows a visualisation of the Star Wars network which was created using the following operations in Gephi:

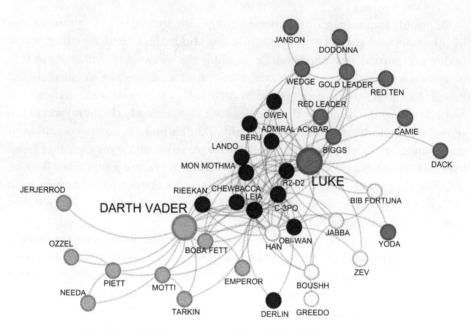

Figure 8.6 Visualisation of the Star Wars network

1 The node names were set as labels on the circles in the visualisation.
2 Node sizes were set to reflect the *betweenness centrality* of each node. This is a node level measure of how important each node is. The simplest form of centrality measure is that of *degree*. The degree of any node indicates the number of direct connections it has with other nodes in the network, thereby indicating how popular or active it is. The *betweenness centrality*, on the other hand, measures the frequency with which a node appears on the shortest path between any two other nodes. This means, in more everyday language, that a node with a high betweenness centrality is one that effectively bridges different parts of the network and that plays an important role in connecting different groups of nodes that are otherwise disconnected. Such nodes can be understood according to sociologist Mark Granovetter's (1973) famous theory about 'the strength of weak ties', arguing that, rather than the strong ties that bind tight subgroups in a network together, the 'weak ties' that bridge different groups are super important due to their role as brokers that are opening up new pathways for information flow, connection, and collaboration within a social network.
3 We included an analysis of *communities* in the network by using Gephi to identify groups of nodes – 'cohesive subgroups', or clusters – that are more tightly connected to each other than to the rest of the network. Such cohesive subgroups come in many forms, where one type is that of the

'clique', which is a group where each node is directly connected to every other node (Tsvetovat & Kouznetsov, 2011: 79). In Figure 8.6, the particular method that Gephi uses for identifying the community structure of networks has been used as the basis for colouring the largest communities into different shades (Blondel et al., 2008).

4   The network was laid out using the Yifan Hu layout algorithm in Gephi (Hu, 2006). When it comes to network layouts, it is crucial to note that one and the same network graph can be laid out in many different ways. Software programs such as Gephi tend to offer certain sets of algorithms for drawing visualisations based on the network data, where different layouts serve different purposes. Some algorithms can, for example, be better at highlighting community structures within the network, while others may be more suitable for identifying central nodes, and so on. A common type of algorithm is that of so-called force-directed algorithms which are designed to produce network images which are as readable as possible with a minimum of crossing lines (Lindgren, 2011). Because of such underlying principles that prioritise readability the relative positions of nodes in a network visualisation most often do not convey any substantial analytic information. More sophisticated forms of network visualisation may, however, be more explanatory.

Analysing Figure 8.6, we can see that the characters that are holding the story together and which are bridging the different parts of the network are Luke Skywalker and Darth Vader. The sizes of their nodes are the largest, meaning that they have the highest betweenness centrality. Vader is at the centre of the light grey subgroup on the left of the network, with characters such as Boba Fett and Tarkin connected to him, while Luke, even though being the centre of the dark grey subgroup, is also connected to several subgroups throughout the network, essentially functioning as a mediator between various characters and groups. Han Solo is in the white subgroup with characters such as Jabba and Greedo, while the droids C-3PO and R2-D2 are in the black cluster with a set of important characters such as Leia and Chewbacca.

The kind of network analysis that we have realised in this way could be a powerful tool in research on digital media and society. Imagine, for example, that these nodes instead represented users of a social media platform and the ties between them represented their interactions. If these users were engaging around a certain political issue, this mapping could give us vital insights into the key actors and groups within the conversation, as well as their level of influence and connectedness. 'Luke' and 'Darth Vader' could be identified as the main protagonists, and we could see who their associates were, and get knowledge about any complexities or unexpected connections among those. It is also very important here to note what it means to use a known example such as Star Wars for the

SNA, which means that the majority of the results will confirm the relationship patterns and dynamics that we already know from the original story. If analysing real-world interaction, however, we don't know any 'original story' in any such way, meaning that the SNA in that case can potentially reveal unknown relationships and dynamics that can feed into further research questions, novel insights and exciting research results.

CONCLUSION

As you have seen in this chapter, social network analysis can be a very useful and exciting tool for researching digital media and society. You will be able to use it to map out different patterns of relationships and interactions between actors on different online platforms, which can give you good insights into how people engage with each other. The method is also informative when it comes to assessing the potential for various messages to spread in different ways, at differing speeds and reach, in different social settings. It is, for example, more likely for content to go viral in a dense and interconnected network than in a sparse one.

Moreover, network analysis can enable you to identify key actors and groups that hold important positions, and that thus potentially have significant influence and power, in communication networks. As we have briefly touched upon, network methods can also be used as a form of text analysis by mapping out connections, not between social actors, but between words and concepts in order to understand how they are connected and structured in a text. Furthermore, as with all methods that we discuss in this book, network analysis can also be fruitfully combined with a variety of other methods to help in getting a rich and nuanced understanding of digital media and society.

9
VISUAL ANALYSIS

Key Questions

- What type of data material can be analysed through visual analysis?
- What is the role of images in the digital society?
- How can analytical concepts be incorporated into a visual analysis?
- What does it mean to interpret different levels of images in unison?

Key Concepts

social semiotics * multimodality * composition * signs * relationality * poses * gazes * power positions

Pictures matter. They make sense of our individual world, as well as our societal conditions. 'Photography and video are not simply recordings of life, but rather they are always emergent from the contingent and continually changing circumstances of life', writes Sarah Pink (2021: 2) in her book *Doing Visual Ethnography*. They are contextually bound to our understandings of specific moments in time, cultures and social conditions, and their ability to become societally important may change over time. Imagine, for example, the role of photographs on a cultural and political level and their ability to change public perception. When 2-year-old refugee Alan Kurdi drowned in the Mediterranean sea in 2015, a photograph of him became synonymous with the ongoing refugee crisis, and the desperate need for aid. As this photograph was given societal and political importance, it was also retweeted, memeified and incorporated into our digital spaces (Mortensen, 2017).

Images are undoubtedly an important part of our cultural condition, as well as our social relationships with each other and society. 'Images are part of how we experience, imagine, learn and know', according to Sarah Pink (2021: 2). Culture and society are in many ways visual, not only on the internet. The critical theorist Guy Debord stated that our contemporary world had turned into a 'society of the spectacle' already in 1967 when he proposed that 'everything that was directly lived has moved into a representation' (Debord, 2012: 107). Images hold significant importance for politics, where 'the socio-political power of images, which make their strategic production and manipulation in important areas of academic inquiry, lies in the emotional impact an image can have' (Lilleker et al., 2019: 2).

Now, in a digital society, images are all around us, and ever as important. Often, however, we tend to view the visual parts of our data as separate from the textual ones, not least when we are dealing with social media data. Why though? When researching, for example, far-right movements in the USA, can we really disregard memes, video clips, and photos if we want to understand them? Probably not.

Why should we incorporate the analysis of visuals into our methods? According to Gillian Rose (2016), there are three reasons for this. First, images hold the capacity to generate rich data, where imagery can expand the depths of our analyses. Imagine, for example, speaking about memes used by Russian dissidents, without also analysing the visual contents of these memes. Second, we are able to explore taken-for-granted experiences and tacit forms of knowledge when analysing images. When we delve into visual representations of society, we are able to uncover layers of common-sense practices derived from societal and political conditions. These conditions can be explored in critical ways when analysing these visual cultural elements. Third, we are able to foster participation and collaboration in our knowledge production, especially when we systematically collect visuals from our research participants.

There are different ways of incorporating images into one's study. During the last half century, visual communication such as illustrations, photographs and images have come to form an increasingly large part of people's communication (Kress, 2010: 6). As explained by Gillian Rose (2016: 15), a researcher may, first, use already existing images as the material for their analysis, or, second, produce images themselves as part of the analytical work, and in a third sense, the researcher may ask research participants to take pictures for the purpose of the study. In this chapter, we will focus heavily on the first way images may be incorporated, through already available imagery from mass media, social media or social contexts that you want to research.

On a technical level, the modes of visual imagery can become more or less important over time. Imagine the role of Ellen DeGeneres' selfie at the 2014 Oscars, which, at the time, became a viral hit. It was the most retweeted photograph ever, passing the previous record held by then-president Barack Obama. Today, this selfie might not feel as enticing. Let's be honest, selfies, while still prevalent, may not hold the same societal importance as a decade ago. Selfies have existed as long as the art of photography. A photograph taken in the mid-19th century by

American photographer Robert Cornelius has at least been called 'the very first selfie', as explored by The Robert Cornelius Daguerreotype Database Project, an online database of his images, led by photograph conservator Rachel Weiss at the Library of Congress (Conversation Center for Art & Historic Artifacts, 2022). But maybe the DeGeneres photograph gained traction for other reasons than it being a selfie. Maybe, the instantaneity of how this photograph was uploaded from the ongoing event, shared on Twitter by Ellen herself, may have been an important part of its success, rather than the format. If we were to analyse it further, the interconnectedness of technology, context and power would be important to relate to. We may want to start by reading previous research on the technological conditions of social media for instant modes of communication, the context of ongoing media events and our parasocial relationship with celebrities, if we were to analyse it further.

In the 2020s, we may feel more enticed to analyse get-ready-with-me-videos on TikTok (GRWM) or maybe the uses of eerie-looking AI filters. What do these modes of visual communication say about ourselves, society and the times we live in?

In sociologist Erving Goffman's (1959) classic book *The Presentation of Self in Everyday Life*, he uses symbolism from the world of theatre to explain how we 'perform' ourselves in different parts of social life. His terminology of 'back-stage' and 'front-stage' ways of being may come in handy when analysing the technological conditions of presenting ourselves on social media. We do present ourselves differently on different sides of the internet. On LinkedIn, we tend, to a larger extent, to use professionally shot photographs for our profile photo, while on TikTok, we tend less to do so – maybe unless we are a big creator making a living off of it. We have many different front-stages in our social lives, where we present our selves in different ways, for different audiences. At home, we may feel more secure with sharing our inner thoughts and feelings, even the difficult

Figure 9.1 Ellen DeGeneres' Oscars selfie (@EllenDeGeneres/Twitter, 2014) and Robert Cornelius' selfie from the mid-19th century (Cornelius, 1839)

ones. But, in a classroom, we put a different front-stage performance on. We present differently; we keep it less personal. By extension, we have many different back-stage selves as well. Some, we might take to the grave. Remember the Carrie Bradshaw-coined term of 'secret single behaviour' from *Sex & The City*? What would you not want anyone to ever see from your own back-stage? On second thought: don't answer that.

It can also be useful to delve into theories of *representation* when talking about photography, for example through the theories of Stuart Hall (1997b). Instead of capturing what we may perceive as a 'reality', photographs are solely arbitrary moments that reflect specific events or something memorable (Machin, 2007). Staying critical to the medium itself, the role of composition, elements and power relations in images may shape not only our understanding of the collected data but also expand our critical mind toward social media representations of everyday life. We will discuss this critical stance in upcoming sections as well.

In another potential study, how might we use AI-generated art as a basis for a study about creativity discourse? While AI art has become a sore subject for contemporary creators, where we have indeed needed to question the role of training data for creating AI systems able to create art, we may also need to reflect upon what role AI may play in our societal understanding of creativity. In Walter Benjamin's essay 'The Work of Art in the Age of Mechanical Reproduction', he argues that the 'aura' of art was lost through technologies of mechanical reproduction (Benjamin, 1969). Aura, he claimed, was the inherent uniqueness and authenticity of a work of art. How might we incorporate such older theories with contemporary research exploring AI art? Perhaps the visuals are but one element in our data collection for such a study, in combination with opinion pieces printed in news media, or interviews with creators themselves.

Imagery is laden with cultural, contextual and political meanings, and these meanings can evolve and change over time. This chapter is dedicated to the analysis of visual material, whether it is static or moving, old or new, and multimodal or not. Given the various forms that your data material may take, it is necessary to cover different methods of analysing these visual aspects.

When teaching students how to analyse visual material, we prioritise concrete analytical concepts derived from traditions such as social semiotics or critical linguistics, over any full application of any of the respective traditions. We refer to these concepts as tools and encourage students to select the appropriate ones for studying a specific image while being transparent and justifying their choices. We should ask you to do the same. Be concrete about the type of visual material you are going to analyse: memes, YouTube videos, journalistic images, user avatars, and so on. Also, be specific about which tools you will use to analyse this material. But, first, let us return to the classical theories that have informed these analytical concepts – social semiotics and multimodal analysis.

Reading images

The way in which meaning is created depends on different levels of *signification*. Here, we will focus on the theoretical model of Ferdinand de Saussure, a founding figure of structuralism and semiotics.

In Figure 9.2, we see, first, that the sign is composed of two elements, the signifier and the signified. When we communicate, we use words ('signifiers') in order to connect different objects or contexts to meanings. We may use the word 'apple' when we talk about apples, but the actual things which we call apples may be very different. There are many different colours, shapes and tastes of apples, as well as different names for each individual apple variety. However, when we use the word 'apple' in order to describe this category of fruit, which de Saussure would call the 'signified', we imagine a figurative apple, which represents the idea of the apple rather than any individual apple itself. For Saussure, the 'signified' is our collective understanding of what constitutes an apple, and how we imagine it. The signifier and the signified, taken together, are what constitute the 'sign'. 'Signification', in the last step, relates to the external reality of the meaning of the object itself. This external meaning is based on cultural and social conditions shaping the interpretation in a myriad of ways.

Images can be understood in different ways, depending not solely on what they represent, but also on how these depictions become interpreted. This two-level way of 'reading' an image is based on Roland Barthes' semiotic theory (1973, 1977). An image, by his terminology, can be understood by analysing, first, what is *denoted*, and second, what the image *connotes*. The first level, then, focuses on what is documented. Images show specific objects, features, events, people, places and things. Colours, light, perspective and other forms of visual representation can be included in this form of analysis. When focusing on what an image denotes, we are asking: who and/or what is depicted here? At a second level of analysis, we focus on what these visuals represent in a broader sense. How can we place them in relation to wider societal, cultural and social contexts and ideas? What messages can be found, and how are these representative of specific understandings? This means that the connotation emphasises which values and ideas are communicated in the image. Thus, the connotation makes visible the underlying messages reflected in the image. By making the connotation visible, it is possible to distinguish which discourses speak through the image. Specific imagery is used to connote specific ideas and concepts. So asking what an image

Figure 9.2 Saussure's theoretical model of signification

connotes is asking: What ideas and values are communicated through what is represented, and through the way in which it is represented?

Representations have different potential meanings. That is true of all qualitative readings of texts, images and concepts. In Machin and Mayr's (2012) multimodal analysis, they have proposed the use of the concept 'meaning potential' rather than 'connotations', as it suggests that meanings are not fixed, but instead present a possibility of meaning, and it encourages us to consider specifically how any visual element or feature is connected to and used with other visual elements, which may serve to modify its meaning. Looking, for example, at a YouTube video, one could consider how it has been directed, cut or manipulated in order to change how it comes across. Often, we see two-person podcasts or talk shows on YouTube where they have added visual elements which may only have been referenced in speech. Sometimes, such shows are even recorded in front of a green screen, in order to edit the content in creative ways, such as the show 'UNHhhhh' by American drag queens Trixie Mattel and Katya Zamolodchikova. These forms of editing can emphasise humorous storytelling by creators, and increase the meaning potential by adding manifest visual denotations.

Meaning potentials depend on these manifest denotations but also on who is doing the looking. This means that we, as researchers, need to be careful when we make claims about the meanings of images that may not be commonsensical to others, or not at all clear to anyone besides yourself. These different 'ways of looking' have been outlined by art critic John Berger (1972), who emphasised the relationship not only between the different parts of an image but also between these parts and our own self. Some may find an image of a gun to be provocative in many ways. If you have never seen a gun in real life but heard of increased gun violence, or are aware of the prevalence of mass shootings, a gun may connote such imagery for you, personally. But somebody who has grown up with guns, or keeps them in their house, may have other – personal – connotations regarding what this gun may represent to them. However, when we do a visual analysis of an image, we try our hardest to place ourselves outside of that reading and look at the social, cultural and societal contexts of what we are seeing. This depends on our ability to be self-reflective (as discussed previously in Chapter 4).

We need to know our own dispositions before we can know how to not be influenced by them. Then we need to ask a series of questions: How are guns normally understood in society? How are things such as violence, discipline, masculinities or fear connected to images of guns in our society? How are things such as social injustice, social movements and protests connected to guns? How can we understand the image of the gun based on these social conditions?

Some people may be sceptical about whether representations matter: 'Why should we be critical when signs in the public bathroom denote a woman changing a diaper rather than a man?' Women have been taking care of their offspring since the beginning of time, so why shouldn't pictures depict social reality as it is?'. Halliday (1978, 1985) explains that specific connotations and imagery become a 'cultural code' that is both shaped by society and shapes our understanding of society. As such, language is not simply a mode of communication, it also becomes constitutive of society itself. This is part of Halliday's social semiotics, where he states that:

> By their everyday acts of meaning, people act out the social structure, affirming their own statuses and roles, and establishing and transmitting the shared systems of value and of knowledge. [...] We have to proceed from the outside inwards, interpreting language by reference to its place in the social process. This is not the same thing as taking an isolated sentence and planting it out in some hothouse that we call a social context. It involves the difficult task of focusing attention simultaneously on the actual and the potential meanings, interpreting both discourse and the linguistic system that lies behind it in terms of the infinitely complex network of meaning potential that is what we call the culture. (Halliday, 1978: 4–5)

Being critical in our visual analysis means that we must be 'concerned with the social effects of the visual material it is studying' (Rose, 2016: 46). Here, we can incorporate the concept of 'myth' as defined by Roland Barthes, who focuses on how signs are used in specific ways that relate to a culture's dominant ways of understanding things (Fiske, 2010: 82). Think, for example, about our idea of motherhood, and the individual mother, and her role in the household, in society, in the workforce. She thinks, first and foremost, of her children and family, not herself. She is proper, not career driven and not dependent on outside appreciation. These myths of mothers recur in societal narratives of mothers, not least in media contexts.

Myths are reproduced both by individuals in society and in mediated forms, and it is key, not only to analyses of language but also to visual analyses that they are able to uncover such myths. When we do a search on Google Images for 'mother', what kinds of imagery come up? Relatedly, what are the image search results for 'scientist'? Thinking back to our previous example of AI art, how would these forms of imagery be incorporated into our AI systems as training data? Timnit Gebru, a computer scientist working on algorithmic bias and data mining, was hired and later famously fired from her position as technical co-lead of the Ethical Artificial Intelligence Team at Google, for raising these kinds of ethical issues around AI models' reproduction of racism and sexism. As explained by

Fiske (2010: 84), the concept of myth can be used to uncover hidden meanings, histories and contexts:

> Barthes argues that the main way myths work is to naturalize history. This points up the fact that myths are actually the product of a social class that has achieved dominance by a particular history: the meanings that its myths circulate must carry this history with them, but their operation as myths makes them try to deny it and present their meanings as natural, not historical or social. Myths mystify or obscure their origins and thus their political or social dimension. The mythologist reveals the hidden history and thus the socio-political works of myths by 'demystifying' them. There is a myth that women are 'naturally' more nurturing and caring than men, and thus their natural place is in the home raising the children and looking after the husband, while he, equally 'naturally', of course, plays the role of breadwinner. These roles then structure the most 'natural' social unit of all – the family. By presenting these meanings as part of nature, myth disguises their historical origin, which universalizes them and makes them appear not only unchangeable but also fair: it makes them appear to serve the interests of men and women equally and thus hides their political effect.

Staying critical in relation to these myths means unpacking them. This goes further than looking at the denotative elements inherent in images and text. We need to reflect upon more than what *is* and relate to what it *means*. This criticality is inherent in theories of discourse (Chapter 6), and discourse analysis can also be implemented for the analysis of images (Rose, 2016). In Machin and Mayr's (2012) *multimodal critical discourse analysis*, they rely on the critical discourse analysis (CDA) framework and combine it with a multimodal perspective on discourse. The method uses a 'social semiotic view of language', which emphasises the way 'we should see all communication, whether through language, images, or sounds, as accomplished through a set of semiotic resources, options and choices' (Machin & Mayr, 2012: 15). They separate different levels of discourse practices: lexical choices and visual semiotic choices. Below, however, we will explain how different modalities of communication should be analysed as a totality.

MULTIMODALITY

Often, students ask where to begin. Looking at the text first? The image first? The angles second? We tend to advise against this stark separation between the parts of visuals. All parts are important and should be analysed in unison rather than separately. In the words of Kress and van Leeuwen (2006: 177):

> The question arises whether the products of the various modes should be analysed separately or in an integrated way; whether the sum of the meanings of the parts, or whether the parts should be looked upon as interacting with and affecting one another [...] It is the latter part we will pursue [...] We seek to be able to look at the whole page as an integrated text. [...] We seek to break down the disciplinary boundaries between the study of language and the study of images, and we seek, as much as possible, to use compatible language, and compatible terminology to speak about both, for in actual communication the two, and indeed many others, come together to form integrated parts.

Photographic images are but one form of visuality, which means that when conducting visual analysis of digital media content, it is necessary to consider multiple modalities of information. The concept of *multimodality* is defined as the use of multiple modes or ways of meaning-making (Kress, 2010). For example, a tweet can combine text, images and emojis to create a multimodal message, and a news story by an online outlet may include pictures, videos and hyperlinks to provide its audience with a broader perspective on an event. Similarly, videos on YouTube or TikTok will typically combine visual, audio and textual modalities. So, if we are to carry out comprehensive visual analyses of digital media content, we must look beyond the surface-level image, and consider more deeply and broadly the various modalities that may be at play in the meaning-making process.

First of all, the omnipresence of video online means that the analysis of visuals becomes much more complex than in the case of still images. When conducting visual analysis of a video, one must, for example, be aware of things such as the audio track, shifting zooms, cuts, camera movements, and edits as well as other properties that are specific only to video. Furthermore, both in the case of still images and video on digital media platforms, the use of other multimodal features such as text overlays, stickers, emojis, hashtags and filters must be taken into account as they can impact strongly on how the content is interpreted.

On the one hand, multimodality is 'the normal state of human communication' (Kress, 2010: 1), as we nearly always draw on more than one mode when we communicate. On the other hand, digital media communication has proliferated multimodal communication. Take the emoji as an example of this. While the origin of the smiley face goes back to the 1950s, its development into our contemporary emoji landscape has been ongoing since then. According to the Emojipedia online resource, there were, as of September 2022, 3,664 different emojis available in the Unicode Standard. And emojis matter (Giannoulis & Wilde, 2019). For example, there has been an increase in disability-centred emojis, such as wheelchair users, in different shades of skin, and in more gender-equal male/female representation in child-rearing emojis, sports emojis, and so on. The use of emojis can itself be an interesting focus for research. For example, if we find that the green heart emoji (♡) is used in an Instagram caption by a famous influencer having taken a long-haul, likely high-emission, trip to the other side of the globe, and this sparks outrage amongst their followers since it may be interpreted as insincere or thoughtless, we may need to look deeper into the way this emoji is often used when speaking about environmental issues such as recycling, sustainability, veganism and other related issues (Ho, 2022).

Symbols mean things. So, when platforms incorporate symbols in their user interface, they shape our means of interaction (see more on ways to study platforms in Chapter 10). In the olden days, Facebook users were only able to 'like' posts by clicking the thumbs-up button. This could be sufficient for interaction purposes, but what happens when a user announces the death of a loved one on Facebook? Are people supposed to 'like' that? In their review of the field of digital mourning, Wagner (2018) highlighted the role of collective norms for utilising technological features on platforms, specifically in times of mourning. Bucher and Helmond (2018) studied the reaction of Twitter users to the new like button feature in 2015. The platform originally offered a star button for 'favouriting' posts but in 2015 they changed the button to a heart. This changed users' perception of what it meant to interact with others' posts, highlighting the importance of visual affordances on social media and how they may affect users' experience on the platform.

Visuals are also an important part of our political communication, especially in digital spaces. In particular, memes have become increasingly important for everyday activists in a variety of contexts, including Russia (Denisova, 2019), Palestine (Zidani, 2021; Cervi & Divon, 2023) and other places. For marginalised communities, visual memes have become an important part of showing resistance against oppressors (Lu & Steele, 2019), and in this way, memes 'stay within the subversive and create frontiers to political elites and the mainstream, but in their playful appropriation of political contexts, they may challenge and push these very same frontiers' (Mortensen & Neumayer, 2021: 2375). However, memes have changed over time and adapted to new features on different platforms. The original internet meme consisted of an image and text alongside each other, but with the rise of platforms like TikTok, memes have undergone an 'aural turn' (Abidin & Kaye, 2021) whereby short musical and sound excerpts, remixes, and so on, are repurposed by users over time. The sound itself may change over these reiterations. For example, the interviewed boy who exclaimed that he loves corn, originally uploaded by the Instagram account @recesstherapy in August 2022, was shortly thereafter remixed into a song by TikTok users, which was later incorporated into over 390,000 TikTok videos.[1] Since memes are no longer limited to mere image and text, Rogers and Giorgi (2023: 2) have emphasised how they are multimodal collections of technical content, shaped by the platforms they inhabit:

> [A]s they spread across different digital spaces, we argue, memes acquire specificities depending on the site where they are constructed. Thus, in our reading, memes are understood as collections of technical content resulting from a combination of digital participatory culture as well as software production practices.

Our visual modes of communicating also shape our own selves in relation to others. By answering a Twitter/X post with a GIF of Forrest Gump quickly running away, we probably want to show ourselves avoiding a certain conversation topic. So, in an internet setting where the body is removed from direct communication the way we use visual images as identifying features of ourselves or our emotions can matter for the way we are perceived. The 'virtual personae' and the 'fragmented self' online, as described by Sherry Turkle (1995) may also be shaped by societal ideals and norms.

Who do we present ourselves as visually? Using avatars as a stand-in for our own bodies is one such way, and as expressed by Taylor (2002: 41), avatars enable users to 'intersect with a technological object and embody themselves, making the virtual environment and the variety of phenomena it fosters real'. In relation to this, scholars and activists have highlighted the need to talk about the use of black bodies in, for example, GIFs as a way of 'sassing up' white users' expressions – as a form of digital blackface. The history of blackface originates from the Jim Crow-era of black minstrelsy in the USA in the early 19th century, where white performers would paint their faces black and act out as black caricatures on stage. In an essay published in *Teen Vogue* in 2017, author Lauren Michele Jackson wrote:

> [W]hile reaction GIFs can and do [express] every feeling under the sun, white and nonblack users seem to especially prefer GIFs with black people when it comes to emitting their most exaggerated emotions. Extreme joy, annoyance, anger and occasions for drama and gossip are a magnet for images of black people, especially black femmes.

GIFs are often essentially an animated form of meme, not technically videos but rather a sequence of images that, just like memes, can visually express emotion, humour or political statements. And while we may be interested in analysing

---

[1]https://knowyourmeme.com/memes/corn-kid-corn-song-tiktok

specific visual entities, we always need to contextualise their usage and historically situate them.

Analytical Toolbox for Visual Analysis

There are, as we have shown, many different ways of analysing images. Gillian
Rose (2016), for example, introduces a framework for what she has called a *critical visual methodology*, which includes within its framework quite a few of the
visual methods approaches available. When it comes to analysing images, Rose
defines four different sites: the site of production, the site of the image itself,
the site of its circulation and the site of its audiencing. Based on this distinction between sites, we can imagine what visual analysis around each of these
might entail. First, analysing the *site of production* would largely be about gaining
an understanding of the context in which the image was created, which might
include the motives of those involved in the creation of the images, and any cultural values or practices that may have influenced the process through which the
image came into being. In the case of an Instagram post, we might, for example,
be interested in who shot the photo, where, what equipment and software they
used, their intentions behind taking and sharing it, and any wider societal factors
that may have led them to do so, and so on.

Analysing the *image itself* would, obviously, be about looking at the content of
the image, including its visual features, and trying to unravel any symbolic or cultural meanings that might be embedded within it. This kind of analysis may also
have to do with the choice of what to depict, from what angle, how the image has
been composed or cropped, whether any filters, text overlays or other elements
were added, and so on. In other words, it is about deconstructing the image to
understand how it was put together and the message it conveys.

Analysing the *site of circulation* would be about studying how and where the
image is shared and disseminated, and furthermore the impact that this might
have on how it is interpreted by different audiences. This analysis would involve
considering the platforms used (see Chapter 10) for sharing the image, as well as
how it is distributed or targeted across different channels and networks through
the use of hashtags, by posting in different communities, and so on.

Finally, analysing the *site of audiencing* could focus on gaining an understanding of how different groups of people might make sense of an image, by taking
into account things such as their cultural background, political views and other
elements that may be pertinent to how the image is rendered meaningful. This,
then, involves trying to analyse how the image addresses or positions the viewer
and how viewers respond. In the following section, we present an analytical
toolbox as guidance for how you might perform a visual analysis of your own. In
general, and for reasons of methodological pragmatism (see Chapter 2), we will

focus on the tools as such, rather than on discussing the broader traditions from which they originate.

COMPOSITION: VALUES, SALIENCE AND FRAMING

An image depends not only on the elements within it but also on how these elements interact with each other in interrelated systems of meaning-making. When we look at magazine covers, for example, we are able to see how different elements are composed in order to create meaning. This process of meaning-making can be analysed along three levels, according to Kress and van Leeuwen (2006: 177):

1 *Information value*: How are elements placed within the image? These placements give the element different informational values, in accordance with the many zones of an image; where information is read, first, from left to right, from top to bottom, from the centre to the margins.
2 *Salience*: How are the elements designed to attract the viewer? This can be done to different degrees, by placing them in the foreground or the background, by their relative size, through contrasts between different tones or colours, their difference in sharpness and blurriness, and so on.
3 *Framing*: How are different framing devices utilised in the picture? Rather than focusing on the elements themselves, we look at how different placements of them, or lines between them, connect or disconnect them from each other. This can show us which elements belong together or are separate from one another.

When analysing composition, especially in magazine covers, we are able to see more of the aspects of the relationship between the placements of text, headlines and images. This can also be true of other, digital, material. Creators are able to incorporate different forms of visual elements in their storytelling when the social media platforms used by these creators allow them to, and TikTok especially comes to mind as a forerunner in this regard. The technical features on offer may allow them to include emojis, GIFs or other visuals. These elements may help to enhance, and sometimes move beyond, the story being told. For example, when a creator may be talking about how they 'love chocolate to death', they might include a tombstone emoji to accentuate this emotion to a point where it becomes humorous. While you would not actually die from your love of chocolate, and indeed need a tombstone for your grave, this makes the connotation funny, and may function as an additional storytelling element. It is important to be aware not only of what elements are included in each video, but also what function they serve in each instance.

DIFFERENT TYPES OF SIGNS

Signs are present within visual material in different ways. Saussure was interested in signs on a quite simplistic level, which was developed over time by the semiologists following him. One of the most important ones was Charles Sanders Peirce who formulated a triadic model of the sign, focusing on its different potential forms: iconic, symbolic or indexical.

An *iconic sign* represents what is being signified by showing its likeness. Returning to Saussure's apple, the apple itself may be represented in a specific style (its shaft, one leaf on the one side, red or green, and so on) which means that the apple itself is represented in relation to our idea of an apple, attempting to visually reproduce it. Such an apple, thus, is an indexical sign – connoting the shape and appearance of a real-life apple, as we have culturally understood it before.

Symbolic signs have cultural meanings that make their understanding contextual and dependent on these cultural conditions. Imagine a wedding ring. The ring is just a piece of jewelery, placed on one of the fingers, preferably. The wedding ring tends to live exactly on the finger that we have culturally decided is where the ring should go: the ring finger. At least in a Western context. This tradition dates back to the Ancient Romans, who believed that this exact finger contained a 'vein of love', Vena Amoris, which ran 'directly to the heart'. In this context, a wedding ring placed on any other finger would be misconstrued as just any other old ring. Remember how Susan Sharon reacted to seeing Carrie Bradshaw's engagement ring sitting in a chain around her neck in *Sex & the City* – it was an awkward moment. Also, did Carrie end up marrying Aidan? Nah.

Returning to the apple, it can also be a symbol of many different things, in which case it would be considered a symbolic sign rather than an iconic sign. For example, in popular culture, apples have been associated with the notion of 'knowledge'. Apples are stereotypically brought to the teacher's desk by their students, often the 'teacher's pet' of the class, in many cultural narratives. We also see the use of an apple in the biblical imagery of Eve eating the forbidden fruit of knowledge, where the apple, that God tells them explicitly not to taste, becomes a symbol of the sought-after knowledge of the first man and woman. The serpent tempts Eve, saying 'Ye shall not surely die: For God doth know that in the day ye eat thereof, then your eyes shall be opened, and ye shall be as gods, knowing good and evil' (Genesis 3: 4–5). Boy, was he wrong. But that is a different story.

Indexical signs, finally, show one thing that connotes something else. The traditional example would be smoke, obviously connoting something else – fire. 'Where there's smoke, there's fire', as the old saying goes.

THE RELATIONALITY OF IMAGES

One part of multimodal critical discourse analysis is to analyse the role of social actors in images. In communication, choices can be made as to whether different people are named and how they are visually represented, and this has an impact on communication. These choices can symbolically place people in a social context and highlight their identities (Machin & Mayr, 2012: 77). The way we are addressed or approached through texts can establish formal, close or distant relationships between the speaker and the addressee (Fairclough, 1995: 58). This is also true for images.

According to Kress and van Leeuwen, specific relationships are built between different forms of participants in images. When we view, interpret and analyse images, we become 'interactive participants' (Kress & van Leeuwen, 2006: 114). While we sometimes are able to interact directly with the producers of images, for example when a friend of ours takes a snapshot of us and we demand to have it 'deleted immediately!!!', we are, most of the time, not able to delve into the backstory of the production or publishing process or the producers' intentions. What do we, then, interact with?

First, relationships are built between the represented participants in an image. In the Ellen DeGeneres selfie, discussed above, we may focus on the way that the celebrities represented in the selfie (Jennifer Lawrence, Meryl Streep, Julia Roberts, to name a few) interact with each other. How are they positioned toward one another, and whose hand is placed on whose shoulder, for example (we will talk more about pose and gaze in the upcoming section)?

Second, the viewer interacts in different ways with specific represented participants. This can be related to their placement in the image itself (we will talk more about positionality in the upcoming section), or be indicative of our imagined relationship to those represented. How does Angelina Jolie's placement, half obscured by her own hand, place her in relation with the other, more central, figures? How does Jennifer Lawrence's red dress allow her increased informational value in the totality of the image?

Third, relationships are built between the viewers of images. As consumers of popular culture in many different forms, we may feel connected in our shared experiences of, emotions toward or relationships to the celebrities in the image. We may be fans of Meryl Streep, but not of Ellen DeGeneres, and connect with others who feel just as closely connected as you to some of the individuals in the image. This may result in sharing the original image on Instagram, or linking to it in a Messenger chat with your friends, and so on.

Furthermore, fonts can be congruent or not with the tone or the affect of the text. In their work on how typeface affects communication, Hazlett et al. (2013) showed that readers could instantly process a certain font's 'personality', and that the given typeface influenced their affective processing of the message. Because of this, when we think about the 'visualities' of an image where text is incorporated into the image, we also have to consider the relevance of the typefaces used to write that text. How would using the font Comic Sans in a corporate newsletter affect the message? How would a child's invitation to a birthday party be affected by using Times New Roman? And, ultimately, what implied social relationships are built into these design choices?

PEOPLE: POSES, GAZES AND POWER POSITIONS

The way that different participants are visually represented in an image corresponds to 'meaning potentials', according to Machin and Mayr (2012). The *gazes* and *gestures* in an image will affect the relationship between the viewer and the represented participants. In particular, a direct gaze demands something from the viewer. What that something is can be different depending on the context. For example, when Uncle Sam gazes directly at us as the text reads 'I want you for U.S. army', his gaze demands more – he wants you to join the army and fight for your country. This is further accentuated by the gesture, leaning in towards the viewer, with his finger pointing at them.

Connecting the role of gaze and gesture to Halliday's (1985) idea of speech acts, Kress and van Leeuwen (2006: 118) suggest that a gaze either creates demands or offers us something, whether it be information, services or goods. In this way, what are solely visualised interactions between us and the portrayed individuals can be understood as a, more formal, form of interaction, where we are expected to do something specific. When a represented participant is not looking at the viewer, on the other hand, there are other effects at play, where we are not demanded to respond (Machin & Mayr, 2012: 71). For example, when an Instagram reel is shot front on, directly at the creator themselves while looking at the camera, we become interconnected not only with them, but also their storytelling. In particular, when a young mother shares a story about the hardships of giving birth, or a man shares the news of a recent cancer diagnosis, we are inclined to lean into the story, rather than back. If shot in another way, such videos might result in a less emotional response.

Furthermore, the camera positions and angles matter for the interpretation of images. The *distance* between the camera and its objects can indicate different forms of relationship. An up-and-close picture of a politician can indicate a level of closeness that they want to try to translate into a real-life relationality with voters. This effect can indicate a willingness to create a more intimate personal relationship with the viewer (Machin & Mayr, 2012: 98). *Angles* can also matter for our perception of closeness to the represented participants. Here, the 'face-to-face' angle, where we are on the same level as the person depicted, versus the 'side-on view' shapes how near, attached or detached we may feel towards them. Additionally, whether the viewer is 'looking up' or 'down upon' the represented participant matters for how power relations are built within the picture (Machin & Mayr, 2012: 98–100). When depicting children, for example, we tend to photograph them from above. Such choices in how images are composed can contribute to shaping our collective ideas of an influential public position, such as that of famous TikTok creator Charli D'Amelio.

Let's consider an example from one of our previous studies (Eriksson Krutrök & Åkerlund, 2023). In that study, we used Machin and Mayr's (2012) *multimodal critical discourse analysis* as a tool for investigating the textual and visual semiotic choices of the top 100 algorithmically ranked TikTok videos that were using the hashtag #BlackLivesMatter. We analysed the most liked video in the data, a video posted by Charli D'Amelio (@charlidamelio) to her, then, 80 million followers (see Figure 9.3). In an article based on that study, we wrote:

> Her video was filmed in a home setting, facing the camera directly, with her gaze centred on the audience watching her through the app. While she was wearing makeup, she was not particularly donned up in fancy attire. Her hair was made in a simple ponytail, and she wore a sweatshirt, tied at the top. The camera was solely focused on her, with a white background, and this simplicity in the background, was also reflected through the lack of use of hashtags and video description: simply *#BlackLivesMatter*. These elements seemed to suggest an urgency of the message and a lack of visibility labour which usually goes into the job practice of influencers, by putting up somewhat of a show. In this video, where she addressed her viewers directly, she stated,
>
> As a person who has been given a platform to be an influencer, I realize that with that title, I **have a job** to inform people on the racial inequalities in the world right now.

Figure 9.3. A screenshot of a video posted by Charli D'Amelio in May 2020

In this transcript and video, we see how influencers may relate to their power position, which, in turn, makes them more visible on the platform. However, there was a lexical absence of a discussion concerning whether she should make statements regarding any situation of racial (in)justice. When claiming she has 'a job' to inform people, she implied that her visible position on the platform *forces* her to make statements on these issues, no matter her relationship to the cause. What is not being said in this statement is just as interesting. There was a lexical absence of a discussion of her privilege in other aspects. Continuing, she said,

A man was killed. His life was ended. 'Don't kill me', George Floyd says, that's his last words. His life should not be over and his name needs to be heard. George Floyd. **A father and a person**. **A human** who lost their life because of the color of their skin. We people of all colors need to speak up at a time like this.

The explicit connections made between the many identity positions of George Floyd are indicative of something that is, in fact, not being said. By addressing George Floyd as a 'father', 'person', and a 'human', the intent of the creator seems to address the ways he has been made illegitimate as a 'real victim'. These indirect meanings of discourse (van Dijk, 2001) show how TikTok users used this space to create a vocabulary of victimisation (Dunn, 2010) that could legitimise their victim status.

Influencers like *@charlidamelio* showcase solidarity with the Black Lives Matter movement. Yet, these videos are not recorded in a setting that would suggest these influencers are themselves out there, actually 'doing something'. As seen elsewhere, self-representation practices can be carefully staged by influencers to appeal to their intended audiences (Lewis, 2020). Ultimately, influencers seem to be leveraging Black people's struggles for increased self-exposure but with little effort to support the actual movement (see also Sobande, 2004). (Eriksson Krutrök & Åkerlund, 2023: 2004-2006)

In the article from which this abstract is taken, we focus on a combination of factors included in the video itself. D'Amelio's hairstyle, clothes and make-up indicate one level of relationship with her viewers. These indications would not be the same for any ordinary user. Seeing as this is a famous TikToker, her physical attributes are usually reflective of a higher form of affluence. By not even bothering, or not to be seen bothering, too much with her physical appearance, she seems to connote an urgency in spreading the message, and, as such, of being politically aware. At a second level, we focus on the connotations of her lexical choices in terms of words both used and not used. For example, she referred to her 'job' of informing others, based on her privileged position as an influencer in the USA. However, she failed to account for her role as a white woman, and the privilege this provides her within American society. At a third level, we placed the video in a relational context within the #blacklivesmatter hashtag on TikTok, as well as the movement at large.

In a visual analysis such as this one, we were able to look at both what is and what is not represented. The symbolic absence of privilege in Charli D'Amelio's video was one such occasion. Kress (2010) also suggests trying out what would happen to the meanings if specific elements in an image were moved, replaced or removed. This is what structural linguistics calls commutation, where we attempt to find out how different elements may be co-creators of an overall signification of an image – which may not be evident from the start. Barthes (1967: 65) writes about something called 'the commutation test' and explains that it 'consists of artificially introducing a change in the plane of expression (signifiers) and in observing whether this change brings about a correlative modification on the plane of content (signifieds)'. If D'Amelio were wearing a cocktail dress out at a restaurant while delivering this message, would we then have found her insensitive to the political issue? Seeing that this was during the pandemic, would we have been raging about her nonchalance towards social distancing as well? Machin and Mayr (2012) call such dimensions the 'setting' of an image, relating specifically to the place, occasion or conditions of an image. The setting of an image creates specific environmental connotations with their own underlying meanings (Machin & Mayr, 2012: 52–53). For example, if we are looking at a wedding photo, it is probably shot outside in a garden and not in a parking lot. And if it was shot in a parking lot, it would definitely alter the connotations. The environment in which, for example, video clips on TikTok are filmed can influence the values and identities that are communicated. Through the commutation test, we are able not only to 'see' what a picture holds, but also how we can make sense of different elements within it.

CONCLUSION

As we have seen in this chapter, it is vital, when researching digital media and society, to incorporate the visual elements in the analysis. This can be done as a method on its own, or in combination with other approaches. It is always important to remember how the visual and other modes of communication may be interconnected, and how together they shape cultural and social meanings in different ways. For example, an emoji can be an interesting object of research in the study of environmentally friendly influencer practices. The pose or gaze of a politician when using Instagram stories can shape their relatability, and thus form the basis for a study of political communication in digital spaces. There are many possibilities to incorporate visual aspects of digital media in your research, and we invite you to use the tools discussed in starting to explore these on your own.

10
PLATFORM ANALYSIS

Key Questions

- How must we shift our focus to bring the logic of *platforms* into view, and why is such a shift useful?
- What are the key ideas in the field of *software studies*?
- What does the term *affordances* refer to, and how can affordances be analysed?
- What methods are available for *platform analysis*, what knowledge can they provide, and how can they benefit digital media and society researchers?

Key Concepts

platforms * methods of the medium * software studies * affordances * algorithm ethnography * walkthrough method * discursive interface analysis * feature analysis * cross-platform analysis

In the previous chapters of this book, the focus has mainly been on analysing digital media content. In this final chapter, however, we will focus on examining the roles and functions of digital media communication platforms – the technological infrastructures enabling digital communication. We live today, many researchers argue, in a *platform society* (van Dijck et al., 2018). This refers to the fact that a significant portion of our social, economic, and cultural activities are mediated and facilitated by digital platforms such as Facebook, X (formerly Twitter), Instagram, Google, YouTube, TikTok, Tinder, Uber, and others. These platforms are not just tools we use to communicate but they also shape and influence our communication practices, social relationships, and even our sense of self. This is why it is meaningful to research them, not only in terms of the content that flows through them but also in terms of their underlying structures and mechanisms. The methods we gather in this chapter, under the umbrella term of *platform analysis*, have in common that they focus on the role of the platforms as such rather than on any particular form of content on them.

A platform, according to van Dijck, Poell and de Waal (2018: 9), is 'a programmable architecture designed to organize interactions between users'. The concept takes into account, on the one hand, that platforms are technological tools with which people do things online – sharing, commenting, buying, watching, listening, booking, and so on. But it also, on the other hand, accounts for the fact that platforms in themselves have a strong impact on how society is organised and, by extension, on how we live our lives. Platforms are ways of seeing the world, and the view differs depending on where one stands. In an anonymous forum such as 4chan, the view might be chaotic and unfiltered, while on a highly curated platform such as Instagram, the view might be more polished and aspirational. Regardless of what types of content we share or are being shown, the platforms through which this happens play a crucial role for the social effects of the interaction that takes place. It matters on which platform we communicate, as each platform has its own set of rules, norms, and values that shape our behaviour and influence how we perceive ourselves and others. Furthermore, every platform is also somewhat unique regarding what technological opportunities they afford users and what limitations they impose. From the perspective of so-called media ecology, platforms are like social structures in the sense that they enable some forms of social action while limiting others.

Platforms get social consequences in a number of ways due to how they are designed and used. And while each platform has its particular characteristics, we often see some rather common traits in platforms, which sometimes form part of the platform analysis. For example, van Dijck and Poell (2013) argue that social media platforms contribute to shaping social life through several different logics, such as:

- *Connectivity*. Platforms make it possible for users to connect and exchange content, including content that is produced by themselves. Users can engage with various individuals, groups, or content on the platform. Additionally, automatic connections may be established through recommendation systems or algorithms implemented by the platform. When analysing a platform, it is crucial to consider the kind of connections that may play a significant role in determining social relations.
- *Programmability*. The underlying software code of the platform, and its algorithms, can steer the user in certain directions, while the user can also, to some degree, contribute to shaping the platform and/or resist its programming. In scenarios where the platform's algorithms steer users, it can, for example, lead to a reinforcement of certain biases or beliefs, creating echo chambers where users are only exposed to information

that confirms their existing views. It might also lead to the exclusion of certain groups or individuals who do not fit into the platform's programmed norms or to the amplification of certain voices over others. The other side of the programmability has to do with how users can leverage direct or indirect knowledge about the algorithmic behaviours of a platform in order to game the system, manipulate the content or influence the outcomes in their favour. Examples of this range from the less refined – such as using certain hashtags, sharing certain links, tagging high-profile users, or attaching content such as images or video based on the expectation that they will receive more likes or views – to the more sophisticated, such as using bots or fake accounts to artificially boost engagement or to manipulate which topics are trending. All in all, the programmability of platforms goes both ways as it can both shape and be shaped by user behaviour.

- *Popularity*. The logic of platforms will make certain users and content more popular and visible according to the laws of virality, by which content that is shared more often and receives more engagement will be promoted to an even wider audience. This all has to do with the fact that the platforms are part of what has been called 'the attention economy' (Simon, 1971; Goldhaber, 1997), which refers to the competition for people's attention in the online sphere where there is an overwhelming amount of information and content available. The interplay between computer algorithms and social and economic factors significantly impacts this process. While the platform may prioritise certain content, users can tap into the attention economy to draw attention to their messages or causes if they are savvy.

The three principles of connectivity, programmability, and popularity will likely be central to how most digital communication platforms work. Take the app Tinder, for example. It uses these principles to connect users, allows them to customise their preferences and interactions, and has become a massively popular way for people to meet potential partners. Another example is Instagram, which uses connectivity to allow users to follow and interact with each other, programmability to enable users to edit and share their photos and videos, and has become a hugely popular platform for sharing and drawing attention to one's visual content. No doubt, however, platforms also have other infrastructural elements of this type, and these may vary depending on the specific platform and its intended purpose. In your own research, if drawing on different approaches for platform analysis, you will be able to discover the unique ways in which each platform is constructed and how it operates. Because of this, you may need to start out by learning more about the previous research done on the platform you have decided to study. If you are, for example, doing a study on Instagram influencers, seek out research that has done this previously. What technical features, which type of communicative patterns and interactions have been evident there, and what can you learn from this moving forward?

Analysing platforms, then, is about directing focus away from the very content to the ways in which the technologies, as such, shape the production, consumption, experience, impact, and distribution of that content. A classic research project that can be inspiring to think about here was documented in a book by a group of scholars who approached the Sony Walkman from a range of perspectives (Du Gay, 2013). For those who may be too young to remember, the Walkman was a portable cassette player that revolutionised the way people listened to music in the 1980s. And for those who may be too young to remember, well, a cassette was a small plastic case containing a magnetic tape on which audio recordings could be stored. The Walkman was a *platform* that enabled people to carry their music with them wherever they went, and this had a huge impact on how people experienced music. Today, when smartphones have made everything portable, this may not sound like much of a thing, but the Walkman was indeed a revolutionary platform when it was first introduced.

Du Gay and colleagues approached the Walkman as researchers in a way that is quite inspiring, also in the case of other platforms, such as the digital ones that we live with today. They wrote that their study was a study of 'a typical cultural artefact and medium of modern culture' and that through analysing it 'one can learn a great deal about the ways in which culture works' (Du Gay, 2013: 2). Similarly, a platform such as, for example, TikTok is indeed a typical cultural artefact and medium of our present time, and there is certainly a lot to learn about how culture works today by analysing it.

First, the authors focus on how cultural meaning is created around the platform through the practice of 'representation' (Hall, 1997a, b). This means looking at how a particular 'image' or aura is created. They look at how different groups or types of people become associated with the platform, thereby also connecting the analysis to issues of identity. In the case of TikTok, to keep with our example here, issues like these may be particularly interesting to delve into as scholars have shown how one of the most defining features of that platform is that it operates according to algorithms that suggest and serve its short videos in a way that is highly tailored to the interests and the locations of users. This means that quite specific 'TikTok' cultures will arise that blend global trending content with regional cultures (Abidin et al., 2023).

Second, the authors of the Walkman study approach issues of how the platform is produced as a cultural object, both in technical and cultural terms. They draw on the key cultural analysis concept of 'encoding' as coined as part of the conceptual pair of encoding/decoding by cultural theorist Stuart Hall (1973). Hall argues that the 'meaning' of media and, by extension, platforms relies, first, on the frameworks of knowledge – i.e. the cultural, social, and historical context – in relation to which the platform exists and is used and interpreted. Second, the structures of production – i.e. the systems and practices involved in producing both the platform and its messages – also contribute to encoding meaning into the platform. Finally, the technical infrastructure as such – i.e. the technologies in terms of networks, hardware, and software that make the platform – also encodes meaning into the platform. In the case of TikTok, frameworks of knowledge to be considered may be the cultural and social norms around self-expression, creativity, and social media use among young people in particular, but also the political climate and the globalised landscape of digital communication more broadly. When it comes to structures of production, TikTok could be seen in the light of the algorithms and content moderation policies that shape what content is promoted and what content is likely to be suppressed, as well as the social practices and behaviours of influencers and other users who create and share content on the platform. Another aspect of the structures of production relates to the ownership of TikTok, which has become a contentious issue due to national security concerns and the involvement of various political actors (Zhang, 2021). As for the technical infrastructure, TikTok could, for example, be analysed in terms of the design of its app and how its different functions and features – such as the role of audio and video editing – shape user behaviour, as well as the role of data collection and processing in creating personalised content recommendations and targeting advertising.

In sum, platform analysis focuses on the platforms as such rather than on the content that circulates through them. In practice, however, you are likely to realise that it is difficult to separate the form and the content. But regardless of that, platform analysis offers a different way of seeing digital media that fits well with media theorist Marshall McLuhan's notion that 'the medium is the message'. He argued that while the content of radio, television, or the internet might be a football game or a political debate, the message is equal to the social changes a medium generates. He wrote that 'the "message" of any medium or technology is the change of scale or pace or pattern that it introduces into human affairs' (McLuhan, 1964: 20). Similarly, one can argue that *the platform is the message*. For a platform analysis, we want to look beyond the content presently at hand to instead look at the technologies and infrastructures through which it is communicated and how these technologies and infrastructures interplay with the social.

At this point in time, however, 'platform analysis' is not an established methodology. There are, however, a set of different, but also overlapping, approaches that have in common that they focus on analysing the materiality and interfaces of digital media and also on their role in producing or maintaining norms and power relations. Throughout the rest of this chapter, we provide an overview of a set of such techniques, hoping that they will inspire you to think more about including these approaches in your analysis of digital media and society.

METHODS OF THE MEDIUM

Richard Rogers (2013: 1) writes about an approach that he describes as using the *methods of the medium*. This is about forms of digital research that have a close relationship to the platforms themselves by focusing on studying and adapting the methods already built into the platforms. Rogers writes that these types of methods:

> strive to make use not only of born-digital data but also the methods that are native to the medium. 'Native' is meant not in an ethnographic or anthropological sense. Rather it is applied in the computing sense of that which is written for a particular processor or operating system, rather than simulated or emulated. Native here is that written for the online medium, rather than migrated to it. (Rogers, 2019: 10)

Rogers' argument is that digital media are already doing research-like things in and by themselves, such as collecting, computing, sorting, ranking, and visualising data. Furthermore, he argues that these activities are often done without clear intentions or explicit research questions, but they still produce valuable insights and knowledge. This is just how the internet functions, and it is not related to anyone developing it this way to be useful specifically for research. Still, he argues, researchers can gain valuable insights by utilising these digital media practices and analysing the already generated data. The central concept of Rogers' approach is to not intervene or interfere very much with these existing 'methods'. Our analyses may, in fact, be more accurate if we respect their integrity, follow them with curiosity, and learn from them. Rogers (2013: 1) writes:

> For example, crawling, scraping, crowd sourcing, and folksonomy, while of different genus and species, are all web techniques for data collection and sorting. PageRank and similar algorithms are means to order and rank. Tag clouds and other common visualizations display relevance and resonance. How may we learn from and reapply these and other online methods? The purpose is not so much to contribute to their fine-tuning and build the better search engine, for that task is best left to computer science and allied fields. Rather, the purpose is to think along with them.

The role of the researcher then becomes to attempt to 'follow the medium' and its methods as they evolve and to find ways of exploiting and recombining them in useful and fruitful ways. This clearly relates to our notion of platform studies, as it emphasises that it is important to understand not just the content that is produced on a particular medium but also the affordances and constraints of that medium in and of itself. In this way, Rogers' approach can be a helpful catalyst to get started with platform analysis because it encourages a focus on the medium (platform) itself and how it shapes the content that is produced and the interactions that take place.

We could, for example, ask ourselves: How can a hashtag be used for social analysis? How can the search function on X (formerly Twitter) be used, not just to instrumentally find tweets but to respond to questions about social dynamics or cultural norms? How can we, as researchers, 'read' a TikTok feed in ways other than those intended by the creators of the service? The aim of thinking and working in this manner is, Rogers (2013: 3) writes, 'to build upon the existing, dominant devices themselves, and with them perform cultural and societal diagnostics; this means that the 'initial outputs' in the research process – a search result, a set of Tweets, a set of Instagram accounts, algorithmic music recommendations, etc. – might well be the same as, or at least very similar to, the things that digital devices output to their users. But with a 'digital methods' approach, Rogers explains:

> they are seen or rendered in new light, turning what was once familiar –
> a page of engine results, a list of tweets in reverse chronological order,
> a collection of comments, or a set of interests from a social networking
> profile – into indicators and findings. (Rogers, 2013: 3)

The main challenge for digital research, in that case, is to develop a mindset as well as a methodological outlook for doing social and cultural research *with* the platforms rather than about them. In sum, then, Rogers argues that to truly understand the impact of digital platforms on society and culture, we must shift our focus away from simply studying these platforms as objects of analysis towards actually engaging them in the research process. This means developing a new mindset that sees these platforms not just as tools but as complex systems that are deeply embedded within broader social and cultural contexts. It also means adopting new methodological approaches that allow us to explore the platforms in more nuanced and detailed ways.

This may sometimes feel challenging, as it appears more interesting to dive down into analysing a certain meme to map what it is about, how it is responded to, and what its impact is. These are, however, all questions of content rather than of infrastructure, and while they are important, they should not be allowed to completely overshadow the value of also analysing the underlying architectures that make memes possible in the first place. Borrowing the words from sociologist Susan Leigh Star, the call to analyse platforms:

is in a way a call to study boring things. Many aspects of infrastructure are singularly unexciting. They appear as lists of numbers and technical specifications, or as hidden mechanisms subtending those processes more familiar to social scientists. It takes some digging to unearth the dramas [and] to restore narrative to what appears to be dead. (Star, 1999: 377)

From this perspective, platforms can be seen as 'embodiments of standards' that can be picked apart and made visible. This potential deconstruction of platforms may also inspire us to engage in various activities of tearing down or breaking things. Star (1999: 382) explains that the infrastructure, or platform, becomes more 'visible upon breakdown'. Infrastructure that simply works as it should is mostly invisible, but as soon as something breaks – a server is down, Instagram does not load, or the screen of our streaming service just shows a spinning wheel – we become acutely aware of the platform's existence, importance, and 'normal' functioning.

In relation to this, one of the methodological approaches suggested by Rogers is that of the *teardown*. This approach was first manifested by Maria Eriksson and colleagues in the book *Spotify Teardown* (2019), where they borrow the notion of teardown from the language of processes of reverse engineering and embark on a project to 'disassemble the way Spotify's product is commonly conceptualized'. In tearing down the platform, however, they emphasise that their teardown 'is meant in an imaginative rather than purely technical sense'. They explain that they will engage in 'interventions' with the platform, which in itself is their research object (Eriksson et al., 2019: 9). Their teardown approach involved techniques such as scraping, analysing network data, and assuming the role of a creator by adding their own music to the platform. But, as explained by Rogers, there are also other – less hacking-oriented – methods for achieving the effect of a teardown to make the platform more visible.

Using YouTube as an example, Rogers suggests a set of approaches to gain insights into the workings of the platform, namely through watching, querying, and subscribing. In terms of watching, one might, for example, take a scholarly interest in what recommendations one receives through which videos are 'up next' and ask questions such as: 'Do they remain on-topic, or even ever come to an end? Do they tend to be more popular (higher view counts), newer (fresher), more niched (thus privileging discoverability) or some combination?' (Rogers, 2019: 256). The approach of querying the platform entails using its search function and receiving the ranked results. Based on this, the researcher can further try to analyse the consequences of such rankings or hierarchies, including questions such as: 'Which videos have the privilege to arrive at the top for viewers of videos concerning the Syrian War? Are there news channels or perhaps micro-celebrities returned as 'authorities'? [...] Are these results relatively consistent over time? Do particular sources persist at the top? Are there voices or points of view that dominate (at certain times)?' (Rogers, 2019: 256). Finally, the act of subscribing will entail receiving recommendations for 'related channels': 'How far away are game walkthroughs from gamergate, and how far is that from the alt-right? Do they overlap?'. Techniques such as these, Rogers argues, can be used to address broader issues and concerns that go beyond the narrow effects of recommender systems to engage analytically with issues such as those of 'algorithmic governance' (Rouvroy & Berns, 2013), 'platform memory' (Chun, 2008), and so on.

No matter if we conceive of these things as reverse engineering, deconstruction attempts, or teardowns, the key point here is to do things to make the platform reveal itself in various ways. This can be through a variety of manipulations that reveal its inner ways of working, such as changing one's location or language settings, creating multiple accounts and playing around with those, or just observing how different types of content seem to be promoted or suppressed. All such attempts may lead to a better understanding of how YouTube and other platforms operate and how they shape our experiences and perceptions of the world.

SOFTWARE STUDIES

Platform analysis is an aspect of the relatively new research field of *software studies*. This area has developed due to algorithms, automation, and artificial intelligence becoming ever more prominent phenomena in culture and society. Software, as in computer code, programmes, and applications, was previously associated rather exclusively with computer scientists and developers, but today it has become a subject of interest for scholars from various fields, including sociology, anthropology, media studies, and cultural studies. This is because software is no longer just a tool or a means to an end but has become a fundamental component of contemporary society, culture, and politics. In today's world, software is a force that structures and enables significant parts of our lives and society. This is, for example, illustrated by the fact that software is now integral to the functioning of everything from social media platforms to financial systems, healthcare services and transportation networks to national and international security. By its narrow definition, software is the set of instructions that tell a computer or other electronic device what to do. It is the set of instructions, the underlying code, that tells technological objects to function in the desired way.

This is the role of software as opposed to hardware, which refers to the physical, technological objects in the form of computer components, such as processors, memory chips, and input/output devices, and stretching further to other things that also run on software such as telephones, televisions, and refrigerators. In 1958, statistician John Tukey published an article where he introduced the term 'software' in relation to computing:

Today the 'software' comprising the carefully planned interpretive routines, compilers, and other aspects of automative programming are at least as important to the modern electronic calculator as its 'hardware' of tubes, transistors, wires, tapes and the like. (Tukey, 1958: 2)

It was Tukey's argument that people that use hardware devices do not necessarily need to have any in-depth understanding of their inner workings, and this notion still holds true today. When we use computers, smartphones, or social media platforms, we seldom think any further about the programming and logic that governs their operations under the hood. This is despite the fact that the details, decisions and rules that are imprinted in the software can significantly impact not only our user experience but also our privacy, security and even our social interactions. In software studies, the idea is that software governs social processes of today in even more far-reaching ways, such as shaping cultural norms and values, influencing political beliefs and behaviours, and affecting the distribution of power in society more broadly. Media theorist Lev Manovich, in his 2013 book *Software Takes Command*, argued that:

Software has become our interface to the world, to others, to our memory and our imagination – a universal language through which the world speaks, and a universal engine on which the world runs. What electricity and the combustion engine were to the early twentieth century, software is to the early twenty-first century. (Manovich, 2013: 2)

Media theorist and literary scholar Friedrich Kittler (1995) emphasised the importance of taking a critical approach to the 'essence' of computers. He wrote that 'software does not exist as a machine-independent faculty'. This points to the importance of focusing on hardware and software as interdependent and that they cannot be analysed in isolation. Second, he claimed 'there would be no software if computer systems were not surrounded any longer by an environment of everyday languages'. Software is not limited to computers and has an impact on society that goes both ways. But research on digital media and society did for a long time overlook software as a crucial component of digital society and tended instead to concentrate on the social and cultural consequences of digital media use as such. Recently, however, more attention has been directed towards the critical examination of how software restricts or facilitates various social practices and relations and how it is both shaped by – and shapes – society.

According to cultural researcher Matthew Fuller (2008), software studies research is important for highlighting that software is not just a technical tool but also a social, cultural, and political phenomenon that shapes our daily lives in many ways. Not only is it mediating our interactions with the world around us and each other, but it also affects how people in today's digitised world think, communicate, act and create. From that perspective, it is easy to see why understanding software is essential for understanding contemporary culture and society. Software studies can cover a wide range of different topics, such as the history and evolution of software, its political and economic implications, its impact on creativity and innovation, its role in shaping identities and communities, its relationship with other media, and its potential for social change. Software studies is about how code, files, copies, visualisations, functions, glitches, interfaces, bugs, and so on 'leak out of the domain of logic and into everyday life' (Fuller, 2008: 1).

Computer philosopher Jaron Lanier gives an example of how software, either as a by-product or by design, can contribute to defining social relations in particular ways. He writes about how the templates, options, functions, and fields to be filled out on social media platforms may indeed be 'user-friendly', but they simultaneously simplify and reduce human identities. He writes:

> The binary character at the core of software engineering tends to reappear at higher levels. It is far easier to tell a program to run or not to run, for instance, than it is to tell it to sort-of run. In the same way, it is easier to set up a rigid representation of human relationships on digital networks: on a typical social networking site, either you are designated to be in a couple or you are single (or you are in one of a few other predetermined states of being) – and that reduction of life is what gets broadcast between friends all the time. What is communicated between people eventually becomes their truth. Relationships take on the troubles of software engineering. (Lanier, 2010: 71)

This example shows how software, which is usually seen as intangible and immaterial, can have real-world effects. Software design impacts how we interact with technology and what we can or cannot do with it. It sets the rules for languages and interfaces and controls what functions are available to us, which is furthermore not without consequence for our social relationships outside of digital media.

Just like dominant political ideas, norms or traditions may be so deeply ingrained in society that they become seen as unquestionable and 'objective', software can also become a transparent or invisible aspect of digital society, despite its crucial role in its functioning. Similar to how dominant powers and beliefs become accepted as natural and unchallenged, software also contains an 'ideological layer' (Fuller, 2008: 3). In other words, software code will always have values and assumptions embedded in them, which can shape and reinforce social norms and power dynamics. For example, algorithms on social media that are used to recommend content to users may reinforce certain biases and perspectives, creating filter bubbles and echo chambers that can help reinforce existing power structures and social hierarchies.

This has to do, on the one hand, with general processes in society by which certain worldviews and ideologies are so ever-present that they seep into any system of knowledge that is deployed. On the other hand, patterns like these can also have to do with the contexts in which software is designed and implemented, as the lack of diversity in the tech industry may lead to a narrow perspective on what problems should be solved and how they should be addressed, leading to a deprioritisation of the needs of marginalised communities. This is why researchers of digital media and society must strive to critique this ideological layer of software. This will help us better understand how digital platforms shape – and are shaped by – our social, political and economic systems.

Software studies, in other words, urge us to look at platforms and apps that we use from a more analytical perspective. When we use apps that are familiar to us, we easily start to take their design, opportunities and limitations for granted. Because we use them so often, they become transparent to us, and we no longer question how they work or how they shape our experiences and interactions. From the perspective of research, however, many questions can be asked, such as: What is the app's intended purpose, and what features does it provide? How could it have been designed differently to achieve other goals or include additional functions? What assumptions does the app make about its users' interests, abilities, and demographic characteristics? Are there any groups of users who are excluded from using the app? Does the app reflect any specific values or beliefs?

AFFORDANCES

In the context of software studies, a crucial concept is that of *affordances*. It was introduced by ecological psychologist James Gibson (1979) to refer to the potential actions that can be taken in response to the physical environment. His main point was that our perception of the environment is not direct and unstructured but rather filtered through the affordances it offers – the potential actions that are available. If we see a doorknob, we see the potential action of turning it, and if we see a ball lying on the floor, we see the potential action of kicking it. In other words, our perceptions of the doorknob and ball, respectively, are based on their affordances as being turned or kicked. Affordances, in that sense, are relational: they establish a relationship between the environment and the individual. In the case of platforms, then, their affordances establish a relationship between the platform and the user. Following Gibson, other writers have developed the concept, and it is often used in social media research to focus on the types of interaction that different features of platforms afford – in terms of both possibilities and constraints – and the social structures that are formed as a consequence (Bucher & Helmond, 2018).

Game studies researcher Adrienne Shaw (2017) has suggested that the notion of affordances is brought together with Stuart Hall's encoding/decoding model that we discussed earlier. Shaw particularly emphasises Hall's (1973) idea that users can decode media in three different ways. First, there are dominant readings of media, which means that users interpret media in the way that was intended – encoded – by the creators. Second, there are negotiated readings, where users interpret media in ways that are partly in line with the intended meaning but that also incorporate their own experiences and beliefs to somewhat alter the encoder's intention. Finally, Hall speaks of oppositional readings that entail users decoding media in ways that go against the intended meaning, often as a form of resistance or subversion.

Shaw (2017) applies this terminology specifically to affordances to devise a critical analysis of how they may operate and be responded to in practice. Platforms will always have ideological meanings encoded in them – they are never entirely neutral. Rather, they can reflect and reinforce existing power structures and social hierarchies. Shaw argues that we can better account for how certain types of interactions and relations are promoted or discouraged by platforms by adapting the concept of affordances to Hall's encoding/decoding model.

Using the terminology proposed by Hall, Shaw (2017) defines the *dominant use* of a platform as using the platform according to the perceptible affordances so that the users' behaviours align with the designers' intentions. The dominant use is the most commonly accepted way of using the platform. *Negotiated use*, according to Shaw, refers to the ways in which users can adapt or modify platforms in order for them to suit their own needs and desires, even if those uses were not intended or imagined by designers. The notion of negotiated use, then, takes into account the power differentials between designers and users by recognising that users may have different interpretations of the affordances of a platform than its original designers. Most interestingly, *oppositional use* refers to cases where users actively resist or subvert the dominant use of a platform, instead using it in ways that are contrary to the designers' intentions and that can challenge existing power structures.

SOME METHODS FOR PLATFORM ANALYSIS

In the following sections of this chapter, we will introduce a set of different methodological approaches that can be used in various ways to gain knowledge about how platforms function socially, culturally, and politically. The first is *algorithm ethnography,* which focuses on studying the algorithms underpinning platform operations and their social implications. The approach is broad and will help you focus on a wide range of aspects of how social relationships and interactions are shaped by algorithms, both within and beyond the platform itself. The second approach is the *walkthrough method*, which involves conducting a step-by-step analysis of the user experience within a platform to understand how it works, what its features are, and how users can interact with it. Finally, we offer an introduction to *discursive interface analysis*, which urges the researcher to 'read' platforms as producers of meaning from the perspective of discourse analysis (see Chapter 6). In combination, we think that these methods will give you an adaptable toolset for starting out exploring and understanding the complexities of platforms and their social, cultural, and political implications.

Algorithm Ethnography

Algorithms are a key element of platforms, as they are the underlying sets of rules and instructions that define how the platform works in use. For example, algorithms are active in sorting and prioritising content based on various factors that they are designed to evaluate, weigh together, and act upon. Such factors may include different metrics for relevance, popularity, recency, and user engagement (Gillespie, 2016; Louridas, 2020). Essentially being a form of software, algorithms are also used to decide which advertisements are shown to which users based on their demographics, interests, and past online behaviour. Additionally, algorithms can also be employed to carry out content moderation and then, for instance, remove or flag content that violates the platform's guidelines or otherwise contains material that is seen as harmful (Gorwa et al., 2020).

Due to the wide use of algorithms on platforms, one methodological approach for platform analysis is to try to get more knowledge about how the often blackboxed algorithms operate. This can, for example, be done through *algorithm ethnography* (Lange et al., 2019; Seaver, 2019; Forberg, 2022). This method is about trying to find ways of mapping out and understanding algorithms in ways that go beyond their mere technical specification. This research is quite different from algorithm audits, which examine the technical specifications and code of algorithms to identify potential biases, errors, or other issues (Brown et al., 2021). First of all, such audits demand that it is possible to get knowledge about those specifications. In practice, this is far from certain, as platforms tend to keep their algorithms secret and do not disclose them to the public. Some researchers may work together with the platform corporations to help them understand and improve their algorithms, but such arrangements can, in turn, come at the cost of signing non-disclosure agreements that make it difficult to publish any results broadly. Second, research of the auditing type may not be what many digital media and society researchers are looking to do, as more problematising and dynamic perspectives may be needed to fully capture the social and cultural implications of algorithms on platforms.

Seaver (2017) writes about seeing algorithms 'as culture', meaning that they are not just straightforward technical tools but that they are also reflective of the values, power structures, and assumptions of the societies that create and use them. He contends that algorithms must be defined in a way that stretches beyond the computer science definition, and that they must be approached as unstable objects that are enacted through a variety of practices. Such a perspective has consequences also for how algorithms are best researched, and Seaver suggests that the researcher should – by contrast to that of the architects and developers of algorithms – assume an outside position and approach the algorithm as culturally embedded. Furthermore, Seaver suggests a number of tactics that the researcher can use to devise the algorithm ethnography:

- *Scavenging*. By creatively gathering information about algorithms from a variety of sources, we can help uncover important knowledge about platform algorithms, without being limited by corporate secrets about the exact and specific configurations. Seaver suggests that things such as off-the-record conversations with coders and engineers, platform corporations' press releases and social media updates, as well as patent applications, and hackathons, can all be ethnographically analysed to give crucial insights into platforms in society, and as culture.
- *Attending to the texture of access*. Seaver also encourages the scavenging ethnographer to not see the limited possibilities of getting access to the field as problems, but as research data in itself. In their interactions with platform corporations, researchers should realise that the obstacles they face when getting access will in fact help in revealing the cultural nature of the algorithmic systems, for example by giving knowledge about what types of information is deemed as being too important to share with researchers. Noting where, and to what, one is granted access provides the researcher with insight into how knowledge about algorithms is disseminated and thus serves as a research outcome in its own right. As Seaver (2017: 7) writes: 'an algorithm's edges are enacted by the various efforts made to keep it secret'.
- *Treating interviews as fieldwork*. Similarly, Seaver argues that in carrying out interviews with people who work with algorithmic systems should not be treated as regular interviews, but as a broader form of fieldwork. This aligns with a view where interviews are seen as being part of everyday life rather than separate from it. Interviewing people who work with algorithms and platforms will mean that we see algorithmic concerns manifested in different ways in the situation of, and around, the interview. Seaver (2017: 8) explains this by writing:

Here is [a] partial list of interviews I conducted during fieldwork: meeting for coffee with an engineer in a San Francisco coffeeshop;

setting up a Skype conversation with an interlocutor who insisted that I send him a Google Calendar invite so that our meeting would show up on his work calendar; interviewing a team of research scientists over lunch in the restaurant next door to their office; chatting in a bar with a former employee of a music streaming service that was slowly going out of business [...] None of these interactions were unusual for my interviewees. They fit me into existing patterns in their lives – often in ways that made my work difficult, giving me only 30 distracted minutes or making it hard to take notes or use my audio recorder. They treated me like a prospective hire, a supervisor, an advisee, a journalist, a friend, or a therapist. In these variously formatted conversations, algorithmic concerns manifested in many ways: as technical puzzles worked out with colleagues over lunch, as sources of anxiety or power, as marketing tools, or even as irrelevant to the real business of a company.

- *Parsing heteroglossia*. Seaver also suggests that the scavenging ethnographer pays attention to documents produced by the platform companies, such as advertisements or press releases. He argues that such documents often speak with many different voices at the same time – this is what heteroglossia means (Bachtin, 1981). The various voices, Seaver writes, can be parsed by the ethnographer to understand how the platform companies construct their image and how they present themselves to their users and the public. This, in other words, is about capturing how corporations that rely on algorithms construct various forms of meaning around their products. Beyond parsing the speech of the corporations as such, Seaver also underlines the importance of analysing the discourses of computer programmers who work with and around algorithms. In connection to this, Seaver (2019: 9) explains:

In my own fieldwork, I met many commercially employed programmers who were deeply ambivalent about their own work or their industry: some had previously been academics or musicians and felt like they had sold out; others felt a moral charge to pursue their own teams' work but felt guilty about broader industry dynamics. This ambivalence often manifested in ambiguous claims or jokes about things like data, markets, or algorithms.

All in all, Seaver's suggested approach to algorithm ethnography is designed to highlight the role of algorithms in culture and society more broadly. This includes a focus on institutions, corporations, people, and other contextual factors that shape how algorithms are created, implemented, and experienced. This approach is therefore more relevant to research on digital media and society than one-sidedly technical approaches to algorithms which neglect the social and cultural dimensions of how they are developed, implemented and used.

Christin (2020) also suggests a set of broader strategies that can be used in algorithmic ethnography, including 'algorithmic refraction' (analysing the complex chains of human and non-human interventions in algorithmic systems), 'algorithmic comparison' (studying algorithms across cases to explain what is unique about each one of them), and 'algorithmic triangulation' (using algorithms themselves as part of the research process), such as by interacting with recommender systems to generate additional qualitative data, and so on. In sum, then, the common idea in algorithmic ethnography is that the researcher must not be held back by the fact that algorithms, in the technical sense, are often inaccessible. Instead, the focus should be on how – to use the terminology of Lee et al. (2019) – algorithms 'fold' and 'unfold' social reality. Beyond the black box view, algorithms can be researched in terms of the many entangled sociopolitical relations and effects that they have (Cellard, 2022).

Walkthrough Method

Apart from analysing the algorithms, another way of approaching platforms is to study the apps that they provide. Apps, as we know, are software applications that run on platforms and that we install on our devices in order to interact with the services provided. Through app analysis, researchers of digital media and society can get insights into the ways in which platforms come into expression through interfaces and functionalities. Through launching what they call the *walkthrough method*, Ben Light, Jean Burgess and Stefanie Duguay (2018) want to address some of the new methodological challenges that apps offer up for socioculturally oriented digital media research. Similar to algorithms, as discussed above, apps are also relatively closed as technical systems. This means, again, that rather than go inside the code or infrastructure of the app as a technological entity, we will be better served as social and cultural researchers by devising other ways to get knowledge about how apps work. One such way is to conduct a walkthrough of the app where we, as researchers, use the app as an everyday user would, and thereby explore its features and functions, and document our experiences along the way.

Light and colleagues describe the walkthrough method as an approach that involves the researcher's direct engagement with the interface of the app under analysis, with the aim of understanding the different cultural aspects and technological mechanisms that contribute to shaping how users experience it. More concretely, the researcher will – while using the app like any user would – observe and document the different screens, buttons, features, and activities step-by-step, and analyse them critically. The method demands that the researcher pays attention to things such as how icons are placed, how visual elements are designed and what they may symbolise. While inspired by common approaches in the field of User Experience Design, where the focus is on the usability of the app, the walkthrough method is grounded in other perspectives, such as cultural studies (cf. Du Gay, 2013) and science and technology studies (STS) (Latour, 2005). The approach aims to map out, first, 'the app's *environment of expected use*' (Light et al., 2018: 883) and, second, its technical elements.

When it comes to analysing the environment of expected use, Light et al. extend the walkthrough to the surrounding context of the app by examining its vision, operating model, and governance. The *vision* can be approached through an analysis of what appears to be the app's purpose, scenarios of use, and target user base. Such things may be gathered from strategic communication, ads, imagery, company blogs, and organisational materials from the platform corporation, through which the app's discursive and symbolic representation is established. Such analysis may show things such as that Tinder references 'a particular view of monogamous intimate relations', while Squirt 'a hook-up app for men who have sex with men', highlights its functionality for communicating with multiple partners at once, disregarding monogamous relationship norms (Light et al., 2018: 889). The *operating model* of the app can be researched through various sources that give insight into the platform's business strategy and how it makes money. This may be through things such as subscriptions, in-app purchases, microtransactions, or by exchanging the users' personal data for services. These things can be gleaned from app stores, tech industry sources, public market information, business media outlets such as Forbes, or company databases such as Crunchbase. Analysing the app's operating model can help reveal its underlying economic as well as political interests. Finally, the *governance* of an app can be analysed through its stated rules and guidelines, as well as any formal Terms of Service documents, alongside knowledge on any informal community norms. This form of analysis will give knowledge about the political economy of the app in question, through for example how the app operates in terms of what user behaviours it allows or prohibits, and how user data is handled. It might be especially interesting in these cases to use tools like the Internet Archive's Wayback Machine, which archives old versions of websites, in order to critically analyse any changes in app governance.

As for the technical walkthrough, Light et al. (2018: 891) explain that the core strategy is that the researcher is 'engaging with the app interface, working through screens, tapping buttons and exploring menus'. The key idea is to assume the position of a user, and from there apply 'an analytical eye to the process of acquiring the app, registering, accessing features and functionalities and discontinuing use'. This whole process should be based in an STS approach, which means that human and non-human agents should be seen as interacting equally with each other in the app's ecosystem. Light and colleagues describe the mindset, activities and goals of the walkthrough researcher in the following way:

The researcher adopts an STS approach of systematically tracing key actors, such as icons and purchase buttons, producing a collection of data by generating detailed field notes and recordings, such as through screenshots, video recordings of the phone screen and audio recordings of one's thoughts while conducting the walkthrough. This involves attention to the app's materiality, including the actions it requires and guides users to conduct, and imaging how users would perceive these as affordances or constraints. It also involves drawing on cultural research skills in textual and semiotic analysis, recognising indicators of embedded cultural discourses, such as how the app constructs conceptions of gender, ethnicity, ability, sexuality and class. (Light et al., 2018: 891)

The approach, then, is much like that of an ethnographer engaging with the world of the app. Some of the key elements to think about this form of analysis include the arrangement of the user interface (button and menu placement), functions and features, textual content and tone (for example, gender categories when creating a user account), and symbolic representation (the look and feel of the app, through colours, font choices, etc.). Importantly, when doing a walkthrough of an app to thus get a feel for its expected uses, this may also help the researcher come across traces of unexpected uses that, consciously or unconsciously, resist or subvert the functions, meanings, and intentions of the app.

Discursive Interface Analysis

The method of discursive interface analysis has some similarities with the walkthrough method but also connects the platform analysis with discourse analysis approaches (as discussed in Chapter 6). Mel Stanfill (2015) introduces a methodological strategy for analysing user interfaces themselves as a form of discourse. Stanfill argues that web interfaces play an important role in shaping and perpetuating various social norms. The point is that, not only do they reflect existing norms, but they also have the potential to actively reinforce them. Using discursive interface analysis, by examining the functionalities, menu options, and page layouts of platforms (websites, apps, and so on), we can gain insight into the underlying meanings and systems of knowledge that they are built upon, and by extension, critically discuss their impact for both technology and its users.

The starting point for discursive interface analysis is that we shall analyse the affordances that platforms offer from the perspective that they both reflect and establish cultural norms about what users should do. This, in other words, means seeing the analysis of affordances as the analysis of normativity. And, importantly, affordances are seen here as something much broader than the mere technical functions of a platform. The interface is seen as an expression of underlying discourses that structure thinking and actions. In developing the approach, Stanfill makes reference to scholars such as Michele White (2006) and Lisa Nakamura (2008) who have it in common that they construe interfaces as contributing to the structuration of knowledge on categorisations, inclusions, and exclusions. The interface 'functions as a meaning producing system' (White, 2006: 106). According to this logic, we can analyse interfaces to find out things about the society and culture within which they are produced and used. The method thereby encourages us to conduct an analysis of interfaces which aims to bring out an understanding of how technology shapes our behaviour, which can in turn inform the design of future platforms that may be more fair and safe. Stanfill suggests that the discursive interface analysis is structured according to three overlapping types of affordances to be analysed:

- *Sensory affordances.* These refer to sensory aspects of the analysed interface, such as font size, colour schemes, and moving or still advertisements. Stanfill argues that these affordances should be included in the analysis as they can affect how users interact with a given interface, and thus also the norms that are constructed through the design. The sensory affordances will give information about how the platform positions, sees and speaks to its users. Basically, the aesthetics of a platform bears witness to if, for example, it targets young children, hackers, or shoppers. Sensory affordances speak to the users' seeing, hearing and feeling.
- *Functional affordances.* This type of affordances consists of the functionalities of the platform that are offered through the interface. This includes what actions or tasks can be performed on the platform – such as applying a filter to a photo and sharing it, watching videos, reading articles, or making purchases. A focus on functional affordances will help bring out information about which types of activities the platform users will do, and desire to do. Functional affordances are about what the platform can do.
- *Cognitive affordances.* These are the aspects of the interface which support the users in their process of making sense of the platform, and producing meaning around it. This includes, for example, the use of language, tonality, and how the user is addressed. When analysing these types of affordances, one finds a clear similarity to discourse analysis, as described in Chapter 6. Stanfill (2015: 1063–1064) explains that cognitive affordances 'relate to naming, labeling, and/or [...] taglines and self-descriptions [...] What a feature or menu or header is called matters, as these statements [...] address particular types of people as Users'. Cognitive affordances are about how users know what the platform can do.

Analysing a platform's interface using Stanfill's approach would then mean asking questions, such as (cf. Carlsson et al., 2021): How do text, image, form and aesthetics interact to produce meaning around the activities on, and identity of, the platform? What functional affordances does the platform have? How do the functions shape (limit and enable) user behaviours and identities? What cognitive affordances are expressed, i.e. what information is provided for the user to produce meaning around the platform? What norms and values are created through this information? How are sensory affordances expressed? How do all of these affordances interact?

CONCLUSION

With this final chapter, we have given an overview of a set of methods that differ from most of the other methods in the book. The main difference is that while the other methods are largely focusing on the content of communication and interactions through digital media, the kinds of approaches that we have bundled together under the umbrella term of platform analysis have it in common that they are more concerned with the infrastructures and architectures that underpin these interactions. As we discussed in the beginning of the chapter, platforms themselves can be quite helpful for us researchers when we are simply trying to figure out where to look for things, and to get help in conceiving and seeing digital media as social structures that may limit or enable different forms of social behaviours, patterns, and relations. By following the platforms – using the 'methods of the medium' – we can be guided along paths from which we may be in a better position to inspect and understand the very architecture of digital media sociality from the inside, gaining insights into the underlying mechanisms that shape our online experiences.

We should also note that, while the platform analysis methods discussed here focus on one platform at a time, there is also much potential for interesting research to be realised if we expand the approaches into *cross-platform analysis*. This means to follow related topical strands or online communities across multiple platforms, in order to gain a more comprehensive understanding of information flows and social dynamics (Burgess & Matamoros-Fernández, 2016; Lindgren, 2019: 432–434; Merrill & Lindgren, 2020). For example, we could examine how conversations about a particular political issue play out on X (formerly Twitter), Facebook, and Reddit, and how users move between these platforms to participate in the discussion. Another example would be to compare the types of content and interactions that happen on a more video-centred platform like YouTube versus an, as of yet, still, more photo-oriented platform such as Instagram, and how these differences shape user behaviour or community norms. Cross-platform analysis could also be useful when analysing memes because they often spread across multiple platforms, and understanding how they are adapted and rehashed in each given context has the potential to give insights into the cultural meanings and values that are attached to them.

Once again, the methods that we have discussed in this chapter will be the most fruitful and powerful in your studies if they are combined with other approaches. Consider, for example, using elements of algorithmic ethnography as an extension of a discourse analysis or network analysis of discussions or interactions that take place on a given platform. Or maybe to expand the walkthrough method, by using digital ethnography to analyse how the broader culture developed among users of a platform takes shape, both online and offline. There are many ways to imagine such methodological combinations in researching digital media and society that will enable more comprehensive and nuanced understandings of the complex and entangled social dynamics that occur in these digital spaces.

REFERENCES

@EllenDeGeneres (2014). If only Bradley's arm was longer. Best photo ever. #oscars. Twitter, 3 March 2023. https://twitter.com/EllenDeGeneres/status/440322224407314432 (accessed 15 June 2023).

Abidin, C. & de Seta, G. (2020). Private messages from the field: Confessions on digital ethnography and its discomforts. *Journal of Digital Social Research*, 2(1).

Abidin, C. & Kaye, D. B. V. (2021). Audio Memes, Earworms, and Templatability: The 'Aural Turn' of Memes on TikTok. In: *Critical Meme Reader*. Amsterdam: Institute of Network Cultures.

Abidin, C., Lee, J., & Kaye, D. B. V. (2023). Introduction to the Media International Australia Special Issue on 'TikTok Cultures in the Asia Pacific'. *Media International Australia*, 186(1), 3–10.

Allen, C. (1996). What's wrong with the 'Golden Rule?' Conundrums of conducting ethical research in Cyberspace. *The Information Society*, 12(2), 175–188.

Althusser, L. (1971). Ideology and Ideological State Apparatuses. In: *Lenin and Philosophy and other Essays*. New York: Monthly Review Press, pp. 121–176. www.marxists.org/reference/archive/althusser/1970/ideology.htm (accessed 8 August 2017).

Anggraini, R., Sawirman, S., & Marnita, R. (2021). The Structures of Trump's Political Discourse. *IJOTL-TL: Indonesian Journal of Language Teaching and Linguistics*, 6(1), 55–72.

Anthony, L. (2019). AntConc [Computer Software]. Waseda University. www.laurenceanthony.net

APA (1953). *Ethical Standards of Psychologists*. Washington, DC: American Psychological Association.

Atkinson, P., Coffey, A., & Delamont, S. (2003). *Key Themes in Qualitative Research*. Oxford: Altamira Press.

Bachtin, M. (1981). *The Dialogic Imagination: Four Essays*. Austin, TX: University of Texas Press.

Bail, C. A. (2021). *Breaking the Social Media Prism: How to Make Our Platforms Less Polarizing*. Princeton, NJ: Princeton University Press.

Barabási, A.-L. (2002). *Linked: The New Science of Networks*. New York: Perseus Books.

Baran, P. (1962). *On Distributed Communications Networks*. Santa Monica, CA: RAND Corporation.

Barley, R., & Bath, C. (2014). The Importance of Familiarisation When Doing Research with Young Children. *Ethnography and Education*, 9(2), 182–195.

Barthes, R. (1967). *Elements of Semiology*. London: Cape.

Barthes, R. (1973). *Mythologies*. UK: Granada Publishing.

Barthes, R. (1977). *Image, music, text*. (Heath, S., Ed.). UK: Fontana Press.

Barton, A. H. (1968). Bringing Society Back in: Survey Research and Macro-Methodology. *American Behavioral Scientist*, 12(2), 1.

Bastian, M., Heymann, S., & Jacomy, M. (2009). Gephi: An Open Source Software for Exploring and Manipulating Networks. *Proceedings of the Third International AAAI Conference on Weblogs and Social Media*, 3(1), 361–362.

Batinic, B., Reips, U.-D., & Bosnjak, M. (eds) (2002). *Online Social Sciences*. Cambridge, MA: Hogrefe & Huber.

Bayer, J. B., Ellison, N. B., Schoenebeck, S. Y., & Falk, E. B. (2016). Sharing the Small Moments: Ephemeral Social Interaction on Snapchat. *Information, Communication & Society*, 19(7), 956–977.

Baym, N. K. (1994). From Practice to Culture on Usenet. *The Sociological Review*, 42(1_suppl), 29–52.

Baym, N. K. (2005). Internet Research as It Isn't, Is, Could Be, and Should Be. *The Information Society*, 21(4), 229–232.

Bechmann, A. & Kim, J. Y. (2020). Big Data. In R. Iphofen (ed.), *Handbook of Research Ethics and Scientific Integrity* (pp. 427–444). Cham: Springer International Publishing.

Bell, D. (1973). *The Coming of Post-industrial Society*. New York: Basic Books.

Benjamin, W. (1969). The Work of Art in the Age of Mechanical Reproduction. In H. Arendt (ed.), *Illuminations*. New York: Schocken Books.

Benkler, Y. (2006). *The Wealth of Networks: How Social Production Transforms Markets and Freedom*. New Haven, CT: Yale University Press.

Benkler, Y., Faris, R., & Roberts, H. (2018). *Network Propaganda: Manipulation, Disinformation, and Radicalization in American Politics*. Oxford: Oxford University Press.

Bennett, W. L., & Livingston, S. (2021). *The Disinformation Age: Politics, Technology, and Disruptive Communication in the United States*. Cambridge: Cambridge University Press.

Bennett, W. L., & Segerberg, A. (2012). The Logic of Connective Action: Digital Media and the Personalization of Contentious Politics. *Information, Communication & Society*, 15(5), 739–768.

Berger, J. (1972). *Ways of Seeing*. TV Mini Series. UK: BBC.

Berger, P. L. & Luckmann, T. (1966). *The Social Construction of Reality: A Treatise in the Sociology of Knowledge*. Garden City, NY: Anchor Books.

Berkowitz, S. D. (1982). *An Introduction to Structural Analysis: The Network Approach to Social Research*. Oxford: Butterworth.

Berners-Lee, T. J. (1989). *Information Management: A Proposal*. Geneva: CERN.

Bhandari, A., & Bimo, S. (2022). Why's Everyone on TikTok Now? The Algorithmized Self and the Future of Self-Making on Social Media. *Social Media+ Society*, 8(1), 20563051221086240.

Bhuta, S. & Doshi, U. (2014). A Review of Techniques for Sentiment Analysis of Twitter Data. *Proceedings of the International Conference on Issues and Challenges in Intelligent Computing Techniques* (ICICT), February. https://doi.org/10.1109/icicict.2014.6781346

Billig, M. (1987). *Arguing and Thinking*. Cambridge: Cambridge University Press.

Billig, M. (2009). Discursive psychology, rhetoric and the issue of agency. [Texte anglais original]. *Critical Discourse Analysis*, 27. https://doi.org/10.4000/semen.8930

Bird, S., Klein, E., & Loper, E. (2009). *Natural Language Processing with Python*. Farnham: O'Reilly.

Blei, D. M. (2012). Topic Modeling and Digital Humanities. *Journal of Digital Humanities*, 2(1), 8–11.

Blommaert, J. & Jie, D. (2010). *Ethnographic Fieldwork: A Beginner's Guide*. UK: Multilingual matters.

Blondel, V. D., Guillaume, J.-L., Lambiotte, R., & Lefebvre, E. (2008). Fast Unfolding of Communities in Large Networks. *Journal of Statistical Mechanics: Theory and Experiment*, 2008(10), P10008. https://doi.org/10.1088/1742-5468/2008/10/P10008

Boehlefeld, S. P. (1996). 'Doing the Right Thing': Ethical Cyberspace Research. *The Information Society*, 12(2), 141–152.

Boellstorff, T. (2010). A Typology of Ethnographic Scales for Virtual Worlds. In W. S. Bainbridge (ed.), *Online Worlds*. London: Springer.

Boellstorff, T. B. A., Nardi, C. P., & Taylor, T. L. (2012). *Ethnography and Virtual Worlds*. Princeton, NJ: Princeton University Press.

Borgatti, S. P., Everett, M. G., & Johnson, J. C. (2013). *Analyzing Social Networks*. Los Angeles: Sage.

boyd, d. (2008). *Taken Out of Context*. Berkeley, CA: University of California Press.

boyd, d. (2014). *It's Complicated: The Social Lives of Networked Teens*. New Haven, CT: Yale University Press.

boyd, d., & Crawford, K. (2012). Critical Questions for Big Data. *Information, Communication & Society*, 15(5), 662–679.

boyd, d., & Ellison, N. B. (2007). Social Network Sites: Definition, History, and Scholarship. *Journal of Computer-Mediated Communication*, 13(1), 210–230.

Braun, V., & Clarke, V. (2006). Using Thematic Analysis in Psychology. *Qualitative Research in Psychology*, 3(2), 77–101.

Braun, V., & Clarke, V. (2022). *Thematic Analysis: A Practical Guide*. London: Sage.

Bridges, D. (2009). Education and the Possibility of Outsider Understanding. *Ethics and Education*, 4(2), 105–123.

Broniecki, P., & Hanchar, A. (2017). Data Innovation for International Development: An Overview of Natural Language Processing for Qualitative Data Analysis. In *Proceedings of the International Conference on the Frontiers and Advances in Data Science* (FADS), October. https://doi.org/10.1109/fads.2017.8253201

Brotherson, M. J. (1994). Interactive Focus Group Interviewing: A Qualitative Research Method in Early Intervention. *Topics in Early Childhood Special Education*, 14(1), 101–118.

Brown, S., Davidovic, J., & Hasan, A. (2021). The Algorithm Audit: Scoring the Algorithms that Score Us. *Big Data & Society*, 8(1). https://doi.org/10.1177/2053951720983865

Bruhn Jensen, K. (2012). *A Handbook of Media and Communication Research: Qualitative and Quantitative Methodologies*. London: Routledge.

Buchanan, E., & Markham, A. (2012). Ethical Decision-Making and Internet Research. AoIR. https://aoir.org/reports/ethics2.pdf.

Bucher, T., & Helmond, A. (2018). The Affordances of Social Media Platforms. In J. Burgess, A. E. Marwick, & T. Poell (eds), *The SAGE Handbook of Social Media* (pp. 233–253). London: Sage.

Burgess, J., & Matamoros-Fernández, A. (2016). Mapping Sociocultural Controversies across Digital Media Platforms: One Week of #gamergate on Twitter, YouTube, and Tumblr. *Communication Research and Practice*, 2(1), 79–96.

Butler, J. (1993). *Bodies That Matter: On the Discursive Limits of 'Sex'*. New York: Routledge.

Button, G. (1991). Introduction: Ethnomethodology and the Foundational Respecification of the Human Sciences. In G. Button (ed.), *Ethnomethodology and the Human Sciences* (pp. 1–9). Cambridge: Cambridge University Press.

Cai, Q., Pratama, M., Alam, S., Ma, C., & Liu, J. (2020). Breakup of Directed Multipartite Networks. *IEEE Transactions on Network Science and Engineering*, 7(3), 947–960.

Campbell, D. T., & Fiske, D. W. (1959). Convergent and Discriminant Validation by the Multitrait–Multimethod Matrix. *Psychological Bulletin*, 56(2), 81–104.

Carley, K. M. (1997). Network Text Analysis: The Network Position of Concepts. In C. W. Roberts (ed.), *Text Analysis for the Social Sciences: Methods for Drawing Statistical Inferences from Texts and Transcripts* (pp. 79–100). London: Routledge.

Carlsson, E., Lindberg, J., & Lundgren, A. S. (2021). Teknografi. In J. Jarlbrink & F. Norén (eds), *Digitala metoder i humaniora och samhällsvetenskap* (pp. 45–69). Lund: Studentlitteratur.

Carpentier, N. (2010). Deploying Discourse Theory: An Introduction to Discourse Theory and Discourse Theoretical Analysis. In I. Tomanić Trivundža, N. Carpentier, & P. Pruulmann-Vengerfeldt (eds), *Media and Communication Studies Intersections and Interventions: The Intellectual Work of ECREA's 2010 European Media and Communication Doctoral Summer School* (pp. 251–265). Tartu: Tartu University Press.

Carpentier, N. (2017). *The Discursive-Material Knot: Cyprus in Conflict and Community Media Participation*. New York: Peter Lang.

Castells, M. (1996). *The Rise of the Network Society*. Oxford: Blackwell.

Castells, M. (2002). *The Internet Galaxy*. Oxford: Oxford University Press.

Cellard, L. (2022). Algorithms as Figures: Towards a Post-digital Ethnography of Algorithmic Contexts. *New Media & Society*, 24(4), 982–1000.

Cervi, L., & Divon, T. (2023). Playful Activism: Memetic Performances of Palestinian Resistance in TikTok #Challenges. *Social Media + Society*, 9(1).

Chadwick, A. (2013). *The Hybrid Media System: Politics and Power*. Oxford: Oxford University Press.

Chandler, D. (2022). *Semiotics: The Basics*. London: Routledge.

Chang, J., Boyd-Graber, J., Gerrish, S., Wang, C., & Blei, D. M. (2009). Reading Tea Leaves: How Humans Interpret Topic Models. NIPS, 22, 288–296. https://proceedings.neurips.cc/paper/2009/file/f92586a25bb3145facd64ab20fd554ff-Paper.pdf

Chaudhari, D. D., & Pawar, A. V. (2021). Propaganda Analysis in Social Media: A Bibliometric Review. *Information Discovery and Delivery*, 49(1), 57–70.

Christakis, N. A., & Fowler, J. H. (2009). *Connected: The Surprising Power of Our Social Networks and How They Shape Our Lives*. London: Little, Brown and Co.

Christin, A. (2020). The Ethnographer and the Algorithm: Beyond the Black Box. *Theory and Society*, 49(5), 897–918.

Chun, W. H. K. (2008). The Enduring Ephemeral, or the Future Is a Memory. *Critical Inquiry*, 35(1), 148–171.

Clark, A., Fox, C., & Lappin, S. (2010). *The Handbook of Computational Linguistics and Natural Language Processing*. Chichester: Wiley-Blackwell.

Clarke, V., & Braun, V. (2006) Thematic Analysis. *Qualitative Research in Psychology*, 3(2), 77–101.

Cohen, L., Manion, L., & Morrison, K. (2018). *Research Methods in Education*. London: Routledge.

Conversation Center for Art & Historic Artifacts (2022). Robert Cornelius Daguerreotype Database Project. https://ccaha.org/initiatives/robert-cornelius-daguerreotype-project (accessed 15 June 2023).

Conway, M., Hu, M., & Chapman, W. W. (2019). Recent Advances in Using Natural Language Processing to Address Public Health Research Questions Using Social Media and Consumer Generated Data. *Yearbook of Medical Informatics*, 28(1), 208–217.

Cormode, G., & Krishnamurthy, B. (2008). Key differences between Web 1.0 and Web 2.0. *First Monday*, 13(6). https://doi.org/10.5210/fm.v13i6.2125

Cornelius, R. (1839). [Robert Cornelius, Self-Portrait; Believed to Be the Earliest Extant American Portrait Photo]. *Library of Congress*. www.loc.gov/pictures/item/2004664436

Correll, S. (1995). The Ethnography of an Electronic Bar: The Lesbian Cafe. *Journal of Contemporary Ethnography*, 24(3), 270–298.

Couldry, N., & Hepp, A. (2017). *The Mediated Construction of Reality*. Cambridge: Polity Press.

Couldry, N., & Mejias, U. (2019). *The Costs of Connection: How Data Is Colonizing Human Life and Appropriating It for Capitalism*. Stanford, CA: Stanford University Press.

Creswell, J. W., & Creswell, J. D. (2018). *Research Design: Qualitative, Quantitative, and Mixed Methods Approaches*. London: Sage.

Creswell, J. W., & Plano Clark, V. L. (2017). *Designing and Conducting Mixed Methods Research*. London: Sage.

Csardi, G., & Nepusz, T. (2006). The Igraph Software Package for Complex Network Research. *InterJournal, Complex Systems*, 1695(5), 1–9.

Dahlberg-Grundberg, M., & Lindgren, S. (2015). Translocal Frame Extensions in a Networked Protest: Situating the #IdleNoMore Hashtag. *IC Revista Científica de Información y Comunicación*, 11.

de Seta, G. (2020). Three Lies of Digital Ethnography. *Journal of Digital Social Research*, 2(1), 77–97.

Debord, G. (2012). The Commodity as Spectacle. In Durham, M. G. & Kellner, D. M. (eds), *Media and Cultural Studies: Keyworks* (2nd edn) (pp. 107–109). UK: Wiley-Blackwell.

Denisova, A. (2019). *Internet Memes and Society: Social, Cultural and Political Contexts*. Abingdon: Routledge.

Denzin, N. K. (1978). *The Research Act: A Theoretical Introduction to Sociological Methods* (2nd edn). London: McGraw-Hill.

Denzin, N. K., & Lincoln, Y. S. (1998). *The Landscape of Qualitative Research: Theories and Issues*. London: Sage.

Digital Rights Watch (2021). Online anonymity and pseudonymity: Why it matters. Virtual roundtable discussion, 30 November. www.youtube.com/watch?v=c_g_hXCW1oY (accessed 24 February 2022).

Djuraskovic, O. (2015). How Jorn Barger invented blogging. firstsiteguide.com. https://web.archive.org/web/20150406031002/https://firstsiteguide.com/robot-wisdom-and-jorn-barger (accessed 24 February 2022).

Drisko, J. W., & Maschi, T. (2015). *Content Analysis*. UK: Oxford University Press.

Du, Y., Li, T., Pathan, M. S., Teklehaimanot, H. K., & Yang, Z. (2022). An Effective Sarcasm Detection Approach Based on Sentimental Context and Individual Expression Habits. *Cognitive Computation*, 14(1), 78–90.

Du Gay, P. (2013). *Doing Cultural Studies: The Story of the Sony Walkman* (2nd edn). London: Sage.

Dunn, J. L. (2010). Vocabularies of Victimization: Toward Explaining the Deviant Victim. *Deviant Behavior*, 31(2), 159–183.

Durkheim, É. (1895). *The Rules of Sociological Method*. New York: Free Press.

Edwards, D., & Potter, J. (1992). *Discursive Psychology*. Thousand Oaks, CA: Sage.

Edwards, D., & Potter, J. (2001). Discursive Psychology. In A. McHoul & M. Rapley (eds), *How to Analyse Talk in Institutional Settings: A Casebook of Methods* (pp. 12–24). London and New York: Continuum International.

Ellis, C., Adams, T. E., & Bochner, A. P. (2011). Autoethnography: An Overview. *Historical Social Research*, 36(4), 138. GESIS-Leibniz Institute for the Social Sciences.

Elo, S., & Kyngäs, H. (2008). The Qualitative Content Analysis Process. *Journal of Advanced Nursing*, 62(1), 107–115.

Eriksson, M. (2018). Pizza, beer and kittens: Negotiating cultural trauma discourses on Twitter in the wake of the 2017 Stockholm attack. *New Media & Society*, 20, 3980–3996.

Eriksson Krutrök, M., & Åkerlund, M. (2023). Through a white lens: Black victimhood, visibility, and whiteness in the Black Lives Matter movement on TikTok. *Information, Communication & Society*, 26(10), 1996–2014.

Eriksson Krutrök, M., & Lindgren, S. (2018). Continued Contexts of Terror: Analyzing Temporal Patterns of Hashtag Co-occurrence as Discursive Articulations. *Social Media + Society*, 4(4), 2056305118813649.

Eriksson, M., Fleischer, R., Johansson, A., Snickars, P., & Vonderau, P. (2019). *Spotify Teardown: Inside the Black Box of Streaming Music*. Cambridge, MA: MIT Press.

Ess, C. (2020). *Digital Media Ethics*. Cambridge: Polity.

Ess, C., & AoIR Ethics Working Committee (2002). Ethical Decision-Making and Internet Research: Recommendations from the AoIR Ethics Working Committee (Version 1.0). AoIR. https://aoir.org/reports/ethics.pdf

Fairclough, N. (1992) *Discourse and Social Change*. Cambridge: Polity.

Fairclough, N. (1995) *Critical Discourse Analysis*. New York: Longman.

Farkas, J., & Schou, J. (2018) Fake News as a Floating Signifier: Hegemony, Antagonism and the Politics of Falsehood. *Javnost: The Public*, 25(3), 298–314.

Fiesler, C., & Dym, B. (2020). Moving Across Lands: Online Platform Migration in Fandom Communities. *Proceedings of the ACM on Human–Computer Interaction*, 4(1), May. https://doi.org/10.1145/ 3392847

Fiesler, C., Beard, N., & Keegan, B. C. (2020). No Robots, Spiders, or Scrapers: Legal and Ethical Regulation of Data Collection Methods in Social Media Terms of Service. *Proceedings of the International AAAI Conference on Web and Social Media*, 14(1), 187–196. https://ojs.aaai.org/index.php/ICWSM/article/view/7290

Fine, G. A. (1993). Ten lies of ethnography: Moral dilemmas of field research. *Journal of Contemporary Ethnography*, 22(3), 267–294.

Fiske, J. (2010). *Introduction to Communication Studies*. London: Taylor & Francis Group.

Forberg, P. L. (2022). From the Fringe to the Fore: An Algorithmic Ethnography of the Far-right Conspiracy Theory Group QAnon. *Journal of Contemporary Ethnography*, 51(3), 291–317.

Foucault, M. (1972). *The Archaeology of Knowledge and the Discourse on Language*. (trans. A. M. Sheridan Smith). New York: Pantheon Books.

Foucault, M. (1981). The Order of Discourse. In R. Young (ed.), *Untying the Text: A Post-Structralist Reader* (pp. 48–78). London: Routledge & Kegan Paul.

Foucault, M. (1989). *The Archaeology of Knowledge and the Discourse on Language* (trans. A. M. Sheridan Smith). Abingdon: Routledge.

franzke, a. s., Bechmann, A., Zimmer, M., & Ess, C. (2020). Internet Research: Ethical Guidelines 3.0. AOIR. https://aoir.org/reports/ethics3.pdf

Freeman, L. C. (1978). Centrality in social networks conceptual clarification. *Social Networks*, 1(3), 215–239.

Freeman, L. C. (1996). Some Antecedents of Social Network Analysis. *Connections*, 19(1), 39–42.

Freeman, L. C. (2004). *The Development of Social Network Analysis: A Study in the Sociology of Science*. Vancouver, BC: Empirical Press.

Froehlich, H. (2015). Corpus Analysis with Antconc. Programming Historian. https:// programminghistorian.org/en/lessons/corpus-analysis-with-antconc

Fuchs, C. (2014). *OccupyMedia! The Occupy Movement and Social Media in Crisis Capitalism*. Winchester: Zer0 Books.

Fuller, M. (ed.) (2008). *Software Studies: A Lexicon*. Cambridge, MA: MIT Press.

Gabasova, E. (2016). Star Wars social network. https://doi.org/10.5281/zenodo.1411479

Garg, S., Panwar, D. S., Gupta, A., & Katarya, R. (2020). A Literature Review On Sentiment Analysis Techniques Involving Social Media Platforms. In *2020 Sixth International Conference on Parallel, Distributed and Grid Computing* (PDGC), 6 November. https://doi.org/10.1109/pdgc50313.2020.9315735

Gee, J. P. (1999). *An Introduction to Discourse Analysis: Theory and Method*. New York: Routledge.

Geertz, C. (1973). *The Interpretation of Cultures*. New York: Basic Books.

Gelir, I. (2021). Can Insider be Outsider? Doing an Ethnographic Research in a Familiar Setting. *Ethnography and Education*, 16(2), 226–242.

George, L., Tauri, J., & MacDonald, L. T. O. T. (2020). *Indigenous Research Ethics: Claiming Research Sovereignty Beyond Deficit and the Colonial Legacy*. Bingley: Emerald Publishing.

Gewin, V. (2021). How to Include Indigenous Researchers and their Knowledge. *Nature*, 12 January. www.nature.com/articles/d41586-021-00022-1 (accessed 24 February 2022).

Ghosh, S., Ghosh, S., & Das, D. (2016). Part-of-speech Tagging of Code-Mixed Social Media Text. In *Proceedings of the Second Workshop on Computational Approaches to Code Switching*. https://doi.org/10.18653/v1/w16-5811

Giannoulis, E., & Wilde, L. R. A. (eds) (2019). *Emoticons, Kaomoji, and Emoji: The Transformation of Communication in the Digital Age*. New York: Routledge.

Gibbs, M., Meese J., Arnold M., Nansen B., Carter M. (2015). #Funeral and Instagram: Death, social media, and platform vernacular. *Information, Communication & Society*, 18, 255–268.

Gibson, J. J. (1979). *The Ecological Approach to Visual Perception*. Mahwah, NJ: Lawrence Erlbaum Associates.

Gillespie, T. (2016). Algorithm. In B. Peters (ed.), *Digital Keywords: A Vocabulary of Information Society and Culture* (pp. 18–30). Princeton, NJ: Princeton University Press.

Gimpel, K., Schneider, N., O'Connor, B., Das, D., Mills, D., Eisenstein, J., Heilman, M., Yogatama, D., Flanigan, J., & Smith, N. A. (2010). Part-of-Speech Tagging for Twitter: Annotation, Features, and Experiments. Defense Technical Information Center. https://doi.org/10.21236/ada547371

Gittleson, B. (2021). Birx on Trump's disinfectant 'injection' moment: 'I still think about it every day'. ABC News. https://abcnews.go.com/Politics/birx-trumps-disinfectant-injection-moment-day/story?id=76474960

Glaser, B. G. (1965). The Constant Comparative Method of Qualitative Analysis. *Social Problems*, 12(4), 436–445.

Glaser, B. G. (1978). *Theoretical Sensitivity: Advances in the Methodology of Grounded Theory*. Mill Valley, CA: Sociology Press.

Glaser, B. G., & Strauss, A. L. (1967). *The Discovery of Grounded Theory: Strategies for Qualitative Research*. Berlin: Aldine de Gruyter.

Goffman, E. (1959). *The Presentation of Self in Everyday Life*. New York: Doubleday.

Golder, S. A., & Macy, M. W. (2011). Diurnal and Seasonal Mood Vary with Work, Sleep, and Daylength across Diverse Cultures. *Science*, 333(6051), 1878–1881.

Goldhaber, M. H. (1997). The Attention Economy and the Net. *First Monday*, 2(4).

Gorwa, R., Binns, R., & Katzenbach, C. (2020). Algorithmic Content Moderation: Technical and Political Challenges in the Automation of Platform Governance. *Big Data & Society*, 7(1), 2053951719897945.

Graham, S., Weingart, S., & Milligan, I. (2012). Getting Started with Topic Modeling and MALLET. *Programming Historian*. https://doi.org/10.46430/phen0017

Granovetter, M. S. (1973). The Strength of Weak Ties. *American Journal of Sociology*, 78(6), 1360–1380.

Grishman, R., & Sundheim, B. (1996). Message Understanding Conference-6: A Brief History. *The 16th International Conference on Computational Linguistics*, 1.

Hagberg, A. A., Swart, P. J., & Schult, D. A. (2008). *Exploring Network Structure, Dynamics, and Function Using NetworkX*. Los Alamos, NM: Los Alamos National Laboratory (LANL).

Hall, S. (1973). Encoding and decoding in the television discourse. Council of Europe Colloquy on 'Training in the Critical Reading of Televisual Language'. https://core.ac.uk/download/pdf/81670115.pdf

Hall, S. (1997a). The Work of Representation. In S. Hall (ed.), *Representation: Cultural Representations and Signifying Practices* (pp. 13–64). London: Sage.

Hall, S. (ed.) (1997b). *Representation: Cultural Representations and Signifying Practices*. London: Sage.

Halliday, M. A. K. (1978). *Language as Social Semiotic: The Social Interpretation of Language and Meaning*. London: Edward Arnold.

Halliday, M. A. K. (1985). *An Introduction to Functional Grammar*. London: Edward Arnold.

Hammersley, M. (1996). The Relationship between Qualitative and Quantitative Research: Paradigm Loyalty versus Methodological Eclecticism. In J. T. E. Richardson (ed.), *Handbook of Qualitative Research Methods for Psychology and the Social Sciences* (pp. 159–174). Chichester: BPS Books.

Hammersley, M. & Atkinson, P. (2019). *Ethnography: Principles in Practice*, 4th edn. London: Routledge.

Hannerz, U. (1969). *Soulside*. New York: Columbia University Press.

Hansen, D., Shneiderman, B., & Smith, M. A. (2010). *Analyzing Social Media Networks with NodeXL: Insights from a Connected World*. San Francisco, CA: Morgan Kaufmann.

Hård af Segerstad, Y. (2021). On the Complexities of Studying Sensitive Communities Online as a Researcher–Participant. *Journal of Information, Communication and Ethics in Society*, 19(3), 409–423.

Hazlett, R. L., Larson, K., Shaikh, A. D., Chaparo, B. S. (2013). Two studies on how a typeface congruent with content can enhance onscreen communication. *Information Design Journal*, 20(3): 207–219.

Highfield, T. (2016). *Social Media and Everyday Politics*. Cambridge: Polity Press.

Hine, C. (2000). *Virtual Ethnography*. London: Sage.

Hine, C. (2005). *Virtual Methods: Issues in Social Research on the Internet*. Oxford: Berg.

Hine, C. (2007). Multi-sited Ethnography as a Middle Range Methodology for Contemporary STS. *Science, Technology, & Human Values*, 32(6), 652–671.

Hine, C. (2012). *The Internet: Understanding Qualitative Research*. Oxford: Oxford University Press.

Hine, C. (2015). *Ethnography for the Internet: Embedded, Embodied and Everyday*. London: Bloomsbury.

Ho, S. (2022). Sustainable Texting? Green Queen's Climate Conscious Emoji Guide. *Green Queen*, 5 January. www.greenqueen.com.hk/sustainable-texting-climate-conscious-emoji (accessed 3 May 2022).

Hollingshead, A. B. (1949). *Elmtown's Youth: The Impact of Social Classes on Adolescents*. Chichester: Wiley.

Honnibal, M., & Montani, I. (2017). spaCy 2: Natural language understanding with Bloom embeddings, convolutional neural networks and incremental parsing. https://sentometrics-research.com/publication/72

Hooley, T., Marriott, J., & Wellens, J. (2012). A Brief History of Online Research Methods. In *What is Online Research? Using the Internet for Social Science Research* (The 'What is?' Research Methods Series, pp. 7–24). London: Bloomsbury Academic.

Hsieh, H.-F., & Shannon, S. E. (2005). Three Approaches to Qualitative Content Analysis. *Qualitative Health Research*, 15(9), 1277–1288.

Hu, Y. (2006). Efficient, High-Quality Force-Directed Graph Drawing. *The Mathematica Journal*, 10. yifanhu.net/PUB/graph_draw.pdf (accessed 28 August 2023).

Hutto, C., & Gilbert, E. (2014). VADER: A Parsimonious Rule-based Model for Sentiment Analysis of Social Media Text. *Proceedings of the International AAAI Conference on Web and Social Media*, 8(1), 216–225.

Idelberger, F., & Mezei, P. (2022). Non-fungible Tokens. *Internet Policy Review*, 11(2). https://policyreview.info/glossary/non-fungible-tokens (accessed 3 November 2014).

Irwin, R. (2007). Culture Shock: Negotiating Feelings in the Field. *Anthropology Matters*, 9(1). www.anthropologymatters.com/index.php/anth_matters/article/view/64/123 (accessed 3 November 2014).

Ito, M. (2008). Introduction. In K. Varnelis (ed.), *Networked Publics* (pp. 1–14). Cambridge, MA: MIT Press.

Jackson, Lauren Michele (2017) We need to talk about digital blackface in reaction GIFs *Teen Vogue*. https://www.teenvogue.com/story/digital-blackface-reaction-gifs (accessed 7 December 2023).

Jackson, S. J., & Foucault Welles, B. (2016). #Ferguson is Everywhere: Initiators in Emerging Counterpublic Networks. *Information, Communication & Society*, 19(3), 397–418.

Jackson, S. J., Bailey, M., & Foucault Welles, B. (2020). *#HashtagActivism: Networks of Race and Gender Justice*. Cambridge: MIT Press.

Jenkins, H. (2006). *Convergence Culture*. New York: NYU Press.

Jewitt, C., Bezemer, J., & O'Halloran, K. (2016). *Introducing Multimodality*. Abingdon: Routledge.

Jick, T. D. (1979). Mixing Qualitative and Quantitative Methods: Triangulation in Action. *Administrative Science Quarterly*, 24(4), 602–611.

Johnson, R. B., & Christensen, L. B. (2014). *Educational Research: Quantitative, Qualitative, and Mixed Approaches*, 5th edn. Thousand Oaks, CA: Sage.

Jones, S. G. (1998). Introduction. In S. G. Jones (ed.), *CyberSociety 2.0: Revisiting Computer-mediated Communication and Community* (pp. xi–xvii). Thousand Oaks, CA: Sage.

Jones, S. (1999). Preface. In S. Jones (ed.), *Doing Internet Research: Critical Issues and Methods for Examining the Net* (pp. ix–xiv). Thousand Oaks, CA: Sage.

Julià, P. (2001). On Norbert Wiener on Language. *AIP Conference Proceedings*, 573(1), 517–533.

Kaplan, A. (1964). *The Conduct of Inquiry: Methodology for Behavioral Science*. Piscataway, NJ: Transaction Publishers.

Katz, G. (2019). Semantics in Corpus Linguistics. In K. von Heusinger, C. Maienborn, & P. Portner (eds), *Semantics: Typology, Diachrony and Processing* (pp. 409–443). Berlin: De Gruyter Mouton.

Kiesler, S., & Sproull, L. S. (1986). Response Effects in the Electronic Survey. *Public Opinion Quarterly*, 50(3), 402–413.

Kincheloe, J. L. (2005). On to the Next Level: Continuing the Conceptualization of the Bricolage. *Qualitative Inquiry*, 11(3), 323–350.

King, S. A. (1996). Researching Internet Communities: Proposed Ethical Guidelines for Reporting of Results. *The Information Society*, 12(2), 119–127.

Kiritchenko, S., Zhu, X., & Mohammad, S. M. (2014). Sentiment Analysis of Short Informal Texts. *Journal of Artificial Intelligence Research*, 50, 723–762.

Kitchin, R. (2021). *Data Lives: How Data are Made and Shape our World*. Bristol: Bristol University Press.

Kittler, F. (1995). There is No Software. *Ctheory*. https://journals.uvic.ca/index.php/ctheory/article/download/14655/5522

Kostoff, R. N. (1993). Co-Word Analysis. In B. Bozeman & J. Melkers (eds), *Evaluating R&D Impacts: Methods and Practice* (pp. 63–78). New York: Springer US.

Kozinets, R. V. (2015). *Netnography: Redefined*. Thousand Oaks, CA: Sage.

Kozinets, R. V. (2020). *Netnography: The Essential Guide to Qualitative Social Media Research*, 3rd edn. London: Sage.

Kress, G. R. (2010). *Multimodality: A Social Semiotic Approach to Contemporary Communication*. Abingdon: Routledge.

Kress, G. R., & van Leeuwen, T. (2006). *Reading Images: The Grammar of Visual Design*, 2nd edn. Abingdon: Routledge.

Krippendorff, K. (1967). An Examination of Content Analysis: A Proposal for a General Framework and an Information Calculus for Message Analytic Situations. www.semanticscholar.org/paper/An-Examination-of-Content-Analysis%3A-A-Proposal-for-Krippendorff/bf48765d53cf5caa792597d7571dda4032efd33e

Krippendorff, K. (2004). *Content Analysis: An Introduction to its Methodology*. Thousand Oaks, CA: Sage.

Krippendorff, K. (2019). *Content Analysis: An Introduction to its Methodology*, 4th edn. Thousand Oaks, CA: Sage.

Laclau, E. (2005). *On Populist Reason*. London: Verso.

Laclau, E., & Mouffe, C. (2014 [1985]). *Hegemony and Socialist Strategy: Towards a Radical Democratic Politics*. London: Verso.

Lange, A.-C., Lenglet, M., & Seyfert, R. (2019). On Studying Algorithms Ethnographically: Making Sense of Objects of Ignorance. *Organization*, 26(4), 598–617.

Lanier, J. (2010). *You Are Not a Gadget: A Manifesto*. London: Allen Lane.

Latour, B. (2005). *Reassembling the Social: An Introduction to Actor-Network-Theory*. Oxford: Oxford University Press.

Leaver, T., Highfield, T., & Abidin, C. (2020). *Instagram: Visual Social Media Cultures*. Cambridge: Polity.

Lee, F., Bier, J., Christensen, J., Engelmann, L., Helgesson, C.-F., & Williams, R. (2019). Algorithms as Folding: Reframing the Analytical Focus. *Big Data & Society*, 6(2), 205395171986381. https://doi.org/10.1177/2053951719863819

Lévi-Strauss, C. (1966). *The Savage Mind*. London: Weidenfeld & Nicholson.

Lewis, R. (2020). 'This is What the News Won't Show You': YouTube Creators and the Reactionary Politics of Micro-celebrity. *Television & New Media*, 21(2), 201–217.

Liddle, D. (2012). Reflections on 20,000 Victorian Newspapers: 'Distant Reading' The Times using The Times Digital Archive. *Journal of Victorian Culture*, 17(2), 230–237.

Light, B., Burgess, J., & Duguay, S. (2018). The Walkthrough Method: An Approach to the Study of Apps. *New Media & Society*, 20(3), 881–900.

Liliequist, E. (2020). *Digitala förbindelser: Rum, riktning och queera orienteringar*. Umeå: Umeå universitet.

Liliequist, E. (2022). Hitta hem: Queer orientering, geografisk plats och tillhörighet. In D. Hundstad, T. Hellesund, R. Jordåen, & M. G. Munch-Møller (eds), *Skeiv lokalhistorie: kulturhistoriske perspektiver på sammekjønnsrelasjoner og kjønnsoverskridelser* (pp. 453–476). Oslo: Nasjonalbiblioteket Oslo.

Lilleker, D. G., Veneti, A., & Jackson, D. (2019). Introduction: Visual Political Communication. In A. Veneti, D. Jackson, & D. G. Lilleker (eds), *Visual Political Communication* (pp. 1–14). Cham: Palgrave Macmillan.

Lindgren, S. (2011). Network Visualization. In G. A. Barnett (ed.), *Encyclopedia of Social Networks* (pp. 619–623). London: Sage.

Lindgren, S. (2016). Introducing Connected Concept Analysis: A Network Approach to Big Text Datasets. *Text & Talk*, 36(3), 341–362.

Lindgren, S. (2019). Movement Mobilization in the Age of Hashtag Activism: Examining the Challenge of Noise, Hate, and Disengagement in the #MeToo Campaign. *Policy & Internet*, 11(4), 418–438.

Lindgren, S. (2020). *Data Theory: Interpretive Sociology and Computational Methods*. Cambridge: Polity.

Louis, A. (2016). Natural Language Processing for Social Media. *Computational Linguistics*, 42(4), 833–836.

Louridas, P. (2020). *Algorithms*. Cambridge, MA: MIT Press.

Lu, J. H., & Steele, C. K. (2019). 'Joy is Resistance': Cross-Platform Resilience and (Re)invention of Black Oral Culture Online. *Information, Communication and Society*, 22(6), 823–37.

Lu, K., Kaluzeviciute, G., & Sharp, W. (2022). Things Can Only Get Stranger: Theoretical and Clinical Reflections on Netflix's *Stranger Things*. *Journal of Popular Culture*, 55(3), 611–631.

Lupton, D. (2016). *The Quantified Self: A Sociology of Self-Tracking*. Cambridge: Polity.

Lynd, R. S., & Lynd, H. M. (1929). *Middletown: A Study in Contemporary American Culture*. London: Harcourt, Brace and Co.

Macbeth, D. (2001). On 'Reflexivity' in Qualitative Research: Two Readings, and a Third. *Qualitative Inquiry*, 7, 35–68.

McEnery, T., & Hardie, A. (2013). The History of Corpus Linguistics. In K. Allan (ed.), *The Oxford Handbook of the History of Linguistics*. Oxford: Oxford University Press.

MacKinnon, K. R., Grewal, R., Tan, D. H., et al. (2021). Patient Perspectives on the Implementation of Routinised Syphilis Screening with HIV Viral Load Testing: Qualitative Process Evaluation of the Enhanced Syphilis Screening among HIV-positive Men Trial. *BMC Health Serv Res*, 21(625). https://doi.org/10.1186/s12913-021-06602-1

McLuhan, M. (1964). *Understanding Media: The Extensions of Man*. Cambridge, MA: MIT Press.

Machin, D. (2007). *Introduction to Multimodal Analysis*. London: Hodder Arnold.

Machin, D., & Mayr, A. (2012). *How to do Critical Discourse Analysis: A Multimodal Introduction*. London: Sage.

Malinowski, B. (1922). *Argonauts of the Western Pacific: An Account of Native Enterprise and Adventure in the Archipelagoes of Melanisian New Guinea*. Abingdon: Routledge.

Malpas, S., & Wake, P. (eds) (2013). *The Routledge Companion to Critical and Cultural Theory*, 2nd edn. New York: Routledge.

Manovich, L. (2013). *Software Takes Command*. London: Bloomsbury.

Marcus, G. E. (1995). Ethnography in/of the World System: The Emergence of Multi-Sited Ethnography. *Annual Review of Anthropology*, 24, 95–117.

Markham, A. (2012). Fabrication as Ethical Practice. *Information, Communication & Society*, 15(3), 334–353.

Markham, A. N., & Baym, N. K. (2009). *Internet Inquiry: Conversations About Method*. London: Sage.

Martino, G. D. S., Cresci, S., Barrón-Cedeño, A., Yu, S., Pietro, R. D., & Nakov, P. (2020). A Survey on Computational Propaganda Detection. *Proceedings of the Twenty-Ninth International Joint Conference on Artificial Intelligence*, July. https://doi.org/10.24963/ijcai.2020/672

Maslow, A. H. (1966). *The Psychology of Science: A Reconnaissance*. New York: Harper & Row.

Mayring, P. (2000). Qualitative Content Analysis. *Sozialforschung/Forum: Qualitative Social Research*, 1(2), Art. 20. http://nbn-resolving.de/urn:nbn:de:0114-fqs0002204

Mayring, P. (2004). Qualitative Content Analysis. *A Companion to Qualitative Research*, 1, 159–176.

Mayring, P. (2014). Qualitative Content Analysis: Theoretical Background and Procedures. In *Advances in Mathematics Education* (pp. 365–380). Dordrecht: Springer Netherlands.

Merrill, S., & Lindgren, S. (2020). The Rhythms of Social Movement Memories: The Mobilization of Silvio Meier's Activist Remembrance across Platforms. *Social Movement Studies*, 19(5–6), 657–674.

Merrill, S., & Lindgren, S. (2021). Memes, Brands and the Politics of Post-terror Togetherness: Following the Manchester Bee after the 2017 Manchester Arena Bombing. *Information, Communication & Society*, 24(16), 2403–2421.

Mikolov, T., Sutskever, I., Chen, K., Corrado, G. S., & Dean, J. (2013). Distributed representations of words and phrases and their compositionality. *Advances in Neural Information Processing Systems*, 26.

Miller, D. (2016). The Internet: Provocation. Blog post. Society for Cultural Anthropology. Published: April 4, 2016. https://culanth.org/fieldsights/the-internet-provocation. Accessed: October 2, 2023.

Miller, D., Costa, E., Haynes, N., McDonald, T., Nicolescu, R. Sinanan, J., Spyer, J. and Venkatraman, S. (2016). How the World Changed Social Media. London: UCL Press. https://discovery.ucl.ac.uk/id/eprint/1474805/1/How-the-World-Changed-Social-Media.pdf

Miller, D. & Horst, H. (eds) (2012). *Digital Anthropology*. Oxford: Berg.

Miller, D. & Slater, D. (2000). The Internet: An Ethnographic Approach. New York: Routledge.

Møller, K. & Robards, B. (2019). Walking Through, Going Along and Scrolling Back: Ephemeral mobilities in digital ethnography. *Nordicom Review*, 40(s1): 95–109.

Moreno, J. L. (1937). Sociometry in Relation to other Social Sciences. *Sociometry*, 1(1/2), 206–219.

Moreno, J. L. (1953). *Who Shall Survive? Foundations of Sociometry, Group Psychotherapy and Sociodrama*. Beacon, NY: Beacon House Inc.

Moretti, F. (2005). *Graphs, Maps, Trees: Abstract Models for Literary History*. London: Verso.

Moretti, F. (2013). *Distant Reading*. London: Verso.

Morozov, E. (2011). *The Net Delusion: The Dark Side of Internet Freedom*. New York: PublicAffairs.

Morse, J. M. (2003). Principles of mixed methods and multimethod research design. In A. Tashakkori & C. Teddlie (eds), *Handbook of Mixed Methods in Social and Behavioral Research* (pp. 189–208). London: Sage.

Mortensen, M. (2017). Constructing, confirming, and contesting icons: the Alan Kurdi imagery appropriated by #humanitywashedashore, Ai Weiwei, and Charlie Hebdo. *Media, Culture & Society*, 39(8), 1142–1161.

Mortensen, M., & Neumayer, C. (2021). The Playful Politics of Memes. *Information, Communication & Society*, 24(16), 2367–2377.

Mustajoki, H. & Mustajoki, A. (2017). *A new approach to research ethics: Using grounded dialogue to strengthen research communities*. New York: Routledge.

Nakamura, L. (2008). *Digitizing Race: Visual Cultures of the Internet*. Minneapolis, MN: University of Minnesota Press.

National Bioethics Advisory Commission (NBAC) (2001). Ethical and policy issues in research involving human participants: report and recommendations of the

National Bioethics Advisory Commission. bioethicsarchive.georgetown.edu/nbac/human/overvol1.pdf

Neri, F., Aliprandi, C., Capeci, F., Cuadros, M., & By, T. (2012). Sentiment Analysis on Social Media. *IEEE/ACM International Conference on Advances in Social Networks Analysis and Mining*, August. https://doi.org/10.1109/asonam.2012.164

Nielsen, F. Å. (2011a). A new ANEW: Evaluation of a word list for sentiment analysis in microblogs, 15 March. https://doi.org/10.48550/arXiv.1103.2903

Nielsen, F. Å. (2011b). AFINN Sentiment Lexicon. sentiment_afinn corpus. http://corpustext.com/reference/sentiment_afinn.html

Nielsen, R. K., & Ganter, S. A. (2022). *The Power of Platforms: Shaping Media and Society*. Oxford: Oxford University Press.

Noble, S. U. (2018). *Algorithms of Oppression: How Search Engines Reinforce Racism*. New York: New York University Press.

Nolan, R. W. (2002). *Anthropology in Practice: Building a Career Outside the Academy* (Directions in Applied Anthropology). Boulder, CO: Lynne Rienner.

Nooy, W. de, Mrvar, A., & Batagelj, V. (2005). *Exploratory Social Network Analysis with Pajek*. Cambridge: Cambridge University Press.

O'Reilly, T. (2005). What is Web 2.0? Design Patterns and Business Models for the Next Generation of Software. Blog post. O'Reilly Media. www.oreilly.com/pub/a/web2/archive/what-is-web-20.html

Papacharissi, Z. (2011). *A Networked Self: Identity, Community, and Culture on Social Network Sites*. Abingdon: Routledge.

Pennington, J., Socher, R., & Manning, C. (2014). GloVe: Global Vectors for Word Representation. *Proceedings of the 2014 Conference on Empirical Methods in Natural Language Processing* (EMNLP), pp. 1532–1543.

Pink, S. (2021). *Doing Visual Ethnography* (4th edn). London: Sage.

Pink, S., Horst, H., Postill, J., Hjorth, L., Lewis, T., & Tacchi, J. (2016). *Digital Ethnography: Principles and Practice*. London: Sage.

Pitts, A. (2016). Polinode: A Web Application for the Collection and Analysis of Network Data. *Proceedings of the 2016 IEEE/ACM International Conference on Advances in Social Networks Analysis and Mining*, pp. 1422–1425.

Pool, I. de S. (1983). *Technologies of Freedom: On Free Speech in an Electronic Age*. Cambridge, MA: Belknap Press.

Purdam, K., & Elliot, M. (2015). The Changing Social Science Data Landscape. In P. Halfpenny & R. Procter (eds), *Innovations in Digital Research Methods* (pp. 25–58). London: Sage.

Rainie, H., & Wellman, B. (2012). *Networked: The New Social Operating System*. Cambridge, MA: MIT Press.

Reed-Danahay, D. E. (1997). Introduction. In D. E. Reed-Danahay (ed.), *Auto-Ethnography. Rewriting the Self and the Social*. Oxford & New York: Berg.

Reid, E. (1991). Electropolis: Communication and Community on Internet Relay Chat. Honours Dissertation, University of Melbourne.

Rheingold, H. (1993). *The Virtual Community: Homesteading on the Electronic Frontier*. London: Addison-Wesley.

Ritzer, G. (ed.) (2007). *The Blackwell Encyclopedia of Sociology*. Oxford: Blackwell.

Rogers, R. (2013). *Digital Methods*. Cambridge, MA: MIT Press.

Rogers, R. (2019). *Doing Digital Methods*. London: Sage.

Rogers, R., & Giorgi, G. (2023). What is a Meme, Technically Speaking? *Information, Communication & Society*. doi: 10.1080/1369118X.2023.2174790

Rose, G. (2016). *Visual Methodologies: An Introduction to Researching Visual Materials*, 4th edn. London: Sage.

Rouvroy, A., & Berns, T. (2013). Algorithmic Governmentality and Prospects of Emancipation: Disparateness as a Precondition for Individuation through Relationships? *Réseaux*, 177(1), 163–196.

Rühlemann, C. (2019). *Corpus Linguistics for Pragmatics: A Guide for Research*. Abingdon: Routledge.

Sandvig, C., & Hargittai, E. (2015). How to Think about Digital Research. In E. Hargittai & C. Sandvig (eds), *Digital Research Confidential* (pp. 1–28). Cambridge, MA: MIT Press.

Schubert, L. (2020). Computational Linguistics. In E. N. Zalta (ed.), *The Stanford Encyclopedia of Philosophy*. Metaphysics Research Lab, Stanford University, CA. https://plato.stanford.edu/archives/spr2020/entries/computational-linguistics

Schwartz, H. A., & Ungar, L. H. (2015). Data-Driven Content Analysis of Social Media: A Systematic Overview of Automated Methods. *The ANNALS of the American Academy of Political and Social Science*, 659(1), 78–94.

Scott, J., & Carrington, P. J. (2011). Introduction. In J. Scott & P. J. Carrington (eds), *The SAGE Handbook of Social Network Analysis* (pp. 1–8). London: Sage.

Seaver, N. (2017). Algorithms as Culture: Some Tactics for the Ethnography of Algorithmic Systems. *Big Data & Society*, 4(2), 2053951717738104.

Seaver, N. (2019). Knowing Algorithms. In J. Vertesi & D. Ribes (eds), *digitalSTS: A Field Guide for Science & Technology Studies* (pp. 412–422). Princeton, NJ: Princeton University Press.

Sera-Shriar, E. (2014). What is armchair anthropology? Observational practices in 19th-century British human sciences. *History of the Human Sciences*, 27(2), 26–40.

Shannon, C. E. (1948). A Mathematical Theory of Communication. *The Bell System Technical Journal*, 27(3), 379–423.

Shannon, P., Markiel, A., Ozier, O., Baliga, N. S., Wang, J. T., Ramage, D., Amin, N., Schwikowski, B., & Ideker, T. (2003). Cytoscape: A Software Environment for Integrated Models of Biomolecular Interaction Networks. *Genome Research*, 13(11), 2498–2504.

Sharma, D., Sabharwal, M., Goyal, V., & Vij, M. (2019). Sentiment Analysis Techniques for Social Media Data: A Review. *First International Conference on Sustainable Technologies for Computational Intelligence* (pp. 75–90). Singapore: Springer Singapore.

Sharp, H., Rogers, Y., & Preece, J. (2019). *Interaction Design: Beyond Human–Computer Interaction*. Chichester: Wiley.

Shaw, A. (2017). Encoding and Decoding Affordances: Stuart Hall and Interactive Media Technologies. *Media, Culture & Society*, 39(4), 592–602.

Shibutani, T. (1966). *Improvised News: A Sociological Study of Rumor*. Indianapolis, IN: Bobbs-Merrill. http://archive.org/details/improvisednewsso0000shib

Simmel, G. (1950). *The Sociology of Georg Simmel* (K. H. Wolff, ed.). New York: Free Press.

Simon, H. A. (1971). Designing Organizations for an Information-Rich World. In M. Greenberger (ed.), *Computers, Communications, and the Public Interest* (Vol. 72, pp. 37–72). Baltimore, MD: Johns Hopkins Press.

Sinclair, J. (1991). *Corpus, Concordance, Collocation*. Oxford: Oxford University Press.

Sinclair, J. (2004). *Trust the Text: Language, Corpus and Discourse*. London: Routledge.

Spärck Jones, K. (1994). Natural Language Processing: A Historical Review. In D. E. Walker, A. Zampolli, N. Calzolari, & M. Palmer (eds), *Linguistica Computazionale: Current Issues in Computational Linguistics – In Honour of Don Walker* (Vol. 9/10, pp. 3–16). Pisa: Giardini editori e stampatori.

Stanfill, M. (2015). The Interface as Discourse: The Production of Norms through Web Design. *New Media & Society*, 17(7), 1059–1074.

Star, S. L. (1999). The Ethnography of Infrastructure. *American Behavioral Scientist*, 43(3), 377–391.

Sumiala, J. & Tikka, M. (2020). Digital media ethnographers on the move – An unexpected proposal. *Journal of Digital Social Research*, 2:1.

Svedmark, E., & Granholm, C. (2018). Research that Hurts: Ethical Considerations when Studying Vulnerable Populations Online. In R. Iphofen & M. Tolich (eds), *The Sage Handbook of Qualitative Research Ethics* (pp. 501–509). Thousand Oaks, CA: Sage.

Tausczik, Y. R., & Pennebaker, J. W. (2010). The Psychological Meaning of Words: LIWC and Computerized Text Analysis Methods. *Journal of Language and Social Psychology*, 29(1), 24–54.

Taylor, T. L. (2002). Living Digitally: Embodiment in Virtual Worlds. In R. Schroeder (ed.) *The Social Life of Avatars: Presence and Interaction in Shared Virtual Environments*. London: Springer-Verlag, pp. 40–62.

Teh, Y., Jordan, M., Beal, M., & Blei, D. (2004). Sharing Clusters among Related Groups: Hierarchical Dirichlet Processes. *Advances in Neural Information Processing Systems*, 17. https://proceedings.neurips.cc/paper/2004/file/fb4ab556bc42d6f0ee0f9e24ec4d1af0-Paper.pdf

Thomas, J. (1996). 'Introduction': A Debate about the Ethics of Fair Practices for Collecting Social Science Data in Cyberspace. *The Information Society*, 12(2), 107–117.

Thomas, L. (2021). Naming Names Won't Stop Abuse on Social Media. *The Strategist*, 8 October. Australian Strategic Policy Institute (ASPI). www.aspistrategist.org.au/naming-names-wont-stop-abuse-on-social-media (accessed 24 February 2022).

Thomas, S. (2006). The End of Cyberspace and Other Surprises. *Convergence*, 12(4), 383–391.

Toffler, A. (1980). *The Third Wave*. London: Collins.

Tomkins, S. S., & Demos, E. V. (1995). *Exploring Affect: The Selected Writings of Silvan S. Tomkins*. Cambridge: Cambridge University Press.

Trow, M. (1957). Comment on 'Participant Observation and Interviewing: A Comparison'. *Human Organization*, 16(3), 33–35.

Tsvetovat, M., & Kouznetsov, A. (2011). *Social Network Analysis for Startups*. Sebastopol, CA: O'Reilly Media.

Tukey, J. W. (1958). The Teaching of Concrete Mathematics. *The American Mathematical Monthly*, 65(1), 1–9.

Turkle, S. (1995). *Life on the Screen: Identity in the Age of the Internet*. London: Simon & Schuster.

Van der Nagel, E. (2021). Online anonymity and pseudonymity: Why it matters. Online webinar. Digital Rights Watch. Youtube. www.youtube.com/watch?v=c_g_hXCW1oY

van Dijck, J., & Poell, T. (2013). Understanding Social Media Logic. *Media and Communication*, 1(1), 2–14 (SSRN Scholarly Paper No. 2309065), 12 August. https://papers.ssrn.com/abstract=2309065

van Dijck, J., Poell, T., & De Waal, M. (2018). *The Platform Society: Public Values in a Connective World*. Oxford: Oxford University Press.

van Dijk, T. A. (1993). Principles of critical discourse analysis. *Discourse & Society*, 4(2), 249–283.

Vander Wal, T. (2007). Folksonomy coinage and definition. www.vanderwal.net/folksonomy.html

Varis, P. (2015). Digital Ethnography. In A. Georgakopoulou & T. Spilioti (eds), *The Routledge Handbook of Language and Digital Communication*. New York: Routledge.

Vicari, S. & Kirby, D. (2023). Digital platforms as socio-cultural artifacts: developing digital methods for cultural research. *Information, Communication & Society*, 26(9), 1733–1755.

Vidich, A. J., & Shapiro, G. (1955). A Comparison of Participant Observation and Survey Data. *American Sociological Review*, 20(1), 28–33.

Wagner, A. J. M. (2018). Do not Click 'Like' when Somebody has Died: The Role of Norms for Mourning Practices in Social Media. *Social Media + Society*, 4, 1–11.

Wasserman, S., & Faust, K. (1994). *Social Network Analysis: Methods and Applications*. Cambridge: Cambridge University Press.

Webb, E. J. (1966). *Unobtrusive Measures: Nonreactive Research in the Social Sciences*. Chicago, IL: Rand McNally.

Weber, M. (1922/1978). *Economy and Society*. Berkeley, CA: University of California Press.

Wellman, B. (2004). The Three Ages of Internet Studies: Ten, Five and Zero Years Ago. *New Media & Society*, 6(1), 123–129.

Wellman, B., & Haythornthwaite, C. A. (eds) (2002). *The Internet in Everyday Life*. Oxford: Blackwell.

Wetherell, M. (1998). Positioning and Interpretative Repertoires: Conversation Analysis and Post-Structuralism in Dialogue. *Discourse & Society*, 9, 387–412.

Wetherell, M., & Edley, N. (2014). A Discursive Psychological Framework for Analyzing Men and Masculinities. *Psychology of Men & Masculinity*, 15(4), 355–364.

White, H. C. (1992). *Identity and Control: A Structural Theory of Social Action*. Princeton, NJ: Princeton University Press.

White, H. C., Boorman, S. A., & Breiger, R. L. (1976). Social Structure from Multiple Networks, I: Blockmodels of Roles and Positions. *American Journal of Sociology*, 81(4), 730–780.

White, M. (2006). *The Body and the Screen: Theories of Internet Spectatorship*. Cambridge, MA: MIT Press.

Williams, M. L., Burnap, P., & Sloan, L. (2017). Towards an Ethical Framework for Publishing Twitter Data in Social Research: Taking into Account Users' Views, Online Context and Algorithmic Estimation. *Sociology*, 51(6), 1149–1168.

Willinsky, J., & Alperin, J. P. (2011). The Academic Ethics of Open Access to Research and Scholarship. *Ethics and Education*, 6(3). www.tandfonline.com/doi/abs/10.1080/17449642.2011.632716

Winther Jørgensen, M., & Phillips, L. (2011). Diskursanalys som teori och metod, 1: 14. Lund: Studentlitteratur AB.

Wittel, A. (2000). Ethnography on the Move: From Field to Net to Internet. *Forum: Qualitative Research*, 1(1), Art. 21. www.qualitative-research.net/index.php/fqs/article/view/1131/2517

Wodak, R. (1997). *Gender and Discourse*. London: Sage.

Wolski, U. (2018). The History of the Development and Propagation of QDA Software. *The Qualitative Report*, 23(13), 6–20.

Zagal, J. P., Tomuro, N., & Shepitsen, A. (2011). Natural Language Processing in Game Studies Research. *Simulation & Gaming*, 43(3), 356–373.

Zhang, Z. (2021). Infrastructuralization of Tik Tok: Transformation, Power Relationships, and Platformization of Video Entertainment in China. *Media, Culture & Society*, 43(2), 219–236.

Zidani, S. (2021). Messy on the inside: internet memes as mapping tools of everyday life. *Information, Communication & Society*, 24(16): 2378–2402.

Zimmer, M. (2018). Addressing Conceptual Gaps in Big Data Research Ethics: An Application of Contextual Integrity. *Social Media + Society*, 4(2). https://doi.org/10.1177/2056305118768300

INDEX

Printed in the USA
CPSIA information can be obtained
at www.ICGtesting.com
LVHW080347100424
776812LV00008B/45

9 781529 605167